The Chinese Path Series

The Road to China's Economic Powerhouse

Zhang Zhanbin
Translated by Lin Jihong

Paths Publishing Group

中国财经出版传媒集团
经济科学出版社
Economic Science Press

Translation Team

Translator: Lin Jihong (Fuzhou University, Fuzhou, China)

Preface

The Chinese path refers to the path of socialism with distinctive Chinese characteristics. As Chinese President Xi Jinping points out, it is not an easy path. We are able to embark on this path thanks to the great endeavors of reform and opening up over the past 30 years and more, and the continuous quest made in the 60-plus years since the founding of the People's Republic of China (PRC). It is based on a thorough review of the evolution of the Chinese nation over more than 170 years since modern times and carrying forward the 5,000-year-long Chinese civilization. This path is deeply rooted in history and broadly based on China's present realities.

A right path leads to a bright future. The Chinese path is not only access to China's development and prosperity, but also a path of hope and promise to the rejuvenation of the Chinese nation. Only by forging the confidence in the path, theory, institution and culture can we advance along this path of socialism with Chinese characteristics. With this focus, *The Chinese Path Series* presents to readers an overview in practice, achievements and experiences as well as the past, present and future of the Chinese path.

The Chinese Path Series is divided into ten volumes with one hundred books on different topics. The main topics of the volumes are as follows: economic development, political advancement, cultural progress, social development, ecological conservation, national defense and armed forces building, diplomacy and international policies, the Party's leadership and building, localization of Marxism in China and views from other countries on the Chinese path. Each volume on a particular topic consists of several books which respectively throw light on exploration in practice, reform process, achievements, experiences and theoretical innovations of the Chinese path. Focusing on the practice in reform and opening up with the continuous exploration since the founding of the PRC, these books summarize on the development and inheritance of China's glorious civilization, which not only display a strong sense of the times, but also have profound historical appeal and future-oriented impact.

The series is conceived in its entirety and assigned to different authors. In terms of the writing, special attention has been paid to the combination of history and reality, as well as theory and practice at home and abroad. It gives a realistic and innovative interpretation of the practice, experience, process and theory of the Chinese path. Efforts are made on the distinctive and convincing expression in a global context. It helps to cast light on the "Chinese wisdom" and the "Chinese approach" that the Chinese path has contributed to the modernization of developing countries and solutions to human problems.

On the basis of the great achievements in China's development since the founding of the PRC, particularly since the reform and opening up, the Chinese nation, which had endured so much and for so long since the modern times, has achieved tremendous growth—it has stood up, become prosperous and grown in strength. The socialism with distinctive Chinese characteristics has shown great vitality and entered a new stage. This path has been expanded and is now at a new historical starting point. At this vital stage of development, the Economic Science Press of China Finance & Economy Media Group has designed and organized the compilation of *The Chinese Path Series*, which is of great significance in theory and practice.

The program of *The Chinese Path Series* was launched in 2015, and the first publications came out in 2017. The Series was listed in a couple of national key publication programs, the "90 kinds of selected publications in celebration of the 19th CPC National Congress", and National Publication Foundation.

Editorial Board of *The Chinese Path Series*

Contents

Chapter 1
The Exploration and Compliance for Developing a Powerful Economy

1.1 National strategy of prioritizing the development of heavy industry in the early days of the People's Republic of China

After World War Ⅱ, many underdeveloping countries successively embarked on the path to independent development. Both the capitalist and socialist countries were exploring how to better realize the industrialization. It is from the industrialization that the People's Republic of China (PRC) made an initial stride in economic development, and thus the national strategy of prioritizing the development of heavy industry was put into practice over a period of time.

1.1.1 Strategic choice of economic development of countries late in developing in the 20th century

Profound changes took place when human history entered the middle of the 20th century. First, the growing international peace forces enabled the colonial and semi-colonial countries and regions in Asia, Africa and Latin America to gain their independence. Consequently, the era when capitalist countries such as Britain, France and the United States relied on colonial plunder for primitive accumulation in the 17th to 19th centuries had passed. Second, the bitter lessons from World War Ⅰ and World War Ⅱ showed that the military hegemony alone could not ensure Germany and Japan to maintain the status as a prosperous country and even made their country and the people pay bitter price for it. Consequently, the era when one country or a nation relied on military force to maintain the prosperity had passed. Third, even if the Marshall's European Recovery Program after World War Ⅱ provided many loans, due to many constraints, it remained inaccessible to many backward developing countries.

In fact, for many relatively backward developing countries, two paths can be mainly learned from the experience. One is the path to industrialization in the early capitalist countries (excluding colonial plunder and wars overseas), which primarily stepped from the development of light industry, and then developed heavy industry with the accumulated elements such as capital and technology. It is actually a path from the gradual development to that of comparative advantage. This path, if chosen, inclines to move towards the market economy with the coexistence and competition of various economic components. Another is the path to developing industrialization rapidly. Take the Soviet Union as an example, with the accumulated elements by the state power weighted towards industry, especially heavy industry, it aims to catch up with the economically developed capitalist countries in a relatively short period of time and to strengthen national defense to resist military threats and aggression. By doing so, it is actually adopting a strategy of prioritizing the development of heavy industry, that is, choosing a development path with the "catch-up" strategy. The division between the two economic systems mainly lies in the different strategies of economic development adopted by many relatively backward developing countries, behind which the decisive element is the choice of different modes of accumulating and allocating economic factors.

Typically, developing countries have strong desire to catch up with and surpass developed countries. As a result, the advocates of radical economic development occupy an important position, and the successful practice of John Maynard Keynes' government intervention in developed countries has a large market in the developing countries as well. Due to these common reasons, not only the socialist countries including China, the Soviet Union and some others in Eastern Europe, but also the non-socialist countries in Asia and the Central and South America, they all formed the similar trinity of planned economy through the choice of economic development strategy, the implementation of macropolicies and the establishment of resource allocation system and micro-management mechanism.[1] That is to say, since the 20th century, especially the middle of the 20th century, many developed capitalist countries and socialist post-developed countries have, early or later, taken the strategy of prioritizing the development of heavy industry, that is, the "catch-up" economic development strategy. Meanwhile, they had

[1] Justin Yifu Lin, Cai Fang, and Li Zhou, *China's Miracle: Development Strategy and Economic Reform*, Shanghai: Truth & Wisdom Press, 1994, pp. 54-57.

gradually implemented planned economy to comply with this economic strategy.

To catch up with and surpass advanced countries in economy is the common "vision" of all the countries and regions late in developing. However, some researches by economists show that nearly all the countries and regions late in developing that implemented the "catch-up" economic strategy plunged into the dilemma, such as the ever-increasing urban and rural poverty, prolonged high inflation and unbalanced economic structure after years of accumulation. Instead, a few developing countries and regions without adopting the "catch-up" economic strategy achieved rapid economic growth. Take Japan, Republic of Korea, Singapore, and China's Taiwan and Hong Kong for example, they ever became highlights known as the "East Asian miracle", or even the "mystery of East Asia".

The success of the Four Asian Tigers that implement the capitalist system, plus the transformed economic system in the countries that develop socialism, it is easy for us to overlook the decisive role of development strategy on economic performance, and to ascribe the different development of economic performances to the different social systems. Some economists such as Justin Yifu Lin et al. pointed out that this conclusion cannot stand scrutiny since it simply abstracts different developments as different social systems without making a detailed economic analysis of different development strategies, macro-policy environment, resource allocation systems and micro-management mechanisms. First, suppose that the success of the Four Asian Tigers owed to the capitalism system, why are many other capitalist countries unable to become emerging industrialized economies? Second, suppose that the economy in the socialist countries were doomed to stagger, why has China achieved remarkable economic changes in the last two decades and created an economic miracle on its coast regions that outperformed the rapid growth of the Four Asian Tigers? Third, suppose that social system were the crux of slow economic growth in the socialist countries, why do the Soviet Union and the eastern European countries remain in dire straits after restructuring their systems?

When examining the experience and lessons from the success or failure of economic development in various countries, Chinese economists Justin Yifu Lin et al. noted that all the countries implementing the "catch-up" strategy failed to achieve success in their economic growth and development. Implementing the "catch-up" strategy, China, the Soviet Union and some eastern European countries with the socialist planned economy failed to achieve their desired goals of "catch-up". It is the case with some developing countries that implement the capitalist system with the "catch-up" strategy or import the substitution strategy. Take the capitalist countries Argentina, Uruguay, Chile and Bolivia Livia in Latin America for example, though their per capita incomes were similar to that in Germany in the late 19th century, these countries remained underdeveloped even after a century later, facing the economic difficulties and extreme polarization of wealth distribution with people's living standards improving slowly. In Asia, the Philippines, once a rising star after Japan in the 1960s, was also in a state of economic chaos and stagnation.

In this regard, Lin et al. repeatedly emphasized that seen from the development experience of Japan and the Four Asian Tigers, these countries and regions can leverage the comparative advantages in factor endowment at each stage of economic development, rather than stray away from the comparative advantages to catch up with or surpass the developed countries. A common law is that with the increasing economic development, capital accumulation and per capita capital ownership, the factor endowment structure has improved, and consequently the leading industries have gradually shifted from labor-intensive to capital-intensive and technology-intensive, even information-intensive mode. This principle of following comparative advantages in the economic development can be called the strategy of comparative advantage.[1]

Why does the strategy of comparative advantage deserve more attention? The reason is that in the early development stage of developing countries or in today's developing countries, its factor endowment structure features serious lack of capital, surplus of labor and backward technology. In the case that promotes heavy industrialization by distorting factor prices and controlling other economies, one thing left to do is to allocate the limited capitals towards a few industries while suppressing the development of other industries and non-state-owned economy. As a result, the suppressed industries and non-state-owned economy cannot provide the original capital accumulation. As the industrial sectors supported by the "catch-up" strategy do not conform to the comparative advantages of factor endowment, they have to rely on distorting prices and on national protective policies, such as financial supports, market regulation, trade barriers and financial subsidies, to survive. Consequently, these industries are inevitably lack of efficiency, competitiveness and self-generating capability. The distorted industrial structure caused by violating comparative advantages

---

[1] Justin Yifu Lin, Cai Fang, and Li Zhou, *China's Miracle: Development Strategy and Economic Reform*, Shanghai: Truth & Wisdom Press, 1994, pp. 54-57.

contradicts the factor endowment structure with abundant labor force, which inhibits the attraction of labor force. This makes it difficult to change the situation that a considerable number of population are in a state of poverty for a long period of time. Actually, the real connotation of economic development lies in improving comprehensive national strength rather than relying on the abrupt and isolated growth of a few heavy industries. To improve the capital intensity of some industries, it has to reduce that of other industries. This means that on the whole it cannot narrow the gap between developing and developed economies in terms of capital and technology. For an economy in a backward position, it should seek the development that follows the principle of comparative advantage and realizes the improvement of factor endowment structure or the increase of capital per capita. From the above analysis, the theory of comparative advantage is logically self-contained and persuasive.

So, does China's economic development strategy follow the principle of comparative advantage? It should be said that the policy of New Democracy, adopted for a relatively short period of time at the early days of the People's Republic of China, was in line with the principle of comparative advantage and adapted to China's realities at that time. Since the starting of the First Five-year Plan (1953-1957) in 1953, the principle of comparative advantage had not been carried on. Instead, the strategy of prioritizing the development of heavy industry was adopted and planned economy gradually took shape. Of course, maybe there was no such a term as "strategy" by the Chinese leaders at that time, but one by the induction of some researchers later. However, from the actual situation, such a priority to developing heavy industry can be summed up as the "strategy of prioritizing the development of heavy industry". The evaluation of China's strategy of prioritizing the development of heavy industry undoubtedly involves the economic policy and strategic orientation before implementing this strategy. Clarifying this issue will provide a frame of reference and basic coordinates for our evaluation.

In fact, in the course of striving for the victory of New Democracy Revolution, the Communist Party of China (CPC) began to design the social development strategy and economic policy after the victory. Especially around 1949, when the Peoples' Republic of China was founded, the CPC's major leaders had claimed on many occasions that it was not the right time to have the socialist revolution immediately after the victory of New Democracy Revolution. Instead, the transition of New Democracy should be first experienced, and then possible efforts should be made to mobilize the initiative of urban and rural private capitalism, so that it could lay good foundation for forwarding the development of national economy and gradually enter socialism by means of peaceful competition and redemption in the near future. It should be said that it is similar to the "dual-track system" in which planned economy coexists with market economy; or else, it can be regarded as market economic system. It is in consistent with the reality of China's economic and social development, comparatively in line with the general law of the development of industrialized countries, and similar to the principle of comparative advantage in economics. Supposed that the constraints of international environment and changes of political and economic power were not taken into consideration, developing economy under this design will undoubtedly play a great promotional role in gradually improving the country's factor endowments and industrial structure as well as the relationship between urban and rural areas, and promoting more stable and rapid economic growth. Then, unnecessary twists and turns may not be experienced by China's economic construction, and small steps can be constantly forwarded without pause and the national strength can be enhanced.

However, if the strategy of prioritizing the development of heavy industry is implemented, the shortage of economic factors is prone to give birth to planned economy no matter what social system a country has. China is no exception. Implementing the strategy of prioritizing the development of heavy industry means to give up market system and change the dual-track system of economic policy of New Democracy—planned economy coexists with market economy—to implement planned economy. The main reasons why the actual transition and the Three Socialist Transformations[1] were carried out in advance and fundamentally completed in China, were to meet the needs of prioritizing the development of heavy industry and building the endogenous planned economy. Here, it can be inferred that adopting the strategy of prioritizing the development of heavy industry is obviously not a simple issue of economic theoretical analysis and economic decision-making, but a more complex and diversified choice after the value evaluation. For one thing, although it did not conform to the factor endowments in China at that time and the principle of comparative advantage, it responded to the special needs of China's military and defense at that time, and the political and economic preferences by decision-makers. For another, China, a country with larger population and areas compared to those with less population and

[1] The Three Socialist Transformations refer to the socialist transformation of agriculture, handicraft industry, and capitalist industry and commerce in the 1950s. —*Tr.*

areas, has both its particularity and comparative advantages and advantages as a latecomer, which give space to its economic development. So, this strategy can be considered as a more realistic and relatively reasonable choice. Considering the international environment at that time and the possible historical experience, it was the most possible and practical choice for China to take the "catch-up" strategy of prioritizing the development of heavy industry, thus accelerating efforts to transition to the socialism of the Soviet model. From this perspective, what China has done is to seek truth calmly from realities without losing the thread. Generally speaking, this choice has both historical effects and historical limitations. The great historical effects were somewhat manifested at that time and could not be denied later; meanwhile, the large historical limitations were gradually experienced and summarized in the process of historical development as they were difficult to be fully recognized at that time. Therefore, both its great effects and large limitations cannot be denied.

1.1.2 Relationship between the strategy of prioritizing the development of heavy industry and planned economy

Heavy industry has three basic features. The first is a huge scale of initial investments and intensive capitals. The second is the relatively high organic composition of capitals, intensive technologies and largely imported equipment. The third is the long development cycle and slow return. These determine that developing heavy industry must have large-scale capital accumulation and supply. However, in the early days of the PRC, when China's agriculture and light industry were backward, the demand of implementing the strategy of prioritizing the development of heavy industry contradicted directly with the resource endowment at that time. It mainly manifested in three aspects: the contradiction between the construction cycle of heavy industry and capital endowment; the contradiction between the investment scale of heavy industry and the capability of capital mobilization; the contradiction between the high technology of heavy industry and the capability of foreign exchange payment. In order to ensure that the accumulated economic surplus flows to the heavy industry sector, a new institutional arrangement is needed. This institution needs to implement the centralized planning in allocating economic resources and build the corresponding micro-management mechanism through the nationalization of enterprises and collectivization of agriculture. That is to say, as long as the strategy of prioritizing the development of heavy industry is adopted, an endogenous trinity of planned economy will come into being according to China's natural endowment. Consequently, the force of planned economy will naturally phase out the market mechanism, which actually means giving up the policy of New Democracy. However, it cannot be said that the emergence of China's planned economy is all due to the strategy of prioritizing the development of heavy industry, apart from the subsequent effects such as unifying finance and economy, supporting the war, resolving the conflicts between state-owned economy and private economy. It is fair to say that implementing the strategy of prioritizing the development of heavy industry was the fundamental reason for China's implementing planned economy.

First, the contradiction between the "catch-up" strategy of prioritizing the development of heavy industry and the extreme shortage of productive factors promoted a high proportion of nationalization of ownership structure. When the "catch-up" strategy of prioritizing the development of heavy industry was implemented, it needed to make great improvement in the ownership and accelerate the proportion of state-owned enterprises. What could be done at that time was to promote this process through the administrative and economic means. In October 1952, entrusted by Mao Zedong, Liu Shaoqi made an explanatory speech to Stalin on the time required for China's transition to socialism and the conditions to be achieved as follows: In the current gross industrial product in China (excluding handicraft industry), state-owned enterprises account for 67.3% while private enterprises only 32.7%. It was estimated that with the help of the Soviet Union in implementing the First Five-year Plan, the share of state-owned economy in industry was to increase more, and that of private capitalist economy was to shrink to less than 20%. In 10 years later, private industry was to have shrunk to less than 10% while state-owned industry would account for more than 90%. Although the share of private industry was to shrink, most of them would keep on developing. Therefore, most capitalists were satisfied to cooperate with the government. Their businesses generally relied on the state for supplies of raw materials, purchasing and marketing finished products, and bank loans, and were included in the state plans rather than independent operations. In this situation, the capitalists' factories were to be expropriated by the state; and in most cases, the adopted approach was to exhort capitalists to give their factories to the state, which retained property for the capitalists to consume, distributed possible jobs to the capitalists to secure their livelihood and paid them a portion of the cost in special circumstances.[1] From this explanation, it can be

---

[1] Bo Yibo, *Review of Some Important Decisions and Events* (Volume II), Beijing: Central Party School Press, 1991, pp. 218-219.

clearly seen that the Chinese leaders had already recognized the link between the industrialization route of prioritizing the development of heavy industry and the change of ownership structure at that time. It can be clearly seen that why the vision of spending 10 to 15 years in transitioning to socialism was put forward in the First Five-year Plan when the policy of New Democracy was abandoned in advance.

Second, the great contradiction between the strategy of prioritizing the development of heavy industry and backward agriculture promoted the process of agricultural cooperation. Prioritizing the development of heavy industry demanded the direct or indirect accumulation from farmers and agriculture. This needed implementing a low-price policy for agricultural products. In this case, the low-price policy reduced farmers' enthusiasm to sell their products to the state, and thus the state-run business sectors were difficult to obtain enough commodity grain, cotton, oil and other products needed by the industrialization. This caused tension in the market, which resulted in unified purchase and sale. The unified purchase and sale made the total volume of agricultural and subsidiary products controlled by the state-owned and cooperative businesses rise from 57% in 1953 up to 70% in 1954, and the total retail sales in rural areas from 44.2% in 1953 up to 60.5% in 1954. Since the supply and marketing of raw materials and products were not largely provided through the market, private enterprises were no longer the real market entities. Bo Yibo pointed out: After implementing the First Five-Year Plan, the large-scale economic development further caused the shortage of supply in the market, which forced the state to adopt the policies and measures like the unified purchase and sale, thus accelerating the transformation of capitalist industry and commerce step by step. Since the implementation of unified purchase and sale, the transformation of private commerce as a link of circulation had gone ahead of that of private industry, which in turn accelerated its pace of transformation. Then, the light textile industry, about two thirds of China's private industry, was heavily influenced by the policy of unified purchase and sale and had to transform itself since it was constrained by supply and marketing. However, the supply-demand contradiction between grain and other agricultural products could not be resolved by the unified purchase and sale. Therefore, the fundamental solution to this contradiction was to accelerate agricultural cooperation, according to Mao Zedong's view that the socialist transformation of agriculture should adapt to prioritizing the development of heavy industry.[1]

In the middle of the 20th century, the "catch-up" strategy of prioritizing the

[1] *Selected Works of Chen Yun* (Volume Ⅱ), Beijing: People's Publishing House, 1995, p. 208.

development of heavy industry was successively implemented in developing countries, such as China, India, Brazil, Argentina, Chile, Egypt, Mexico and Eastern European countries. And a trinity of planned economy system (a trinity of macro-policy environment, resource allocation system and micro-management mechanism) was gradually formed to promote this strategy. Under this system, to enhance the capability of economic mobilization and strengthen the demand for economic surplus, the state has to artificially distort the relative price of productive factors by means of policy. The available means was mainly as follows: to lower the level of interest rate, to hold down the exchange rate, to implement a unified low-salary policy; meanwhile to implement a highly centralized financial monopoly mechanism, the centralized and unified management of foreign trade and exchange, the unified supply of important materials and the unified purchase and sale of agricultural products. By controlling the economy artery to promote economic nationalization and the high proportion of state-owned economy, the government participated in allocating scarce resources, enforced trade monopoly, made the industrial policy weighted toward or propping up the heavy industry, set up barriers to control financial industry, effectively reduced the capital threshold of industrial economy through raising funds by administrative power, and improved the profits of enterprises. To hold residual control and flow of accumulation and make it utilized in the strategic sectors of national economic development, it is necessary to realize the nationalization of enterprises to the maximum and establish a planned system of unified mandatory production and a financial system of unified collection and expenditure on this basis. Accordingly, the system of agricultural collectivization was formed to match the policy of unified purchase and sale of agricultural products. This was a looped policy chain. Although Justin Yifu Lin et al. did not directly discuss the relationship between the strategy of prioritizing the development of heavy industry and the abandonment of the policy of New Democracy, such a logical sequence implied that the economic policy of New Democracy naturally came to an end.

1.1.3 Differentiation and analysis of the strategy of prioritizing the development of heavy industry from the international perspective

In the late 1980s, under the influence of "new thinking", the historian academia in the Soviet Union had ever launched a campaign of reappraising the Soviet history. When it came to developing industrialization during the Stalin period, most of them believed that the artificial emphasis on the speed of development of heavy industry, which had forced the development of agriculture and light industry to pay a price, hindered the process of social modernization. However, based on the practical testing after the disintegration of the Soviet Union, the mainstream view on behalf of the government and the majority of Russian historians has changed. According to a history textbook *A History of the Motherland in the Twentieth Century*, reviewed and approved by the Ministry of Education of the Russian Federation and edited by A Shestakov et al. in 2002, it said, "In the 1930s, the country faced a new threat of war... To win the war, a strong industry is needed. It is a matter of life or death for the nation." But the Soviet Union had no colonies, no foreign investments, backward industries... It was also impossible to follow the traditional path of industrialization, which started with light industry and was relatively slow. Therefore, it was compelled to implement the centralized planned management and reduce the role of market, and obtain funds from the "super-economic coercion" of agriculture, which made people "tighten their belts" in finance. The book also argues, agricultural collectivization is the most important precondition to accelerate the realization of industrialization.[1]

Then, how to evaluate the strategy of prioritizing the development of heavy industry in China? From a historical and international perspective, there are at least four favorable factors that deserve our value for China's implementing the strategy of prioritizing the development of heavy industry.

First, it speeded up the economic base for building socialism. Carrying out the strategy of prioritizing the development of heavy industry, which resorted to the mobilization and organizational strength of the new state power as well as the love and loyalty of the people to the new state, involved that the socialist transformation was completed by peaceful means and the economic foundation for building socialism was laid. From 1953 to 1956, the national gross industrial output value was up by an average of 19.6% and 4.8% of gross agricultural output each year. In a relatively short period of time, the relatively rapid economic development and better economic results had been achieved. The achievements in industrial production during the First Five-year Plan period had far surpassed those in old China in the last hundred years.[2] Meanwhile, it made Chinese people see the strength and capability of the new country and rebuild the confidence to develop the Chinese nation.

---

[1] Wu Siyuan, "Keep Fair to History: Russia's Reflection on the Total Denial of Soviet History", *Theoretical Front in Higher Education*, 2004 (8).

[2] Liu Suinian, Wu Qungan, *A Brief History of China's Socialist Economy*, Harbin: Heilongjiang People's Publishing House, 1985, p. 182.

Second, it rapidly improved the capabilities of national defense and military defense. Implementing the strategy of prioritizing the development of heavy industry had enhanced its capabilities of national defense and military defense in a relatively short period of time, and successfully launched atomic bombs, hydrogen bombs and satellites, which raised China's international status and ensured its national security and sovereignty. For a new independent power with sovereign unification, it was great to use its own factor resources and construction strength to break the "nuclear" monopoly of the western powers in the period of Cold War, improve the comprehensive capability in the world community rapidly, end the hundred years' humiliation history, and maintain the dignity of the country and the people's life safety completely. This is a "big event" and "big transition" with far-reaching political significance and international influence, far beyond the scope of economics.

Third, it accelerated efforts to promote the process of national socialist industrialization. Implementing the strategy of prioritizing the development of heavy industry enabled the completion of 150-plus projects assisted by the Soviet Union, which helped establish a relatively complete national economic and industrial system rapidly and provided a prerequisite for developing comprehensive and integrated industrial capability after the reform and opening up. As what is said, "The national socialist industrialization is both a sure and a must for national independence and prosperity." The First Five-year Plan enabled China to establish a number of basic industries, which were necessary for national industrialization but very weak in the past. It changed the once backward heavy industry, which had a very weak base and relatively low level of production. Therefore, an independent and relatively complete industrial system and national economic system was established. This primarily resolved the problem of weak base in the national economy, laid foundation for becoming a major industrialized power, and provided the premises for the rapid development of China's industry and the rapid rising of China's manufacturing industry as the world's manufacturing center after the reform and opening up.

Fourth, it promoted in-depth cooperation between Chinese industry and international advanced countries. Through the strategy of prioritizing the development of heavy industry and learning the experience from the Soviet Union, China has accumulated rich experience in building great industry and greatly deepened the understanding of industrialization, which provided valuable experience for introducing industrial projects and cooperating with international advanced countries. So, at the beginning of reform and opening up, China began to introduce foreign capitals and equipments on a large scale and proposed multi-level economic cooperations with international advanced countries. Today, our successful cooperations in heavy industry and other projects owe much to the practical achievements and accumulated valuable experience.

However, there needs an objective understanding of the disadvantages of the strategy of prioritizing the development of heavy industry despite the remarkable achievements, since the comprehensive evaluation may go beyond the scope of economics. From the perspective of economics, Justin Yifu Lin et al. made a comprehensive analysis and interpretation of problems difficult to be solved under the strategy of prioritizing the development of heavy industry. Here, some more explanations on a few important issues.

First, the seriously imbalanced proportion of national economy between agricultural industry, light industry and heavy industry was difficult to resolve. As is known, the continuous progress in prioritizing the development of heavy industry may cause the issues such as the imbalanced economic relations and rigid economic system, the seriously imbalanced proportions of national economy between agricultural industry, light industry and heavy industry, the rigid problem of urban-rural separation and governance, and the heavy cost to solve the problem facing agriculture, rural areas and farmers. In order to learn lessons from the Soviet Union and Stalin, Mao Zedong proposed in his speech On the Ten Major Relationships in 1956: The issue should be avoided such as paying one-sided attention to heavy industry and neglecting agriculture and light industry like the Soviet Union and some Eastern European countries, and more investments should be put in agriculture and light industry with heavy industry as the main player. In 1957, in his article On the Correct Handling of Contradictions Among the People, he proposed the principle of developing industry and agriculture side by side. In 1959, he put forward the idea of developing national economy in order of agriculture, light industry and heavy industry, and pointed out, it did not violate Marxism since the proposal suggests prioritizing the development of materials of production. Regrettably, it was not fully applied into practice as the crux of "catch-up" strategy remained. In addition, the "leftism" had gradually prevailed, which required the accelerated efforts to develop industry and evolved into an absolute indicator during the Great Leap Forward period (1958-1960) —the "high" index of rapid development occupied. As a result, there brought about the serious imbalanced proportion of national economy between agricultural industry, light industry and heavy industry; it was hard to change the urban-rural dual economy and difficult to transfer the labor force of agriculture.

There even appeared the phenomenon of counter-urbanization that the urban population devolved to the countryside. All of these made the comparative advantage suppressed and out of play, which led to the serious backwardness of agriculture, rural areas and rural people.

Second, it inevitably caused the recession of non-state-owned economy. The strategy of prioritizing the development of heavy industry led to the embarrassing status of non-state-owned economy, which competed with state-owned economy for the economic surplus in the market, and was strictly restricted or even banned. As time passed, the recession of non-state-owned economy was inevitable. Just as the Soviet Union gave up the New Economic Policy (NEP) during the Stalin period, the policy of New Democracy was abandoned for the "catch-up" strategy of prioritizing the development of heavy industry, which resulted in the sharp contraction and severe recession of non-state-owned economy. Therefore, during the period of Great Leap Forward and Cultural Revolution (1966-1976), non-state-owned economy was fundamentally suppressed and individual economy and private economy were even mistaken as capitalist economy. As a direct result, the trend of "leftism", hit or even suppressed the non-state-owned economy. All of these had brought about many difficulties to social employment, commodity circulation, commodity supply, people's livelihood and so on.

Third, it directly caused the lack of vitality and competitiveness of economy entities of micro-market. Due to lack of market competition mechanism and the absence of non-state-owned economy, micro-organized state-owned enterprises and rural cooperatives are inefficient and uncompetitive. Despite of good results achieved in implementing the "catch-up" strategy of prioritizing the development of heavy industry in its initial stage or in a certain period of time, the disadvantages accumulated by excluding market and competition had been revealed and gradually deteriorated in many developing countries. In particular, lack of competition from non-state-owned economy, and supported and aided by the state in many aspects, state-owned enterprises dominated national economy. On the one hand, the paternalism of the state tended to equate state-owned enterprises with government and public institutions. In this case, state-owned enterprises had no enthusiasm for more profits and operated in severe low efficiency, which caused its lack of self-production capability. On the other hand, due to lack of the incentives and the inability to solve the supervision problem, rural cooperatives had gradually become a sector with weak force and low agricultural output. As a result, the entire national economy gradually became undynamic and uncompetitive.

Fourth, the unbalanced development brought about economic stagnation and deterioration. In the absence of national factor endowment, the long-term strategy of prioritizing the development of heavy industry made economic stagnation and deterioration inevitable. Seen from the lessons, the practice, after decades of accumulation, not only failed to catch up with the developed countries, but even widened the distance between developing countries and developed countries. Ample evidence had been found from the painful cost by the Soviet Union, China, India, Brazil and Eastern European countries. However, Japan and the "Four Asian Tigers", which did not implement the "catch-up" strategy and gave priority to the factor endowment and comparative advantage of their own countries and regions, had successively achieved economic take-offs. The repeated comparisons enabled more and more countries to realize that the "catch-up" strategy of prioritizing the development of heavy industry, as a distorted industrial policy, was actually taking risks despite of various reasons for implementing it. Due to the severe ignorance of national factor endowments and comparative advantage, the artificial distorted law of value for being eager for quick success, and the suppression of non-state-owned economy, it was not reasonable to implement the "catch-up" strategy in the long-run even if all national powers were put to carry on. It should be gradually adjusted to improve the proportion of economic structure. Otherwise, the economic stagnation and deterioration will inevitably happen as time passes.

Although the strategy of prioritizing the development of heavy industry had once made the Soviet Union the only great power to compete with the United States after World War I, the decline and final collapse of the Soviet Union ironically revealed its failure to timely adjust the industrial development strategy. After building a developed system of heavy industry and a strong foundation for national industrialization, it failed to timely adjust its industrial development strategy from heavy industry to light industry and constantly improve people's living standards. Nor did the economic growth timely shift from extensive to intensive mode. In this sense, lessons mean wealth as they pay off decades later. Any mode has its historical background and timeliness. It is essential to reform once its advantages have come to the extreme, or the development strategy has completed its historical mission. In this sense, the reform should keep pace with the times and is an ongoing process.

Even if necessary to implement the strategy of prioritizing the development of heavy industry for a certain period of time, it did not mean "necessary and effective" for a long time. A long-term strategy of prioritizing the development of heavy industry and the ignorance of adjusting its factor endowments would ultimately lead to the distorted industrial structure. Thus, lack of harmonious economic growth was bound to cause the failure of industries to cooperate with each other. The industry standing head would fall into a dilemma of isolated development, hard to shoulder the responsibility for promoting the overall economic development. For one thing, achieving high accumulation and low consumption by restricting non-state-owned economy failed to resolve the problem of capital accumulation and regeneration, which accordingly failed to expand its reproduction in the long run and led to the extremely difficult life for people. For another, the long-term division between the governance of urban and rural areas and the acute backwardness of agriculture, rural areas and farmers failed to be alleviated for a long time. Thus, social contradictions gradually spread in many aspects and on many levels and social stability became a serious problem, which in turn repeatedly postponed the goal of realizing modernization. Therefore, it was not wise to keep the industrialization strategy of prioritizing the development of heavy industry immobilized.

On the whole, the strategy of economic development can be theoretically an alternative choice as it depends on the decision-makers. However, can it be possible as a substitute when it comes to the practice of different periods in different countries? Here, a distinction must be made. Take China's situation at that time for example, although another choice of development strategy was possible even with some base in the CPC, it seemed not comprehensive enough to only take economy into consideration, and perhaps more practical to take politics, economy, military and other aspects into consideration. In terms of "catching up with and surpassing the developed countries", all the countries that implemented the "catch-up" strategy failed to achieve economic growth and development. This conclusion is reasonable and should be learned from. However, China's economic growth and development was undoubtedly far more successful and comparable than that of major developing countries like India even before the reform and opening up in 1978.

From China's practical situation at that time, there seemed to be an alternative development strategy, as the development strategy of comparative advantage could be theoretically analyzed for the advantages of economically backward countries. However, under the circumstance when the world was still in the smoke of war, it remained unpredicted what was to happen even if the development strategy of comparative advantage was adopted. Therefore, even if an alternative development strategy was theoretically possible, it remained difficult to carry out the practice at the time and critically difficult to resolve the constraints. Obviously, implementing the strategy of prioritizing the development of heavy industry did not mean that all the issues could be resolved. In particular, when factor endowment is relatively deficient, first, priority should not be given to the long-term development of heavy industry and adjustments should be periodically made to ensure the balanced development of agriculture, industry and commerce, which is easy to recognize and hard to carry out; second, it is not simply assumed that implementing the strategy of prioritizing the development of heavy industry means implementing planned economy without some gaps and channels for other coexisted economic modes; third, even if there is free political and diplomatic environment, some conditions remain essential to resolve economic issues. Anyway, we have encountered some difficulties and failures on these issues.

In the era of global economic integration when peaceful development are the theme of today's world, each state has the environment to exert its comparative advantage for a long time. Therefore, the economic development should not improve in a rush for quick success, and its strategy should be chosen from its practical situation in line with the principle of comparative advantage to seek balanced development between agriculture, industry and commerce and form their own competitive advantages through the innovations in some areas. This is much more for China. In the era when the international community was in war or in the Cold War period, the political factors played more roles than the economic factors in doing this. For a major country like China, under the international environment at that time, it was realistic and necessary to implement the strategy of prioritizing the development of heavy industry. Anyway, choosing this strategy did not necessarily follow that it was correct all the time and forever. Nor did it follow that agriculture and commerce should be neglected or abandoned. This meant to adjust their deficiencies based on the change of political economy and social development. If not, even if the choice is correct for the economic development, it may go to the extreme.

1.2 Exploring arduously from planned economy to market economy

After the founding of People's Republic of China, China gradually built and implemented the system of socialist planned economy, which is a new system at that time. Although the system mode by Marxist classics and the Soviet Model could be for guidance and reference, the practical effects were actually not satisfactory and there were profound lessons. After the launching of reform and opening up in 1978, Deng Xiaoping, as the chief architect, played a crucial role in promoting the economic system restructuring from planned economy to market economy. The establishment of socialist market economy has overcome the deficiencies in a highly centralized planned economy, which is a major innovation in the economic system restructuring. It has stimulated the vitality of China's economy and is of great significance to build China's economic powerhouse.

1.2.1 Advancing the system from planned economy to market economy

In the traditional socialist theory, the socialist society should implement planned economy, since it can achieve "planned, proportionate" development to escape the periodical crises in the capitalist market economy. However, nearly 100 years of development of planned economy in the socialist system failed to realize the superiority from the theoretical deduction. In competing with the market economy adopted by those countries, the weaknesses and deficiencies of planned economy were becoming increasingly apparent. Therefore, most socialist countries made the common choice to reform socialist planned economy and take the path of market economy.

1.2.1.1 Discussions on the relationship between planning and market in the early days of the People's Republic of China

In China's economic academia, the first climax of discussions on planning and market as well as commodity and value under the socialist system was during the year of 1956 to 1957, just before and after the fundamental completion of Three Socialist Transformation, the socialist transformation of agriculture, handicraft industry and capitalist industry and commerce. At that time, the social and economic relations were undergoing major changes with socialist economy gradually acting as the sole economic base of the whole society. The theory of commodity production and commodity exchange explained in terms of various coexisted economic components, popular in the early 1950s, was challenged by the real economic life.[1] Among Chinese economists, there arose the discussions on whether commodity production and commodity exchange are compatible with socialist production relation and on the relationship between

[1] Zhang Zhuoyuan, *Historical Perspective on Chinese Economics (1949-2011)*, Beijing: China Social Sciences Press, 2012, pp. 60-62.

commodity production and socialist public ownership and distribution according to one's performance. Generally speaking, these discussions centered on the objective necessity of socialist commodity production and the relationship between planned economy and the law of value.

At that time, the economic theory in the book *Economic Problems of Socialism in the USSR* by Stalin prevailed in China. The discussions broke through the framework of traditional socialist economic theory and clearly put forward the views that was proved valid by later practice. The first is the view by Chinese economist Sun Yefang in 1956 that planning must be based on the law of value. In his view, the basic content and function of the law of value, that is, to promote the development of social productive forces, regulate social production or distribute social productive forces by determining the value through the average of socially necessary labor, are practicable in both socialist and communist societies. That is to say, the planning of socialist economic development must be based on the law of value. Thus, the role of the law of value in socialist economy was put to an unprecedented height, which widened the vision of understanding this issue. The second is the view by another Chinese economist Gu Zhun in 1957 that socialist economy regulates production by economic accounting. In his view, this regulation keeps the material rewards of laborers in extremely close contact with the profits and losses of enterprises, which makes price the main tool to regulate production. Due to the enterprises' spontaneous pursuit of production at a favorable price, it will lead to the spontaneous fluctuations of prices, which in turn regulates production. Therefore, it is the essential factor of socialist market economy to regulate production through the spontaneous fluctuations of prices. In this sense, Gu Zhun was said to be the first who advocated the theory of socialist market economy in China. The third is the view by Chen Yun, a leader of the state and the CPC at that time, that market regulation must be conducted in the socialist planned economy. He pointed out that a major proportion of national industrial and agricultural products were produced as planned and meanwhile some were freely produced in pace with market changes and within the state planning. That is to say, planned production is the main body of industrial and agricultural production, while free production within the state planning and in pace with market changes is a supplement to planned production. The free market, led by the state as a supplement to national market, is an integral part of the socialist unified market. What's more, some economists, from the perspective of the principle of material interests in the socialist society, demonstrated the existence of commodity relations in the socialist society, especially within the state ownership, which affirmed that the means of production being exchanged within the state ownership also belonged to commodities.

1.2.1.2 Discussions on commodity economy and law of value in the early phase of the reform and opening up

After the end of Cultural Revolution, China stepped into the era of reform and opening up, and the discussions on planning and market were activated again. In the middle of the year of 1977, articles were drafted on commodity production by the Finance and Trade Group of the State Council. In May 1978, the article about Refute the Fallacy of Four Gangs' Slandering Socialist Commodity Production organized and written by Deng Liqun was published in *People's Daily*. This was an important theoretical article about planned economy and market economy in the ideological and theoretical circle at the very beginning of reform. It analyzed the objective basis of developing socialist commodity production and commodity circulation and put forward the strategy of developing commodity production at the macro level.

In December 1977, a notification, issued by the State Council on convening meetings for promoting urban and rural commerce by learning from Daqing and Dazhai, clearly pointed out: The socialist commodity production and commodity circulation fundamentally differentiate from that of capitalist. It must be justifiable to promote socialist commodity production and develop commodity circulation in China. Then, series of articles were published in *People's Daily* to rectify the situation of mistaking commodity economy for capitalist economy.[1] Although the writing carried the trace of that era, it was typical enough to prove that the development of commodity economy was acceptable at that time.

In the good atmosphere of discussions on the standards of truth, Chinese economist Sun Yefang reiterated his view that "the law of value goes first before thousands of other economic laws". Another Chinese economist Xue Muqiao proposed that the advantage of market must be taken to activate circulation to facilitate long-distance trafficking. An article, entitled Acting with the Economic Law, Accelerating the Realization of Four Modernizations by Hu Qiaomu, demonstrated the objectivity of economic law and put forward many proposals on economic reforms.

In 1978, based on the needs of China's socialist modernization and the reality of

---

[1] Zheng Yougui, *The Economic History of the People's Republic of China (1949-2012)*, Beijing: Contemporary China Publishing House, 2016, p. 130.

the development of capitalist economy in the world, Chinese economist Zhuo Jiong rethought the commodity economy and the law of value and pointed out: Under the circumstance that capitalist relations of production no longer adapt to the development of productive forces, the capitalist production remains a considerable development and even faster than that in some countries which has changed capitalist private ownership. What is the reason behind it? Zhuo further pointed out: Under the capitalist system, there is neither the basic economic law of socialism nor the law of planned proportional development. Nevertheless, their productions develop further and faster than China's. What is the reason behind that? The only reason is that they attach importance to commodity production and the law of value in practice, while we are in great confusion as to the issues on commodity production and law of value. The problem goes to that some conclusions about Marxism are put into application as a rigid dogma rather than through a serious study.[1] In connection with the reality of China's socialist economy, Zhuo's research had made a complete investigation on Marx's demonstration on the law of value. As the slow development of socialist economy is due to inadequate understanding of commodity production and the law of value, the correct choice goes to vigorously develop commodity production. As Zhuo put it, "what is being done is to reform the economic management system in order to accomplish the four modernizations". To give full play to the law of value, the basic direction of economic reform was to recognize that what socialism implemented was the commodity system.

Reflecting on the lessons from the history, some Chinese economists realized that market economy must and could be implemented in socialism. Some economists then conducted in-depth discussions on the proposal of "planned economy as a main body with market economy as a supplement". In their view, this proposal put planned economy in opposition to market economy, as if planned economy excluded market economy and market economy worked without planning, which was not in accordance with the basic principles of Marx. In the socialist economy, planned economy and market economy are not opposed to each other, since socialist economy is a commodity economy, which is bound to have the existence of market that differentiates from free market in the capitalism, a market planned into the state's track.

In 1979, Lin Zili, another Chinese economist with active thoughts, put forward a preliminary proposal for economic reform in his article entitled Building Economic Forms and Economic Laws in the Socialism Period. In his view, the development of

---

[1] Zhuo Jiong, *On Socialist Commodity Economy*, Guangzhou: Guangdong People's Publishing House, 1981, p. 267.

commodity economy is a natural and historical process, which no one or not any social system can stop or restrict. Enterprises are business entity, namely commodity producers. Planned economy is a direct, imperative planning and must be transformed into an indirect, instructive planning through the market mechanism. Therefore, to implement commodity economy, the constraints of competition must be broken and a wide range of equal competition should prevail among producers.[1]

In 1979, Chinese economist He Wei pointed out in his article in *Economic Perspectives*: Commodity economy is the product of the development of human society at a certain historical stage. If the economic development of human society can be divided into three phases, namely natural economy, commodity economy and planned economy, then the whole world now remains in the phase of commodity economy.[2] He also pointed out: Natural economy had been backward and out of date, and the conditions for planned economy were not quite ready, especially in some developing socialist countries. If commodity economy was artificially restricted, the development of social productive forces would inevitably be hindered.

In 1980, Chinese economist Xue Muqiao made a speech on What on earth is revisionism? in a theoretical symposium. He put forward: Political economy and scientific socialism adopted the perspective of historical materialism to analyze the capitalist society; as to socialism, Karl Marx's socialism must be constantly developed, since Marx had no practical experience, and the view of historical materialism is needed to analyze the socialist economy and then to distinguish what is scientific socialism and what is revisionism. He further pointed out that the decision by the Third Plenary Session of the 11th CPC Central Committee to combine planned regulation with market regulation to promote the development of commodity economy and large-scale socialized production was conducive to building socialism. In the past, the development of commodity economy and market regulation was not recognized, but was criticized as revisionism for developing self-sufficient natural economy that impeded the economic development.[3]

During this period, the ideological and theoretical workers had heated discussions on planned economy and market economy. The most important theoretical research in the 1980s was embodied in the document The Preliminary Opinions on the Economic

---

[1] Chen Jing, *Economic Theory for Recent Twenty Years: Interviews with Eminent Economists*, Changsha: Hunan People's Publishing House, 1999, p. 381.

[2] *Selected Works of He Wei*, Taiyuan: Shanxi Economy Press, 1992, pp. 3-9.

[3] Xue Muqiao, *Some Current Problems of China's Economy*, Beijing: People's Publishing House, 1980.

System Restructuring proposed by the Office of Economic System Restructuring of the State Council in September 1980. The document clearly pointed out that "China's socialist economy at the current phase is commodity economy in which the public ownership of means of production is dominant and various economic components coexist. Under the circumstance that the public ownership of means of production is dominant, the principle and the development direction of China's economic system restructuring should meet the requirements of developing commodity economy and promoting socialized mass production, consciously apply the law of value and give full play to market regulation under the guidance of planning rather than merely planned regulation". This is an important document in the historical process of market-oriented reform in China. Different from the general research articles in academia, it was put forward by the specialized department of the State Council and discussed at the meetings attended by the first Party Secretaries of the provinces, autonomous regions and municipalities and held by the Central Committee of the Communist Party of China. Later, Xue Muqiao recalled and said that it was a pity that the idea of the reform had not yet been a consensus among the leaders in charge of economic developments at that time and had not been determined as a governmental decision.

1.2.1.3 Deng Xiaoping's talks on market economy

Seen from the public literature, Deng Xiaoping, as the important advocate and architect of China's socialist market economy, was surely aware that market economy can speed up national economic development, and the market-oriented reform in China's economy had its necessity and was in urgency, though he just made a few comparisons between planned economy and market economy.[1] From *The Chronicle of Deng Xiaoping and The Biography of Deng Xiaoping* compiled by the Party Literature Research Center of the CPC Central Committee, the whole process of Deng Xiaoping's contemplations on market economy can be reviewed.

In 1978, Deng wrote in a manuscript, "The contradiction between autonomy and state planning can be adjusted mainly through the law of value and the relationship between supply and demand." It can be seen that Deng had already attached importance to the role of market economy.

In 1979, Deng pointed out for several times, "It is certainly an incorrect argument that market economy exists only in a capitalist society and that there is only capitalist

[1] Zhong Xiangcai, *Contemporary China Economic Reform*, Shanghai: Shanghai Academy of Social Sciences Press, 2016, p. 117.

market economy. Why can't market economy be there in socialism?" It shows Deng's resolution to promote market economy in China at that time.

In 1980, Deng pointed out, "Planned regulation must be combined with market regulation". This shows Deng had a distinctive market economy in mind.

In 1982, Deng said: "How to solve the issue between the role of planning and that of market? If well solved, then it will be beneficial for economic development and vice versa." This shows Deng's urgent mood to promote the socialist market economy.

In 1984, Deng viewed that The CPC Central Committee's Decision on Economic Restructuring, which proposed "planned commodity economy based on the public ownership", was the first draft of socialist political economy, which combined the basic tenets of Marxism with Chinese socialist practice.

In 1985, Deng said in a talk with American entrepreneurs: "There is no fundamental contradiction between socialism and market economy. If planned economy is combined with market economy, it unleashes more productive forces and accelerates the economic development." This is an important exposition by Deng on China's development of market economy with more mature and firm thinking.

In 1987, Deng pointed out that "Both planning and market are methods, which can be utilized if they are beneficial to the development of productive forces. If it serves socialism, then it is social practice; and if capitalism, the capitalist practice." Clearly, both "planning" and "market" are regarded as means of economic development by Deng.

In 1989, Deng stressed, "The integrated regulation between planning and market must continue to be promoted and can not be changed. In practice, to make it more flexible, more planning can be made or strengthened in the period of adjustment and at another time more market regulation." It shows that Deng is pragmatic and flexible in striking a balance between the role of "planning" and that of "market" as long as it is beneficial for the economic development.

In 1990, Deng pointed out in a talk with the State central leaders in charge of development, "It should be theoretically understood that the differentiation between capitalism and socialism is not an issue between planning and market. The simple reason is that market economy can be implemented in socialism while planned or controlled economy can also be carried out in capitalism. It is not believed that implementing market economy refers to taking the path to capitalism. Both planning and market are needed since disengagement in market involves falling behind willingly without observing what happens in the world." What stated here is a warning that we will lag behind if we do not develop market economy.

In 1992, Deng Xiaoping pointed out in "South Tour Speeches", "The essential difference between socialism and capitalism does not lie in more 'planning' or more 'market'. Planned economy is not equal to socialism as capitalism also has 'planning'; while market economy is not equal to capitalism as socialism also has 'market'. Both planning and market are economic means. To gain the advantages of socialism compared with that of capitalism, it should absorb and draw upon all the civilized results created by human society, for example, all the advanced operation and management methods which reflect the law of modern socialized production in all the countries including the developed capitalist countries." The socialist market economy advocated by Deng, the chief architect of China's reform and opening up, not only ensures the correct direction of economic system restructuring, but vigorously promotes the theoretical research on market economy in China.

1.2.1.4 The CPC's literature on promoting efforts from planned economy to market economy

In the phase from the Third Plenary Session of the 11th CPC Central Committee in 1978 to the 12th CPC National Congress in 1982, traditional planned economy made a breakthrough. In 1982, the 12th CPC National Congress formally approved the mode of "planned economy with market regulation as a supplement". At this phase, market regulation was for the first time recognized to have a share and no longer excluded in the economic system. During this period, the rural household contract responsibility system was carried out, the autonomy of urban state-owned enterprises was reformed, the autonomy of economic entities was expanded and the price control was released. Gradually, a new pattern took shape, in which the government dominates in fostering the market and opened the door for what had long been restricted in planned economy. Generally speaking, it was the period when the development remained in the framework of planned economy, the government played the dominant role in regulating economy around its mandatory planning and the market mechanism could not play its due role.

In the phase from the 12th CPC National Congress in 1982 to the 14th CPC National Congress in 1992, both the government and the market alternatively played a dominant or subsidiary role. In 1984, the Third Plenary Session of the 12th CPC Central Committee for the first time proposed and made the "planning of commodity economy" clear, which pushed the relationship between planned economy and commodity economy from mutual opposition and exclusion to mutual unity. In a talk in February 1987, Deng Xiaoping denied the proposal of "planned" as a dominant role. In 1987, based on the "planning of commodity economy", the 13th CPC National Congress further proposed the "system of internal unity between planned economy and market economy", which weighted toward the role of market. In 1989, due to the severe international and domestic situations, such as the drastic change in the Soviet Union and East Europe, and the failure of price breakthrough, "planning" was reemphasized and the mechanism of economic operation which combined planned economy with market regulation gradually returned.[1] Generally speaking, it was the period when the mode of "government regulating market along with market guiding enterprises" was established, marking that China's market-oriented economic system restructuring was still on the way forward for development.

In the phase from the 14th CPC National Congress in 1992 to the Third Plenary Session of the 16th CPC Central Committee in 2003, it was generally stated in the documents on market economy that market played a fundamental role. The 14th CPC National Congress decided that the goal of economic system restructuring was to build socialist market economy, in which the market played a fundamental role in allocating resources under the macro regulation and control. The 15th CPC National Congress proposed that the market should play a fundamental role in allocating resources under the country's macro regulation and control. The 16th CPC National Congress proposed that market played a fundamental role in allocating resources to a greater extent. It was not until the Third Plenary Session of the 16th CPC Central Committee that the socialist market economy was announced to be fundamentally built. Generally speaking, it was the period when the reform of market system made major breakthroughs in many areas and the role of market was more prominent.

In the phase from the Third Plenary Session of the 16th CPC Central Committee to the 18th CPC National Congress in 2012, the socialist market economy has steadily improved. The understanding of the fundamental role of the market in allocating resources has been gradually deepened. From "better leverage the fundamental role of the market in allocating resources" proposed by the 17th CPC National Congress to "let the market play the decisive role in allocating resources and let the government play its functions better" proposed by the 18th CPC National Congress, it is clear that the government has gradually withdrawn from the planning of intervening the market and shifted to the role of macro regulation and control. In this phase, at the micro level, the

---

[1] Shi Liangping, Shen Kaiyan et al., *Research on the Market Model in the Primary Stage of Socialism*, Shanghai: Shanghai Academy of Social Sciences Press, 2016, p. 9.

reform of state-owned shareholding enterprises have been accelerated, and the institutional environment for the development of non-state-owned economy continued to improve. At the medium level, the capital market has been standardized and developed, the price system of productive factors continued to be reformed and perfected, and the protection of intellectual property rights has been gradually strengthened. At the macro level, the system of financial transfer payments and the system of public finance has gradually improved, the reform of the investment and financing systems continued to deepen, and steady progress has been made in transforming state-owned commercial banks into joint-stock commercial banks. In general, the market has become the basic mechanism of economic and productive operation, and dominated the function of prioritizing the resources allocation.

In November 2013, Decision of the Central Committee of the Communist Party of China on Some Major Issues Concerning Comprehensively Deepening the Reform, adopted by the Third Plenary Session of the 18th CPC Central Committee, proposed to let the market play the decisive role in allocating resources and let the government play its functions better. This is a major innovation and breakthrough in striking a balance between the role of the government and that of the market, which sets a new direction for the evolution of China's market mode. Comparatively speaking, the operation mechanism of the fundamental role of market is that the government regulates the market and the allocation of resources and the market allocates resources, while the operation mechanism of the decisive role of the market is that the market allocates resources and the government regulates the market. The latter emphasizes that the government has a free hand on the market's allocating resources and no longer puts a hand on allocating resources directly. Through years of efforts and practices, an effective form of public ownership, especially state-owned ownership had been explored—mixed ownership economy.

1.2.2 Historical progress of developing China's market economy

Over the past 40 years of reform and opening up, China has theoretically and practically adhered to the socialist market economy, firmly advanced the great cause of reform and opening up and fully motivated the enthusiasm and creativity of hundreds of millions of its people. A great historical impressive transition has been made from the highly centralized planned economy to the vigorous and vital socialist market economy and from being a largely closed society to one that is open to the world in all respects.

This has greatly unleashed and developed productive forces. A prosperous socialist China, oriented toward modernization, the world and the future, has stood tall and firm in the world stage. [1]

1.2.2.1 Fundamentally establishing the system of socialist market economy

The socialist market economy can mainly manifest itself as follows. First, the basic economic system has been built in the primary stage of socialism. The ownership structure evolved from the ownership by the whole people and collective ownership in overwhelming superiority, to a pattern in which maintains public ownership as the dominant role and promotes the common development of enterprises under diverse forms of ownership. The public ownership economy has been unswervingly strengthened and actively developed with diverse forms, and its vitality, control power and influence have been enhanced through deepening reform. Also, the development of non-state-owned economy, such as the individual sector and private sector, has been unswervingly encouraged, supported and guided, and the proportion of the non-state-owned economy has been greatly increased. Second, the vitality of microeconomic entities of enterprises has been remarkably strengthened. The majority of state-owned enterprises was transformed into joint-stock enterprises, gradually building the modern enterprise system to change the operational mechanisms and playing as the main entities of market competition with independent management and responsible for their own profits, losses and risks. Then, market access was expanded, and the market environment for fair competition was created to enable non-state-owned enterprises to develop rapidly. Third, a modern market system has gradually taken shape. The market played an increasingly important role in allocating resources. The reform of price system continued to improve, and a mechanism that market determines price was fundamentally developed. Fourth, a pattern of all-round opening up to the outside world has taken shape. The government adheres to implementing a win-win strategy of opening up, pursues development with doors wide open, fully utilize domestic and international markets and resources, actively expands import and export trade, continues to attract foreign investments and makes great efforts to develop overseas investments. Thus, it is making new ground in pursuing opening up on all fronts in a comprehensive, wide-ranging and multilevel way. With the continuous improvement of open economy in China, the Chinese market has become an important part of the world market. Fifth, the

---

[1] Wei Liqun, "The Rich Connotation and Great Contribution of Deng Xiaoping's Theory of Socialist Market Economy", *Journal of Chinese Academy of Governance*, 2014 (5).

macro regulation and control system has continued to improve. Through constantly deepening reform in planning, fiscal, financial and investment, the macro regulation and control has been transformed from direct regulation and control to indirect regulation and control, which mainly utilizes economic and legal means along with necessary administrative means to promote the balance of economic aggregate and structural adjustment and the coordinated development between economy and society. Then, a relatively healthy system of macro regulation and control under the market economy and opening up has basically taken shape.

1.2.2.2 Remarkable achievements in building socialist modernization

Since the reform and opening up, China has gradually implemented the mechanism of market economy. In 1992, the socialist market economy was further established as the goal of economic system restructuring, making it clear that developing a socialist economy with Chinese characteristics meant developing a socialist market economy. With the continuous advancement of market-oriented reform, China's economy has taken off rapidly, with an average annual economic growth of 9.6 percent from 1979 to 2015, which created a new miracle of long-term rapid economic growth in human society. It has proved correct and effective to develop the socialist market economy in accordance with China's national conditions. In this context, the theory of socialist market economy has become the main pillar of socialist political economy with Chinese characteristics. Since the core of the theory of socialist market economy is the integration of socialism with market economy, it naturally becomes the main line of political economics of socialism with Chinese characteristics.[1] The building and improvement of socialist market economy has greatly stimulated the great potentials of economic and social development. Thus, great progress has been made in economy, politics, culture, society and ecological civilization in all areas and at all levels, comprehensive national strength has been sharply developed, people's living standards have greatly improved, and its international status and influence have significantly increased. Since the reform and opening up, the national economy has maintained a rapid growth with its economic aggregate ranking second in the world, which creates an unparalleled miracle in the history of world economy. China has grown into the largest trading country in goods, the second largest in foreign direct investment and exporter of capital, and ranked first in foreign exchange reserves. Infrastructure such as

---

[1] Zhang Zhuoyuan, "To Realize the Organic Combination of Socialism and Market Economy", *People's Daily*, Nov. 21, 2016.

transportation, energy, telecommunications, and water conservancy has made substantial progress. A modern industrial system with a wide range of sectors has been basically established. The output of over 200 important industrial products, including steel, coal, cement, and cotton cloth, now ranks first in the world. Due to the vigorous rise of high-tech industries and the continuous construction of developing an innovative country, a large number of scientific and technological results with independent intellectual property rights have been achieved. The proportion of the service sector has significantly increased, and the level of information technology in the national economy and society has continued to improve. Urban and rural areas have been greatly improved, and people's lives have greatly improved. With 7 percent of the world's arable land, China has been able to feed one fifth of the world's population, lifting over 700 million people out of poverty. The implementation of socialist market economy has also greatly promoted the development of democracy, the rule of law, culture and education, social construction, ecological progress and other fields. These achievements fully demonstrate the powerful force by implementing the socialist market economy, and proves that the reform of establishing a socialist market economic system is completely correct.

1.2.3 Internal logic between China's market economy and building an economic powerhouse

Xi Jinping pointed out, "Both theory and practice have proved that the allocation of resources by the market is the most effective means to this end. It is a general rule of the market economy that the market decides the allocation of resources, and a market economy in essence is one in which the market determines resource allocation."[1] Seen from the course of rising economic powers in the world, they all rely on the development of market economy to achieve economic rise. Market is the most efficient way to allocate resources. It is due to this reason that through the operation of price mechanism, competition mechanism and interest mechanism, it can stimulate the internal vitality, endogenous momentum and economic creativity for economic development to the maximum, thus providing strong drive for a state to achieve the strategic goal toward building an economic powerhouse.

1.2.3.1 Market providing internal vitality for building an economic powerhouse

As mentioned above, the price mechanism, the competition mechanism and the

[1] Xi Jinping, *The Governance of China*, Beijing: Foreign Languages Press, 2014, p. 84.

interest mechanism can play a full role under the market economy. These three mechanisms can well support the general law and basic regulations of market economy, such as the law of "the supply and demand determines the price and the price adjusts to supply and demand", the law of "survival of the fittest" and the law of "maximizing the interest of the individual". It is these general laws and basic regulations that can fundamentally stimulate the internal vitality of national economic development, ensure the optimal allocation of social resources, which ultimately promotes the realization of the strategic goal toward building China's economic powerhouse.

Generally speaking, an economic powerhouse has its connotation and features in six aspects. First, it has an economic scale ranking top in the world and higher per capita income. Second, it has a strong innovation capability in science and technology and masters the core technology. Third, it has a high-level and ecological industrial structure that occupies a favorable position in the global industrial division of labor. Fourth, it has a high degree of urbanization and forming a number of influential urban agglomerations in the world. Fifth, it has a freely interchangeable international currency and a developed and stable financial system. Sixth, it has an important and influential status in the international economic system.[1]

To realize the connotation and features of an economic powerhouse, the most important way is to stimulate the development vitality of national economic entities. In fact, under the market economy in which market can play a decisive role, each economic entity is free in the market, where the environment can provide equal competitive opportunities and access threshold, and price signals can reflect the scarcity of resources and the supply and demand of commodity at any time with flexible transmission mechanism. Thus, under the guidance of price mechanism, competition mechanism and profit mechanism, the internal vitality of each economic entity can be constantly stimulated to create social wealth, which can optimize the allocation of resources. This is the exact mechanism that gives full play to the decisive role of the market and the internal vitality of economic development needed to build an economic powerhouse.

In an economy where the market plays a decisive role, the utilization and distribution of productive factors are fully guided by the price mechanism, competition mechanism and interest mechanism, and the access threshold of competitive production territories is fair and equal for all operators. Thus, productive factors, such as labor force,

---

[1] Wei Liqun, "Development Strategy for the Transformation from Largest Economy to Economic Powerhouse", *Xinhua Digest*, 2013 (18).

capital, information and technology, can flow freely and be flexibly allocated among various industries. In this process, this economy is bound to have strong vitality and competitiveness in promoting technological innovation, optimizing industrial structure and building a developed financial system.[1]

1.2.3.2 Market providing endogenous momentum for building an economic powerhouse

The term "endogenous momentum" stems from the "human capital spillovers" model proposed by Robert E. Lucas Jr. and the "knowledge spillovers" model proposed by Paul Romer in the theory of New Economic Growth. The core concept of "endogenous power" entails two connotations: one is technological innovation progress and the other is human capital accumulation. It can be safe to say that the continuous technological innovation progress and the accumulation of abundant human capitals is an important way to ensure the realization of the strategic goal of being an economic powerhouse.

From the perspective of the progress of technological innovation, the course of rising economic powers in the world has proved eloquently that innovations in science and technology play an important role in the rising of an economic power. It is a requisite path for a state to rise in the world by relying on the continuous scientific and technological innovations and constantly transforming them into productive forces. With the steam engine invented by Watt as the lead, Britain set off a tidal wave of technological inventions and improvements in the 18th century, which laid a solid technical foundation for its industrialization and economic rise. With Edison's inventions as the lead, the United States became the birthplace of electrical revolution in the 19th century as well as electronic information revolution in the 20th century. The United States had built a sound system and mechanism to encourage technological innovations and scientific and technological inventions, and various inventions sprung up like the bamboo shoots. With its strong scientific and technological strengths, the United States had taken the lead in the global economy. Relying on the technological introduction, improvement and innovation, Japan had built an independent scientific and technological system, by which it rapidly caught up with and surpassed the advanced countries.

When a careful analysis is made on the process how these economic powerhouses achieve technological innovations, it can be found that market also plays a decisive role in the technological innovations. Whether it is the invention of British steam machine

[1] Gao Shangquan, "Let the Market Play a Decisive Role in Allocating Resources", *Frontline*, 2013 (12).

in the 18th century, or it is that of American electromotor in the 19th century, the starting point is to enable the enterprises to raise the productivity of labor and win more market shares and profits in the fierce market competition, which inspires the inventors' internal motives of personal wisdom and intellectual to gain the success of their inventions by the continuous experiments and efforts, and eventually brings about the industrial revolution in the whole industry and the substantial growth of economic and social wealth. Under the modern market economy, the best way for a state to achieve the progress of technological innovations is to improve the market-oriented mechanism for technological innovations, and give full play to the market's guiding role in the direction of technological research and development, the choice of routes, the price of factors and in allocating various innovative factors.

From the perspective of human capital accumulation, the theory of human capital put forward by the American economist Theodore William Schultz in the 1960s had been widely valued by western countries. The United States, Japan, Germany and other economic powerhouses all rely on huge investments in human capital to create a high-level education system and cultivate high-quality talents, thus providing steady stream of drives for the scientific and technological innovation and strong supports and necessary conditions for their economic rise. Thus, the United States became an economic powerhouse as well as a country rich in human resources, taking the lead in the number of high-level universities and research institutions in the world. One secret of Japan's rebuilding its economy from the ruins after World War II was that the Japanese government attached great importance to education and the investment and accumulation of human capital, which laid a foundation for its economic take-off. Relying on the government's strong investments in education, Germany made rapid development of basic science and applied science after the Second World War, which provided talents and intellectual supports for its economic rise.

It is true that market plays a decisive role in allocating resources. It should be said that all economic powerhouses value the role of market mechanism in accumulating human capitals. Take the United States for example, in its higher education system, Harvard University, Chicago University, Stanford University are all established by social forces, and fully leverage the decisive role of market mechanism in allocating human resources, oriented to market demand in talent cultivation, education funds and student employment. Of course, adhering to the decisive role of market in accumulating human capitals does not mean denying the important role of the government. On the whole, it is necessary to adhere to the principle of public welfare in education, improve the systems of government subsidy, government purchase service, student loan, fund reward and donation incentive, encourage social forces to run education, and guide the social capital and market forces into the field of education in diverse way. All of these can not only provide important guiding principles for the market to play the decisive role and the government to play better role, but ensure vigorous institutional supports for accumulating human capitals toward building an economic powerhouse.

1.2.3.3 Market providing economic creativity for building an economic powerhouse

Giving full play to the decisive role of the market in allocating resources means allowing all elements such as labor, knowledge, technology, management and capital to fully function, bringing forth all surging sources of social wealth, and full exerting the creativities conducive to the economic prosperity. Generally speaking, the economic development of a country depends on the productive factors such as resource endowments, science and technology and human capitals. However, without a strong guarantee for systems and mechanisms, the productive factors would be unable to play due roles in economic efficiency. The course of rising economic powers shows that the innovation of system and mechanism in the economic and social development is not only an importance aspect in stimulating economic creativity, but also a prerequisite for a state to rise.

From the history of world economy, whether Portugal's innovation of fund mechanism for maritime exploration or Spain's reform of the system of individual property rights, whether Dutch's innovation of monetary and financial system or the UK's reform of the democratic political system by the Glorious Revolution, and whether the United States' establishment of free market economy or Germany's exploration for social market economy, they well prove that the ongoing reform and innovation of institutional system is one important inspiration of the rising of an economic power.[1] Thus, the focus on the reform of system and mechanism is to fully leverage the decisive role of the market in allocating resources. Only in this way can it provide the economic creativity needed by building an economic powerhouse.

Currently, as the international flow of capital, goods, technology, information and services is accelerating, all the countries are adjusting their industrial structure. The world's economic powerhouses are accelerating efforts to transfer traditional industries and modern service industries to developing countries with better labor quality and

---

[1] Wei Liqun, "Development Strategy for the Transformation from Largest Economy to Economic Powerhouse", *Xinhua Digest*, 2013 (18).

lower costs. Any country who develops market economy can obtain more productive factors from the outside to upgrade their industrial structure and promote their technological progress. Under this background, the gain from external factors of production by a country or region can not only effectively allocate various domestic productive factors, but significantly stimulate the creativity of the domestic economy and promote the growth of economic wealth.

Therefore, under the modern market economy, a high-level and ecological industrial structure in a country can be effectively created by stimulating the creativity that is needed for economic development, thus upgrading the transformation of its economic structure and helping occupy a favorable position in the global industrial division of labor system. By participating in the division of labor in the global value chain, it can significantly improve the economic aggregate and per capita income level of a country or a region, which is obviously an important way for an economy to become powerful.

1.2.3.4 Firmly implementing market economy in the era of big data

The Internet is now fully integrated into human society in every corner at all levels from the micro to the macro level. All human behaviors and activities in the traditional society, including politics, economy, society, culture and personal communication, have been changed and reconstructed due to the emergence of the Internet. When the network society reconstructs the whole social structure, economic activities are greatly reconstructed and changed as the main type of human social activities as well.[1] Due to the big data generated by the Internet, some people renewed the hope for planned economy, feeling that the conditions for promoting new planned economy were gradually available.

In the traditional economy, economic system can be generally divided into planned economy and market economy. How will big data affect the two economic modes? Some believed that big data has enabled human beings to enter the era of the interconnection among one another, that the ability to reprocess data was far more than that in the past, and that the understanding of the world should be then lifted to a new height for the reason that big data can make prediction and planning possible. Therefore, it was suggested that planned economy and market economy should be redefined, and market economy not be necessarily better than planned economy.[2] From the search in the CNKI, the similar views were suggested several years ago, which was criticized by many

[1] He Zhe, "The Network Economy: Beyond Planning and Market", *Comparative Economic & Social Systems*, 2016 (2).

[2] See Ma Yun's Speech at the China International Big Data Industry Expo in Guiyang, May 26, 2017.

economists in China. For example, Wu Jinglian pointed out that planned economy cannot be implemented even with the help of big data.[1] Zhang Weiying believed that it was completely wrong to have the idea that the emergence of big data made planned economy feasible again, because the data-based decisions were made only by science instead of by entrepreneurs.[2] So, how to understand this issue?

In the 20th century, planned economy was neither endogenous nor unique to China. As an economic system that has once been widely practiced by the socialist countries in the world, it has its own ideological source and theoretical support. The planned management in social economy was first proposed by the Utopian socialists in Europe, and became an important part of this trend of thought. Marxist classical writers critically inherited the ideological achievements of Utopian socialism. They did not elaborate on how to implement planned economy in socialism, but obviously advocated the tendency to replace the economic operation of capitalism with planned system. With the occurrence of the capitalist economic crisis in the 1920s, the free competitive market economy was questioned, and the Soviet planned economy had achieved effectiveness. This made planned economy recognized by the socialist countries.

After the founding of the People's Republic of China in 1949, its economic system was not planned economy at the very beginning. From the recovery of national economy destroyed by the war, to the implementation of socialist planned economy, there experienced the evolution of several economic developments and decision-makings. Justin Yifu Lin et al. believe that as long as the strategy of prioritizing the development of heavy industry is implemented, planned economy would come into being based on China's natural endowment and the force of planned economy would naturally phase out the market mechanism.[3] In terms of economic decision-makings and its implementation, the decision-makings by the central planning departments were based on the understandings of local information. Due to the one-sided, deviated and lagged information collection, coupled with many links and long chains of information transmission, as well as off-site decision-makings and the delay of implementing plans, it was difficult to realize the idea of scientifically planned development in proportion. In order to realize the "catch-up" development strategy, China had adopted the highly centralized mandatory planned

[1] See Wu Jinglian's Speech at SAIF-CAFR Distinguished Speaker Series, Apr. 19, 2017.

[2] See Zhang Weiying's Speech at the Opening Ceremony for EMBA, National School of Development at Peking University, Apr. 28, 2017.

[3] Justin Yifu Lin et al., *China's Miracle: Development Strategy and Economic Reform*, Shanghai: Shanghai SDX Joint Publishing Company, 1994.

economy, which excluded market mechanism for quite a long period.

In this system, the decision-making structure was centrally controlled, and the state allocated economic resources according to a detailed plan, focusing scarce resources on the key sectors as a priority for development by the country. In terms of dynamic structure, the state directly issued plans mainly through the various administrative organizations to the economic activities of various departments and enterprises, implementing the principle of equalitarianism distribution and relying on the administrative forces to implement the strategy of national economic development. In terms of information structure, the vertical transmission of planned orders was implemented, so that all economic activities were on the track of planning and enterprise behaviors were not restricted by market signals. Affiliated by the government's administration, state-owned enterprises had soft budget constraints with no independent interest goals and management, did not bear the consequence of decision-makings, which resulted in passively executing the planed orders and completing the output value index.[1] Although planned economy can pull social resources together for economic development, that is, pull forces together to achieve the goal, however, in the long run, this highly centralized administrative intervention would make the whole economy lose its creativity with too much rigid planning that enterprises had no independence and low efficiency and were lack of competition and vitality.

Due to the irreparable deficiency in the information collection of planned economy, it affects the decision-makings and leads to the low efficiency of allocating resources and the slow development of national economy. This is the fundamental reason for China's reform of planned economy. In the new era, some people hope to make up for this deficiency through the function of big data and abandon the chaos of market economy to carry out "new planned economy". Some even hope to associate this "new planning" with the "new planned economy" proposed by American and British scholars which reconstructed market models based on computer technology. In our opinion, planned economy has its deviation and lag in the information sources, as well as its unscientific calculation and even deficiencies, and its essence is mainly an economy of power, that is, a system of power control that the state dominates all economic resources and organizations. Here, the key that planned economy was reviewed lies in that planned

---

[1] Yang Ruilong, "The Relationship between Government and Market under the Logic of Political Economy of Socialism with Chinese Characteristics". In *15 Lectures on Socialist Economics with Chinese Characteristics*, Beijing: China Renmin University Press, 2016, pp. 96-97.

economy is a complete institutional arrangement instead of a pure economic model or an economic operation mechanism, no matter whether east European economists realized planned economy through theoretical calculation or through big data.

The essence of planned economy is the total control of power. It is meant that people have no power to control the economy, and nor have the society and enterprises. The biggest difference between market economy and planned economy is that people can gain the power of economy under the market economy, and so it is with the society and the enterprises. The practice of market economy in many countries has proved that the communities that acquire its power have the capacity to create. It is pointed out by some scholars that the more scientific, big data and detailed the plan is, the more mandatory it is. Big data can just meet some conditions for economic development, making decisions more scientific and information of decision-makings more accurate. It is by no means sufficient and necessary for the development of planned economy. In a modern society, to develop economy, what really counts is competition since it brings innovation and innovation reversely brings development. Only market economy can provide this environment. To sum up, it stands scrutiny that planned economy becomes feasible again in the era of big data.

1.3 Reform and opening up boosting China's development from a major economy to a powerful economy

Reform and opening up defines contemporary China and is the most prominent feature of the Communist Party of China. Deng Xiaoping, the chief architect of China's reform and opening up, pointed out that it was China's second revolution and China's development should not be separated from the world. This is the most important practical viewpoint of Deng's thought of reform and opening up, which has long-term guiding significance for China's development.[1] General Secretary Xi Jinping stressed that reform and opening up was an important approach for the Party and the people to stride ahead to go along with the times, the only path to uphold and develop socialism with Chinese characteristics, a game-changing move in making China what it is today, and a game-changing move for us to achieve China's Two Centenary Goals and its great

---

[1] Xu Yaotong, "Deng Xiaoping's Thought of Reform and Opening up", *Studies on Socialism with Chinese Characteristics*, 2014 (4).

national rejuvenation.[1] Following the path of reform and opening up firmly is a great process of promoting China's development from a major economy to a powerful economy.

1.3.1 Historical position of the reform and opening up

Since the Third Plenary Session of the 11th CPC Central Committee in 1978, China has achieved rapid economic growth due to the domestic reform and opening up to the outside world. Through over 40 years of the reform and opening up, a firm focus has been kept on the economic development as the central task and on unleashing and developing the productive forces. China's GDP has grown from RMB367.9 billion to RMB82.7 trillion in 2017, with an average annual growth of 9.5% in real terms, much higher than that of the world of around 2.9% in the same period. Its GDP accounted for 15.2% of the world, up from 1.8% at the beginning of the reform and opening up. Over the years, China has contributed more than 30% to global growth. It is fair to say that in the human history there has rarely been seen anywhere else in the world for such a high-speed or rapid growth of development in such a large country for a long period.[2] Now, China has become the world's second largest economy, the largest manufacturing country, the largest trading nation in goods and services, the second largest consumer market, and the second largest in foreign capital inflow. China's foreign exchange reserves have ranked first in the world consecutively for many years, and the foreign direct investment second with real GDP per capita of more than US$12,000. All these achievements attribute greatly to the reform and opening up, which has injected vitality into China's development and added impetus to building China's economic powerhouse. Since the reform and opening up, over 700 million Chinese population has been alleviated out of poverty, and the life quality and standards of over 1.4 billion Chinese people has been greatly improved. It took just a few decades for China to complete the development course that developed countries took several hundred years to do.

1.3.1.1 Reform and opening up leading to the path to accelerating China's economic development

Deng Xiaoping pointed out that the reform and opening up has showed a path to

---

[1] Xi Jinping, *Speech at the Conference Celebrating the 40th Anniversary of Reform and Opening Up*, Beijing: People's Publishing House, 2018.

[2] Justin Yifu Lin, "The Belt and Road Initiative and Free Trade Zone: New Measures of China's Reform and Opening Up", *New Economy*, 2016 (34), pp. 5-9.

building socialism with Chinese characteristics. This exposition suggests that the path of socialism with Chinese characteristics is the Chinese path to the development, which is different from the modernization development path of the western for hundreds of years. It provides an alternative path for developing countries that account for the vast majority of the world's population to realize modernization. Over 40 years of reform and opening up has made China the world's second largest economy and striving to build itself into an economic power. Those far-sighted men in the West have mostly seen this fact and regarded China's reform and opening up as one of the most important events in the world history between the late 20th century and the early 21st century. The reform and opening up has widened the path to building China's economic powerhouse. Looking back at the historical process of the reform and opening up, from rural areas to cities and from the economy to all other areas, a great historical impressive transition has been made from the highly centralized planned economy to the vigorous and vital socialist market economy. Opening to the outside world has continued to expand. A great historical impressive transition has been made from the building of special economic zones and new economic zones to free trade zones, from the large-scale "bringing in" to the great stride of "going global", and from being a largely closed society to one that is open to the world in all respects. All demonstrate that a right path leads a country and a nation to a bright future, and its people to happiness. It is the reform and opening up that leads China to the right path of economic development, and has created a miracle in the human history of economic and social development. China's economic aggregate has risen by several major steps and its comprehensive national strength has greatly improved. On the whole, Chinese people have enjoyed a moderately prosperous life. Both urban and rural areas have taken on a new look. The development path of China's reform and opening up was different from free mode of capitalist development in the West. Taking the economic development as the central task, China has adhered to the Four Cardinal Principles and the reform and opening up, and constantly unleashed and developed the productive forces. Meanwhile, it has gradually achieved common prosperity for all the people and promoted all-round development of the people.

1.3.1.2 Reform and opening up playing a major role in promoting China's poverty eradication

The essential requirement of socialism is to eradicate poverty, improve people's well-being and gradually realize common prosperity for all people. Since the reform and opening up in 1978, China has carried out large-scale poverty alleviation through development, lifted 700 million rural people out of poverty, which had made great achievements and attracted worldwide attention with a glorious chapter in the history of anti-poverty. The reform and opening up has enabled China to address the issues of poverty gradually. Starting from the approval and transfer of the Minutes of the National Conference on Rural Work in 1982, the central government has consecutively issued the No.1 Document for six years, affirming that the household contract responsibility system is a great creation of Chinese farmers under the leadership of the Party. The reform of household contract responsibility system has greatly aroused the initiative of hundreds of millions of farmers. It is a great achievement that agricultural production has rapidly increased, and the living conditions of the poor population in rural areas have greatly improved. In May 1986, the first plenary session of the State Council's leading group for overall development of poverty-stricken areas put forward how to meet the basic needs of the vast majority of people in the poverty-stricken areas during the Seventh Five-year Plan (1986-1990) period. It clarified 10 points on implementing the new economic development mode in the poverty-stricken areas, which focus was on the organized, planned, large-scale development-driven poverty alleviation in China. Thus, a great battle against poverty alleviation for hundreds of millions of poor people has officially started in China. Since 1994, China has formulated, promulgated and implemented the Priority Poverty Alleviation Program (1994-2000) and the Outline of Development-driven Poverty Alleviation in Rural Areas (2001-2010). By 2010, except that a small number of social security targets, people living in extreme poverty areas with poor natural environments, and some disabled people, the problem of food and clothing for the impoverished rural population has been basically solved, which fulfilled years of aspirations of rural people in poor areas to have enough to eat and warm clothing. This has played an important role in promoting China's economic development, ethnic unity, consolidation of border areas and social stability. In 2011, the Outline of Development-driven Poverty Alleviation in Rural Areas (2011-2020) was promulgated and implemented in China. It raised the standards of poverty alleviation and set out the goals of "Two Assurances and Three Guarantees"[1], thus entering a new stage of alleviating poverty through development. Since the 18th CPC National Congress, the Central Committee has incorporated the work of alleviating poverty through development

[1] It refers to assurances of adequate food and clothing, and guarantees of access to compulsory education, basic medical services and safe housing for impoverished rural residents.

into the Four-pronged Comprehensive Strategy[1] and put it in a more prominent position as the key work to achieve the First Centenary Goal. Xi Jinping attaches great importance to the development-driven poverty alleviation. He has conducted numerous investigations in impoverished rural areas, delivered a series of important speeches on development-driven poverty alleviation, and put forward important theories and practical issues, such as targeted poverty alleviation, poverty alleviation through an effective approach, endogenous poverty alleviation, and the reform and innovation of mechanisms of poverty alleviation. This formed the thought of the development-driven poverty alleviation in the new era. Meanwhile, the 19th CPC National Congress stressed the commitment to ensuring and improving people's livelihood through development, carrying out intensive poverty alleviation efforts, ensuring that all people have a greater sense of gain from joint development and shared development, and promoting all-round human development and common prosperity for all people. Over the past 40 years of reform and opening up, China has embarked on a path to poverty reduction with Chinese characteristics, which adheres to the reform and opening up, the government's leadership, the open policy of poverty alleviation, mobilizing the participation of the whole society and the combination of inclusive and preferential policies.

1.3.1.3 Reform and opening up creating a new model for the peaceful development of major countries

As a super-large country, China faces unprecedented contradictions, difficulties and pressures that have never experienced by the human development of modernization. However, China did not follow the path of foreign expansion or war as other rising powers did, but has embarked on a new path of peaceful development, which the scale and speed of development have caught the worldwide attention. In terms of international trends, the West has dominated the historical basis of the past 500 years. However, China's development is now changing the world's pattern at many levels. The global political and economic center gravity will gradually shift to Asia and the Pacific region. China's rapid development is breaking the stereotype that western civilization is monistic. The western model that was regarded as the only one to realize industrialization had met the challenge of the path of socialism with Chinese characteristics. All of these has been achieved in a state of peaceful development. By pursuing open, cooperative and win-win development and expanding common interests

[1] That is, comprehensively build a moderately prosperous society, comprehensively deepen reform, comprehensively implement the rule of law and comprehensively strengthen Party self-governance.

with other parties, China has blazed a new path of working together in common cause for win-win cooperation. Through the launching of reform and opening up, China has resolved the basic social contradictions between relations of production and productive forces, and the superstructure and economic base, the relationship that exists in the socialist society as well, thus finding the inexhaustible driving force for social progress and development. Since the launching of reform and opening up, Chinese leaders have repeatedly declared that China will never seek hegemony or engage in expansion, even if it achieves national rejuvenation, reaches the level of developed countries and becomes a real world power. Since the 19th CPC National Congress, the CPC Central Committee with Xi Jinping at its core has stressed that we must adhere to promote building a community with a shared future for mankind, coordinate the domestic and international situations, unswerving follow the path of peaceful development, and pursue the strategy of opening up for win-win results. We must adhere to the correct concept of justice and benefit and set up a new concept of common, integrated, cooperative and sustainable security. We must seek the prospects of an open, innovative, inclusive and mutually beneficial development, promote exchanges among civilizations that seek harmony without uniformity and inclusiveness, and build an ecosystem that respects nature and promotes green development. We must keep committed to building the world peace, contributing to the global development and upholding the international order. All of these have boosted China's building an economic power in a peaceful development environment.

1.3.1.4 Reform and opening up strengthening the confidence in developing a powerful economy

To achieve the great rejuvenation of the Chinese nation, we must maintain firm confidence in the path, theory, institution and culture. Xi Jinping pointed out that in today's world, the Communist Party of China, the People's Republic of China and the Chinese nation have the most reason to be confident if any political party, country or nation can be. The path of socialism with Chinese characteristics is the only path to socialist modernization and a better life for the people. The theory of socialism with Chinese characteristics is the right theory to guide the Party and the people to realize national rejuvenation, a scientific one that stands at the forefront of the times and keeps pace with the times. The system of socialism with Chinese characteristics provides the fundamental institutional guarantee for the progress and development in contemporary China, since it is an advanced system with distinctive Chinese characteristics, obvious institutional strengths and strong self-improvement capacity. All of these stem from the great reform and opening up, which ensures China a correct path of development. Through pushing forward reform and opening up, China will be able to overcome difficulties and achieve more success on the journey to realize the great rejuvenation of the Chinese nation.

1.3.2 Reform and opening up entering a new historical stage

Since the socialism with Chinese characteristics has entered a new era, the CPC Central Committee with Xi Jinping at its core has unswervingly consolidated and developed socialism with Chinese characteristics, held courage to practice and innovate, deepened the understanding of the laws that underlie the Party's governance, the development of socialism, and the evolution of human society, and formed a series of new concepts, new ideas, and new strategies for governance. It provides theoretical and practical guidance for deepening reform and opening up, and accelerating the socialist modernization under the new historical conditions.[1] In recent years, though confronting a complex international environment and the arduous tasks of reform and development, the Party has led the people to advancing reform and opening up across the board, and sparing coordinated efforts to promote economic, political, cultural, social and ecological progress, thus creating a new pattern for the cause of socialism with Chinese characteristics.

1.3.2.1 More emphasis on the top-level design for reform and opening up

A major issue that has been repeatedly stressed by the central government in recent years is to advance reform and opening up with top-level design and unswervingly deepen reform and opening up. Deepening reform and opening up is an extremely complex and systematic project, as it involves not only the productive forces and relations of production, but the economic base and superstructure. It is a complex and arduous task, especially in the stage of tackling tough issues head-on. To achieve this, it needs the top-level design, overall planning and coordination to make reforms more relevant, integrated and coordinated. In order to better the overall design and planning of the reform and opening up, the Third Plenary Session of the 18th CPC Central Committee adopted the Decision of the CPC Central Committee on Some Major Issues Concerning Comprehensively Deepening the Reforms, which set out the strategic objectives, major principles, major tasks, major measures, as well as the roadmap and timetable for comprehensively deepening the reform and opening up. Xi Jinping has

[1] Wei Liqun, "Reform and Opening Up Broadens the Road of China's Development", *Qiushi*, 2015 (21).

particularly stressed the needs to strengthen the top-level design for the reform and opening up, which is dialectically integrated with cautious advance. The thought of Xi Jinping's top-level design has exerted an important influence on advancing the reform and opening up correctly. From a practical perspective, the top-level design means reform itself and that the central government must have authority while the local government must set up the concept of "coordinating all the activities of the nation like moves in a chess game." This is undoubtedly correct. The central government must keep the reform in the right direction, and put value on the combination of reform measures so that all reform measures constantly move closer to the central goal.[1] The reform under the top-level design puts more value on its integrity and synergy. Local governments must uphold the unity and seriousness of major policies and principles of the CPC Central Committee in combination with measures adapting to local conditions, and give full play to their subjective initiatives. They should not only act firmly in accordance with the direction, goals, and principles set by the CPC Central Committee, but have the courage to explore and make innovations. To this end, in December 2014, the central government decided to set up the Central Leading Group for Comprehensively Continuing Reform, responsible for the overall design, coordination, promotion and supervision of the implementation of the reform. In addition, the Central Conference on Economic Work held at the end of 2017 stressed that reform and opening up should be intensified, economic system restructuring be further accelerated, the focus be on improving the property rights system and market-based allocation, and breakthroughs be made in the reform in the fundamental and key areas. Efforts should also be made to open wider to the outside world, and significantly relax market access to accelerate a new pattern of all-round opening up.

1.3.2.2 More emphasis on comprehensively deepening reform in accordance with the general goal

The Third Plenary Session of the 18th CPC Central Committee set improving and developing the socialist system with Chinese characteristics and modernizing China's governance system and capacity as the overall goal of comprehensively deepening reform. The 19th CPC National Congress also stressed that the country must uphold and improve the system of socialism with Chinese characteristics, continue to modernize China's governance system and capacity, have the determination to remove all outdated

[1] See Main Problems and Reform Suggestions on the Structure of Central and Local Administrative Power (A Research of Chinese Administrative System Reform Research Institute led by Zhang Zhanbin), 2016.

thinking and ideas and all institutional ailments, break impediments of vested interests, draw on the achievements of other civilizations and develop a set of systems and institutions that are comprehensive, procedure-based and effective. The reason is that a country's governance system and capacity are the concentrated embodiment of a country's institution and of its capacity to implement the rules and regulations. This is an overall perspective to consider and answer the question of what the reform in various areas is for and what the overall results are to achieve. That is to say, deepening reform in all respects should be a comprehensive and systematic reform and improvement, a linkage and integration of that in various areas, and an overall effect and result in modernizing China's governance system and capacity. It is in this sense that continuing to advance reform must keep committed to this overall goal and must be innovation-oriented in theory, practice, institution and other fields to make systems more mature and better-defined, development in higher quality, governance more advanced, and more importantly, the people have a better sense of fulfillment.

1.3.2.3 More emphasis on people-centered reform and opening up

The Report to the 19th CPC National Congress clearly pointed out that committing to a people-centered approach. We must ensure the principal status of the people, and adhere to the Party's commitment to serving the public good and exercising power in the interests of the people. We must observe the Party's fundamental purpose of wholeheartedly serving the people, and put into practice the Party's mass line in all aspects of governance. We must regard as our goal the people's aspirations to live a better life, and rely on the people to move history forward. The people-centered development philosophy is committed to bettering the people's lives, improving the people's well-being. Development is of the people, by the people and for the people to pursue the goal of common prosperity. Xi Jinping pointed out: We must respond to the people's aspiration for a better life and adhere to the people-centered philosophy of development. The reform and development need to embody shared development for all, and continue to expand the coverage of shared development so that everyone can enjoy their share. We must demonstrate comprehensive sharing, constantly enrich its content of shared development to fully protect the legitimate rights and interests of the people in economic, political, cultural, social, ecological and other fields. We must promote joint contribution and shared benefits, expand the channels for shared development, and create a dynamic environment in which everyone participates, contributes, and has a sense of achievement. We must demonstrate gradual sharing and promote shared development from a low level to a high level and from unbalanced to balanced. To sum up, the focus must be on ensuring and improving the people's well-being, developing various social services, strengthening regulation of income distribution, winning the battle against poverty, ensuring the people's right to equal participation and equal development, and ensuring that the fruits of reform and development benefit all the people in a more equitable way, so that the people will have a greater sense of achievement and fulfillment.

1.3.2.4 More emphasis on resolving major contradictions and issues in China's development

It is fair to say that existing problems have forced Chinese to reform, and reforms are deepened once problems are tackled and solved. The salient feature of comprehensively deepening reform is to remain problem-oriented, face up to and identify the issues, and then resolve them, especially the prominent contradictions and issues facing China's development. Currently, the main framework of reform in all fields with "multiple pillars" has been basically established with a clear problem-oriented direction. Since the Third Plenary Session of the 18th CPC Central Committee, the overall pattern and context of comprehensively deepening reform have become increasingly clear. Comprehensive efforts have been made to reform the economic, political, cultural, social, ecological civilization and the Party's construction systems. After several years of efforts, the main framework of reform has been spread in the major fields such as the state-owned enterprises, tax and finance, scientific and technological innovation, land system, opening up to the outside world, cultural education, public judicial administration, environmental protection, social pension and employment, medical care and health, and the Party's construction and discipline inspection. The iconic and multi-pillar reforms have been primarily established, further deepening the reform.[1] Based on the new context, the Report to the 19th CPC National Congress gave a new description of the main contradiction in China's society and emphasized that as socialism with Chinese characteristics has entered a new era, the principal challenge facing Chinese society has evolved. What we now face is the challenge between unbalanced and inadequate development and the people's ever-growing needs for a better life. It is of great and far-reaching significance to fully understand the new historical juncture that China's development has entered and the

[1] Department of Economics Teaching and Research, National Academy of Governance, *New Orientation of China's Economy*. Beijing: People's Publishing House, 2017, p.147.

Chinese dream to build a powerful socialist economy and to realize the great rejuvenation of the Chinese nation in the new era under the leadership of the CPC Central Committee with Xi Jinping at its core. This requires us to further deepen reform in an all-round way and resolve the main contradictions in the current economic development, especially through the supply-side structural reform to optimize the allocation of factors, adjust the industrial structure, improve the quality and performance of supply system, stimulate market vitality and promote coordinated development.

1.3.2.5 More emphasis on making judgments during the tough stage of reform and critical period of development

During the tough stage of reform and crucial period of development, the central government put forward a series of important measures on reform and development to promote sustained and sound economic and social development. Most of measures target at common and universal issues, which need to be creatively resolved by all regions, sectors and organizations based on their own realities. This requires leading cadres at all levels to have a strong sense of commitment to reform, a strong sense of devotion to the cause, and a strong sense of responsibilities, and to be confident enough to resolve problems and make decisions on key issues. It should be noted that the reform aims at resolving issues. To resolve the issues, it needs to shoot the arrow at the target and put forward targeted measures. This will touch upon the deep-seated contradictions, which needs to balance the complex interests. However, as long as it meets the requirements of the CPC Central Committee, the realities at the grassroots level and the needs of the people, the reform must be resolutely carried out and daringly carried on. If leaders fear to take responsibility, lack decisiveness, are overtaken by misgivings and fear, and slow down and hesitate to press forward in the face of difficulties, it will result in acting through meetings and documents instead of taking real actions, and fail to bring good measures of reform and development into effects. It should also be noted that leading cadres who brave making decisions at the critical stage should adapt to the different times and circumstances rather than making decisions anytime and anywhere at random. To say, prompt and bold decisions should be made when the directions, requirements and bottom lines are clear in the actual work and arrangement. This is an important test to their leadership and understanding of policies.

1.3.2.6 More emphasis on deepening reform through all-around and high-level opening up

With the deep development of economic globalization, China's economy and the world's economy has become more interconnected and interdependent. This requires China to open even wider and deeper to the outside world and to promote domestic reform and development in an all-round way and at a high level. In recent years, an important strategic guideline for comprehensively deepening reform has been advancing the reform of system and mechanism through wider opening up, modernizing China's governance, promoting stable growth, upgrading the growth model and structural structure and increasing efficiency. It has been also highly innovative to establish pilot free trade zones, promote the transformation of government functions, improve the reform of foreign investment management system, implement the negative list system, expand the opening up of service sectors and facilitate the free flow, efficient allocation of domestic and foreign production factors, and deep integration of the market. In particular, the measures such as the Belt and Road Initiative and the establishment of the Asian Infrastructure Investment Bank, have not only promoted all-round opening up under the new historical conditions but facilitated strategic plans to comprehensively deepen reform and promote China's economic transformation and upgrading. This has produced and will continue to bring about positive results. Meanwhile, China has more proactively participated in the global economic division of labor and the reform of the governance mechanism of international organizations, thus effectively expanding its influence in the regional economic cooperations.

1.3.2.7 More emphasis on leveraging the guiding and driving role of law-based governance to escort reform and opening up

To reform and to govern by law, they function as the two wings of a bird or the two wheels of a car. Without further deepening reform, our development will lack impetus and our society will be devoid of vitality. The Report to the 19th CPC National Congress stressed ensuring every dimension of governance is law-based. We must exercise Party leadership at every point in the process and over every dimension of law-based governance, and be fully committed to promoting socialist rule of law with Chinese characteristics. We must improve the Chinese socialist system of laws, at the heart of which is the Constitution, establish a Chinese system of socialist rule of law, build a socialist country based on the rule of law, and develop Chinese socialist rule of law theory. We must pursue coordinated progress in law-based governance, law-based exercise of state power, and law-based government administration, and promote the integrated development of rule of law for the country, the government and the society. Without advancing the rule of law, state affairs and social life cannot run in an orderly manner, and social harmony and stability will be difficult to achieve. Throughout the modern history of the world, all the countries that successfully realized modernization have well resolved the problem of rule of law and rule of man. On the contrary, although some countries have achieved rapid development, there is no threshold for them to move smoothly towards modernization. Instead, they have fallen into one trap or another. Therefore, we must ensure that every reform is based on the law. During the whole process of reform, the guiding and driving role of law-based governance must be fully leveraged and the rule of law comprehensively must be advanced. We must adhere to the path of socialist rule of law with Chinese characteristics, speed up the construction of a socialist system of rule of law with Chinese characteristics and build a socialist country practicing the rule of law. We must ensure that everyone in the country honors the authority of the Constitution and the law, and uphold the Constitution. We must ensure that all organizations and individuals conduct activities within the scope of the Constitution, and that no one has the privilege to exceed the Constitution and the law. Besides, the rule of law must be combined with the rule of virtue to ensure that they are put equal emphasis.

1.3.3 Open development boosting China's building an economy powerhouse

The concept of open development, proposed by The Fifth Plenary Session of the 18th CPC Central Committee, further makes clear the new goals, new tasks and new requirements for open development. This is a major deployment made by the CPC Central Committee. Xi Jinping pointed out that we must unswervingly implement the basic national policy of opening to the outside world, carry on a more proactive opening-up strategy, improve the level of open economy, introduce foreign capitals and foreign technology and continue to develop the mechanism and system of opening up, so that it can deepen reform by expanding opening up and expand opening up by deepening reform. Historical experience has proved that openness can bring prosperity and progress.

Here, the focus should be on some points as follows: First, China's economy should be considered in the context of global development. China has now entered the World Trade Organization (WTO) and fostered a strong manufacturing capacity. Its trade has continued to expand and its quality and efficiency constantly improved. Through adapting to and guiding the transfer of international industries, it can form an open economic system to release huge human resources and market advantages, and provide necessary capital, technology, management experience and institutional arrangements for sustainable economic development. Second, open development must focus on fostering new comparative and competitive advantages. Openness brings reform. The perfection of the socialist market economic system cannot be separated from the mutual learning of international experience, rules and routes as well as its practical applications. There needs to build a new system for an open economy to constantly enrich the institutional content of socialism with Chinese characteristics, and provide institutional guarantee for raising the level of an open economy. Third, open development must focus on mutual benefits and build a community with a shared future. With the deepening of economic globalization, countries in the world have become more interconnected and interdependent. To expand opening up, it needs to foster the consciousness of building a community with a shared future, help supply each other's needs and complement each other's advantages, achieve mutual benefits and win-win results through strategic cooperation, accommodate the legitimate concerns from other countries while pursuing one's own interests, promote common development of all countries while pursuing one's own development, and constantly expand the convergence of common interests.

1.3.3.1 Taking the Belt and Road Initiative as the guide to build a new pattern of all-round and proactive opening up

In September 2013, when visiting the Central Asian countries, President Xi Jinping proposed an initiative to jointly build the Silk Road Economic Belt for the first time. In October 2013, when visiting the Southeast Asian countries, he proposed an initiative to jointly build the 21st Century Maritime Silk Road. The two initiatives constitute the Belt and Road Initiative. Advancing the Belt and Road Initiative is the great strategic concept made by the CPC Central Committee with Xi Jinping at its core. It is the major strategic decision, made by the CPC Central Committee, to proactively respond to the global changing situation, the new situation, task and requirements that China is facing, as well as the overall international and domestic situations. It is the top-level design for building a new system of an open economy. It is generally believed that three events are particularly memorable when it comes to 40 years of reform and opening up. One is Deng Xiaoping's proposal of building economic special zones, which made China open the door to the outside world. One is China's entry into the WTO, which has completely changed China's development. Another is the Belt and Road Initiative, which makes China open even wider based on the two previous opening. From 2013 to 2017, more than 100 countries and international organizations have proactively supported and participated in the Belt and Road Initiative. Its content has been absorbed by the important resolutions of the United Nations General Assembly and the United Nations Security Council. The Belt and Road Initiative has gradually transformed from concept to action and from vision to reality. It has achieved fruitful results.[1] With policy communication, road connectivity, unimpeded trade, currency circulation and people-to-people connectivity as the core, and supported by international cooperation in production capacity and equipment manufacturing, the Belt and Road Initiative will promote an all-round cooperation between China and countries along the Belt and Road to achieve common development and prosperity. It will also bring new opportunities for China to better utilize the international market and resources, accelerate the open economic development in the central and western regions and border areas, encourage domestic capital and production capacity to go global and accelerate the internationalization of renminbi. It is of great significance to expand the space for development, and consolidate and prolong the important period of strategic opportunities. The Report to the 19th CPC National Congress clearly pointed out that making new ground in pursuing opening up on all fronts. We should pursue the Belt and Road Initiative as a priority, give equal emphasis to "bringing in" and "going global", follow the principle of achieving shared growth through discussion and collaboration, and increase openness and cooperation in building innovation capacity. With these efforts, we hope to make new ground in opening China further through links running eastward and westward, across land and over sea.

1.3.3.2 Coordinating "bringing in" with "going global" to foster new strengths in international cooperation and competition

Since China's economy has been deeply integrated into the world economy, an open approach must be adopted to foster new strengths in international cooperation and competition, rather than "build a car behind closed doors". Efforts are needed to better coordinate "bringing in" with "going global", and cultivate new strengths in technology, brands, quality and services. Over the years, China has made great progress in utilizing foreign capitals, and foreign-invested enterprises have made important contributions to the growth of China's economy, tax collection and employment. On the one hand, in the new situation and environment, the level of China's industrial technology continues to

[1] Xi Jinping, "Work Together to Build the Silk Road Economic Belt and the 21st Century Maritime Silk Road: Speech at the Opening Ceremony of the Belt and Road Forum for International Cooperation", *People's Daily*, May 14, 2017.

improve and the competitive advantage of traditional cost tends to weaken. On the other hand, the United States and other developed countries are vigorously attracting manufacturing industries return, and many developing countries are taking advantage of low costs to utilize international capitals. In the future, to better leverage the role of foreign investments and boost the supply-side structural reform, we must actively relax the restrictions on foreign investment access in the service sector and other areas, support foreign investments to involve in implementing innovation-driven development strategy and transforming and upgrading the manufacturing industry, further improve the legalized, international and convenient business environment, and improve the work of attracting investment. Currently, China has formed a strong manufacturing capacity and international competitiveness in many industries, such as electric power, tele-communication, petrochemical, railway, automobile, aviation, construction machinery and so on. Some leading enterprises in the industry have gradually shifted to the high-end links of international division of labor, such as research and development, design, marketing, brand building, etc. China has formed the primary capacity of "going global" to build an industrial chain and international division of labor system with China as its main body on a global scale. In the future, essential comprehensive measures should be taken to encourage and support powerful enterprises to "going global", set up research and development centers, production bases and marketing networks overseas, support the development of Chinese multinational corporates with global influence, and enhance China's status in the global division of labor and international competitiveness.

1.3.3.3 Accelerating efforts to implement the free trade zone strategy and achieve new breakthroughs in reform and opening up at a higher level

Building pilot free trade zones is a major measure taken by the CPC Central Committee and the State Council to advance reform and opening up under the new circumstance. In September 2013, China's first pilot free trade zone was established in Shanghai. In April 2015, Guangdong Pilot Free Trade Zones, Tianjin Pilot Free Trade Zones and Fujian Pilot Free Trade Zones were approved and established. In March 2017, the State Council approved the establishment of seven new pilot free trade zones in Liaoning, Zhejiang, Henan, Hubei, Chongqing, Sichuan and Shaanxi. In November 2015, the 18th Conference of the Central Leading Group for Comprehensively Continuing Reform adopted Several Opinions of the State Council of the People's Republic of China on Accelerating the Implementation of the Strategies for Free Trade

Zone Strategy, and put forward the overall requirements, basic principles, goals and tasks, and strategies for building free trade zones. It marked that the theoretical system of China's free trade zone has taken shape.[1] Pilot Free Trade Zones are the experimental fields for deepening reform and opening up in China. Its purpose is to take the lead in accelerating the transformation of government functions, building a legalized business environment, and building a new system of open economy, so as to form a batch of institutional achievements that can be duplicated and extended, and to accumulate experience for comprehensively deepening reform. Therefore, it should open wider to the outside world at a higher level, further form a compelling effect on the institutional reform, and form a more international, market-oriented, law-based transparent and standardized institutional environment. For example, the negative list management system embodies the concept of "Everything which is not forbidden is allowed", which is fundamentally different from the past management mode that is mainly based on administrative examination and approval. As China has become the world's second largest economy, its economic development has entered a new normal state and moved to the higher end of the global industrial chain and value chain. There is an urgent need to further improve the level of openness, actively build a new system for an open economy, and accelerate efforts to build the high-level free trade zones. Under the new situation, we should fully leverage the important and unique role of free trade zones, take free trade zones as an important platform for China to actively participate in formulating international economic and trade rules, strive for the institutional power of global economic governance, and speed up priorities to build high-quality and high-standard free trade zones in the new round of opening up.

1.3.3.4 Building a community with a shared future for mankind and improving global governance

The Report to the 19th CPC National Congress stressed that China called on the people of all countries to work together to build a community with a shared future for mankind, to build an open, inclusive, clean, and beautiful world that enjoys lasting peace, universal security, and common prosperity. We should respect each other, discuss issues as equals, resolutely reject the Cold War mentality and power politics, and take a new approach to developing state-to-state relations with communication, not confrontation, and with partnership, not alliance. It is clear that building a community with a shared future for mankind is China's goal and philosophy for improving global governance

[1] Li Guanghui, "Speed up the Implementation of China's Strategy to the Free Trade Zone", *Study Times*, Apr. 21, 2017.

now and for a long time to come. In today's world, all the countries are interdependent and share weal and woe. In this context, the countries in the world are more interconnected, interdependent, cooperative and mutually reinforcing than ever before. Meanwhile, countries in the world are all facing some global challenges, and no country can stay aloof from them. It can be said that the interests of all countries in the world are highly integrated with a mutual stake. To build a community with a shared future for mankind, three aspects need to be advanced. First, promote multi-cultural exchanges and integration. Cultural exchanges and integration provide an important spiritual support for the development and progress of human society. Practice has proved that only by strengthening exchanges and mutual learning can different cultures thrive and develop in advancing human social progress and safeguarding world peace. Culture is enriched by exchanges and mutual learning. Cultural exchange and mutual learning is an important driving force to promote the progress of human civilization and the development of world peace. Human history is a magnificent picture that shows mutual exchanges, learning and integration between different cultures. Second, build a platform for common development. Building a community with a shared future for mankind means that all the countries in the world pursue development on an equal basis and respect each other. The key to China's development is that it has blazed a development path adapts to China's national conditions, a path that seeks common development through opening up. Currently, we should pursue equitable development and make development opportunities more equal, so that it can enable all countries to be participants, contributors and beneficiaries of the world development. We should stay committed to open development, oppose all forms of protectionism, pursue extensive consultation, joint contribution and shared benefits, and ensure that the fruits of development benefit the people of all countries better. Third, establish a partnership of win-win cooperation. Since the end of World War Ⅱ, the achievements of mankind in resolving differences of interests through cooperation have shown that cooperation has become the rational choice of all countries. Practice has proved that as long as all the countries hold high the flag of win-win cooperation, deliver the thinking of "mutual benefits and win-win results", take the development demands and common development of other countries into account in the pursuit of their own interests and development, a community of shared future for all mankind can be built on a new type of global development partnership with a more equal and balanced basis.

1.4 Completing the building of a moderately prosperous society in all respects to lay foundation for developing a powerful economy

Completing the building of a moderately prosperous society in all respects is a major decision made by the Communist Party of China and serves as the significant base of developing a powerful economy, as China has attained the objectives of the first two steps of the Three-step Development Strategy for the modernization drive and the people have by and large become prosperous. By 2020, the completion of building a moderately prosperous society in all respects as scheduled will broaden the way forward to building China into a great modern socialist country.

1.4.1 Proposing the goal of building a moderately prosperous society and the Three-step Development Strategy

It is the important experience for the Communist Party of China to undertake the development and reform by putting forward inspiring goals according to the will of the people and the requirements of developing the cause during the different historical periods. The Three-step Development Strategy, based on Deng Xiaoping's thought on bringing about a moderately prosperous society, constitutes an important part of Deng Xiaoping's Theory. It specifies the goal of fulfilling the great rejuvenation of the Chinese nation and is the first modernization strategy made by the Party since the launching of the reform and opening up in 1978.

1.4.1.1 Exploring the development of modernization by the first-generation leaders of the PRC

To build a modernized country is the dream of several Chinese generations. In 1953, China began to launch massive economic development campaigns after completing various reforms and restoring the national economy. In September 1953, the Party set forth the general line for the transitional period to achieve the country's socialist industrialization gradually over a quite long period. In June 1954, in the speech on the Draft of the Constitution of the People's Republic of China, Mao Zedong called for laying foundations for the socialist industrialization by implementing three five-year plans. In September 1954, Zhou Enlai proposed in the report on the work of the government to build the country with strong modern industry, agriculture, transportation and national defense. These are the CPC's initial expositions on the Four Modernizations.[1]

In 1956, before the opening of the Eighth CPC National Congress, Mao Zedong put forward a detailed vision for building China's socialist modernization in two steps. The first step was to achieve basic industrialization by three five-year plans and the next step was to approach or keep pace with the level of developed countries through several decades. In September 1956, during the Eighth CPC National Congress Mao Zedong specified the time of fulfilling the goal of the second step by 50 to 100 years.

From the late 1950s, the Party's guiding thought was stuck in the "Leftist" mistakes, posing great impediments to building the socialist modernization. With efforts to remedy the erroneous principles and making proper adjustments, by around 1963, the Party continued to follow the objectives and steps of the socialist modernization development proposed at the Eighth CPC National Congress in 1956. In September 1963, the CPC Central Committee Conference on Economic Work proposed to achieve the development strategy of Four Modernizations by a two-step approach. The first step was to establish an independent and complete industrial system and national economic system within 15 years. At this stage, China's industrial system would approach the advanced world level. The next step was to develop the country's industry and economy into the forefront of the world and fully modernize China's agriculture, industry, national defense, and science and technology within 50 to 100 years. To this end, the four-modernization objective was defined as a whole.

Unfortunately, the Cultural Revolution (1966-1976) diverted the focus of the Party to the erroneous principle of taking class struggle as the key, leaving the two-step modernization strategy abandoned. In November 1974, Mao Zedong called for boosting the national economy. In January 1975, Zhou Enlai reaffirmed the objective of the Four Modernizations and the two-step strategic deployment at the First Session of the 4th National People's Congress. Not long after the closing of the 4th National People's Congress, Deng Xiaoping who was reinstated his job in 1973 led the work of rectifying the country's economy, gaining insight into the goal of accomplishing the Four Modernizations by the end of the 20th century. In June 1975, Deng Xiaoping described the modernization development which was put forth at the Fourth CPC National People's Congress when he met the delegation of the American Society of News Editors.

---

[1] Research Group on Moderately Prosperous Society, Literature Research Office of the Central Committee of CPC, *Theory and Practice of Building Moderately Prosperous Society for Recent 30 Years*. Beijing: Central Party Literature Press, 2009, p. 78.

He explained that the modernization of China was to approach or relatively approach that of the developed countries; it was unrealistic for China to pursue the neck-and-neck development with the developed countries during the period because of its own national conditions with the large population as a prominent one. In September 1975, Deng Xiaoping pointed out at the Conference of Learning Dazhai in Agriculture that China was still beset with poverty and backwardness in industry and agriculture, so it could take the country a few decades to catch up with the developed countries. [1]

1.4.1.2 Proposing the goal of building a prosperous society

In the Third Plenary Session of the 11th CPC Central Committee in 1978, the Party made the historic decision to shift the Party's focus to the modernization drive. Then, Deng Xiaoping contemplated that priority should be given to how to push forward the modernization based on the people's desires and the country's needs.

To develop modernization, it is essential to understand the gaps between China and developed countries. To this end, with the advocate of Deng Xiaoping and other political leaders, China reopened its door around 1978 after the over ten-year isolation from the world, and sent business delegations and overseas study groups to Japan, western Europe, the United States and other developed countries. So, Officials which were sent abroad for investigations were deeply impressed by the world's rapid development and the advanced modernization of those countries. Deng Xiaoping himself also frequently visited other countries where he truly perceived the development level of the contemporary world's modernization as well as the gaps between China and the outside world thorough the on-the-spot investigation. Therefore, Deng Xiaoping contemplated China's future and resolved to set a goal for building a modernized China by the end of the 20th century.

In September 1978, when Deng Xiaoping met the visiting Japanese journalists, he said that China was to achieve its Four Modernizations by the end of 20th century, yet it would not as wealthy as Japan by then. In March 1979, Deng Xiaoping clarified the concept of China's Four Modernizations for the first time when he met the delegation of the Sino-British Cultural Association. He explained that China was to complete the goal of Four Modernizations by the end of the 20th century, and why he called it China's Four Modernizations was that its concept was different from that of the western countries. Later, he replaced "China's Four Modernizations" with "China's Modernization" at the

---

[1] *A Chronicle of Deng Xiaoping's Life* (*1975-1997*) (Volume Ⅰ), Beijing: Central Party Literature Press, 2004, pp. 97-98.

Meeting of the Political Bureau of the CPC Central Committee in March 1979. As a new concept, what does China's modernization differentiate from the Four Modernizations? In July 1979, Deng Xiaoping specified the new concept for the first time when he interviewed the governors of Shandong Provincial Committee and Qingdao Municipal Committee. He described that China would see the per capita income reach US$1,000 and the people lead a decent life when China's Modernization was achieved by the end of the 20th century.

In December 1979, when he met then Japanese Prime Minister Masayoshi Ohira, Deng Xiaoping envisioned that China were to build a prosperous society in an all-round way by the end of the 20th century. The well-known vision has exerted far-reaching influences on China's development in the following decades. He explained that China's modernization aimed to build a moderately prosperous society, which was different from that of Japan. He added that even though China realized the Four Modernizations in some aspects as scheduled, the goal of the per capita Gross National Product (GNP) of US$1,000 would take strenuous efforts to reach but be much lower than that of developed countries, so China would only be a moderately prosperous society by then.[1]

Based on China's conditions and the experience of the developed countries' modernization, Deng Xiaoping proposed the goal of building a prosperous society in an all-round way. It is the major adjustment and modification on the objective of comprehensively accomplishing the Four Modernizations by the end of the 20th century, which was proposed by the CPC since the 1950s. The goal has far-reaching significance for the CPC to properly formulate and improve the strategic objectives of building China's modernization.

1.4.1.3 Establishing the Three-step Development Strategy

To achieve the goal of building a prosperous society in an all-round way, Deng Xiaoping made an elaborate design and planning. He pointed out many times that efforts should be made to double the Gross National Product (GNP) of 1980 by 1990 and quadruple it by 2000, so that at the end of the 20th century, per capita GNP will be up by US$800 to US$1,000, and China will step into a moderately prosperous society. His conception was written into the "*Report on the Work of the Government*" adopted at the Fourth Session of the Fifth National People's Congress in November 1981. According to the Report, efforts should be made to quadruple the total industrial and agricultural output value in 20 years so that people's consumption can reach a prosperous level.

---

[1] *Selected Works of Deng Xiaoping* (Volume Ⅱ), Beijing: People's Publishing House, 1994, p. 237.

In September 1982, the Report to the 12th CPC National Congress formally defined Deng Xiaoping's conception of achieving a prosperous society in an all-round way at the end of the 20th century as the strategic plan for China's economic development in the next twenty years. That is, to quadruple the total industrial and agricultural output value from RMB710 billion in 1980 to RMB2.8 trillion by 2000. The Report pointed out that if this goal was to achieve, China's total national income and the output of major industrial and agricultural products would be in the front ranks of the world. By that time, great progress would have been made in modernizing national economy, the income of urban and rural people would have been boosted manyfold, and the material and cultural progress will have reached a prosperous level.[1]

While formulating and constantly improving the goal of realizing a prosperous society at the end of the 20th century, Deng Xiaoping continued to ponder over the goal of China's development in the next century. In April 1984, he pointed out that the first development goal involved ensuring the people a moderately prosperous life by 2000. The second goal was to reach or approach the level of developed countries within 30 to 50 years. In February 1987, when meeting foreign guests, Deng Xiaoping proposed that by the middle of 21st century China was to build a moderately developed socialist country. Then, his previous goal of reaching or approaching the level of developed countries by the middle of 21st century was revised to build a "moderately developed country" by the middle of the 21st century, which undoubtedly made the goal of development more realistic and better to achieve.

In April 1987, when Deng Xiaoping held meetings with then Vice-Premier of Spanish, he summarized for the first time the Three-step Development Strategy of the Chinese nation in the one hundred years from the founding of the People's Republic of China to the middle of the 21st century. He pointed out that according to the original goal, the first step was to double the GNP by the end of the 1980s. Based on the figure in 1980, per capita GNP would be doubled from US$250 to US$500. The second step was to double the per capita GNP to US$1,000 by the end of 20th century. Achieving this goal meant to build a moderately prosperous society and make China out of poverty and into a moderately prosperous country. Then, the GNP would exceed one trillion US dollars, and national strength was strong enough to make more progress despite of a relatively low level in per capita terms. More importantly, the third step was to take 30

[1] *Selected Important Works since the 12th National Congress of the CPC* (Volume Ⅰ), Beijing: People's Publishing House, 1986, p. 14.

to 50 years to quadruple the per capita GNP to US$4,000 in the 21st century. By doing this, China will have entered a moderately developed society.[1]

In October 1987, the Three-step Development Strategy proposed by Deng Xiaoping was officially confirmed at the 13th CPC National Congress. The first step was to double the 1980 GNP by the end of the 1980s and ensure that the people would have adequate food and clothing. This goal has been achieved now. The second step involved doubling the 1990 GNP by the end of the 20th century and ensuring the people a moderately prosperous life. The third step was to increase the per capita GNP level to that of moderately developed countries, ensuring the people a relatively affluent life, and realizing basic modernization by the middle of the 21st century. Then, China should continue to move forward on that basis.

The Three-step Development Strategy combines the grand goal of national modernization with the real life of more than one billion people, ensuring that the people will have adequate food and clothing as the first step and then a moderately prosperous life as the second and a relatively affluent life as the third, so that the people can truly feel and experience the change and the development of the country. At this point, Deng Xiaoping has completed the design of the Three-step Development Strategy.

1.4.1.4 The significance of Three-step Development Strategy to China's modernization

Deng Xiaoping's Three-step Development Strategy is a modernization goal for development based on the actual situation of China's economic and social development, which is of great significance to China's modernization.

First, the Three-step Development Strategy enriches the thought of developing China's modernization. To Mao Zedong, Zhou Enlai and other first generation of Chinese leaders, the understanding of modernization centered on industrialization. In 1953, when Mao Zedong planned for the general line of the transitional period (from 1949 to 1956), he set the industrialization as the goal of China's economic development and put forward the slogan of "striving for the socialist industrialization". In September 1956, building a complete industrial system in the next three Five-year Plans was proposed at the Eighth CPC National Congress, which was a tentative plan to achieve the "Four Modernizations" based on industrialization. Then, Deng Xiaoping's Three-step Development Strategy shifted the focus from industrialization to the modernization of industry, agriculture, national defense and science and technology. The Three-step Development Strategy also added an important content, that is, to build China a highly

[1] *Selected Works of Deng Xiaoping* (Volume Ⅲ), People's Publishing House, 1993, p. 226.

civilized and democratic socialist country. This is vital to the country's modernization.

Second, the Three-step Development Strategy conforms to the modern economic development theory. In general, a country may undergo many stages before becoming a modernized one, including traditional society stage, primary development stage, fast development stage, and mature developed stage, high-consumption stage and a stage of pursuing for a high-quality life. Conformed to the long-term and phased development of modernization depicted in the modern growth theory, the Three-Step Development Strategy demonstrates that China's modernization is to be a long-term process with clear phased goals. As the "three-step" itself includes three stages and steps, each stage contains many small development steps. So, Deng Xiaoping stressed on many occasions that development was the absolute principle, and every available opportunity should be seized to reach a new level, so as to make a leapfrog development every 10 years to enter a new stage.

Third, the Three-step Development Strategy contains the goal of realizing a common prosperity for all. In this strategy, not only the goal of doubling the national economy is put forward, but also the concepts of "having adequate food and clothing", "moderately prosperous society" and "moderately developed society" are included to directly describe the improvement of the people's lives. Compared with previous economic development strategies, it better reflects the inherent laws and essential requirements of China's modernization and pays more attention to the people's livelihood. The Three-step Development Strategy shifts the emphasis of China's modernization from attaching importance to national strength to the improvement of people's living standards, which greatly enhanced the enthusiasm and initiative of people's participation in building a modernized China.

1.4.2 Core connotations and new characteristics of completing the building of a moderately prosperous society in all respects

Through the efforts by the whole Party and all people of the country, by 2000, China has successfully realized the first two steps of the "three-step development", becoming a moderately prosperous society on the whole. In 2002, the 16th CPC National Congress put forward the goal of building a prosperous society at a higher level to benefit more than 1 billion people. In 2007, the 17th CPC National Congress proposed new requirements for building a prosperous society in an all-round way. In 2012, the 18th CPC National Congress adjusted "building a prosperous society in all respects" to "completing the build of a moderately prosperous society in all respects". Building a moderately prosperous society in all respects emphasizes not only "prosperous", but also "in all respects" which is more important and more difficult to achieve. The concept "prosperous" is about the level of development, and the concept "in all respects" is about the balance, coordination and sustainability of development.[1]

1.4.2.1 Core connotations of completing the building of a moderately prosperous society in all respects

First, completing the building of a moderately prosperous society in all respects covers more areas. Based on the focus on economic development and people's living standards at the beginning of this proposal, the 18th CPC National Congress clearly outlined the grand goal of building a moderately prosperous society in all respects, with the ideological connotations of a moderately prosperous society having been transformed from the "Three-sphere Integrated Plan"[2] to the "Four-sphere Integrated Plan"[3], and then to the "Five-sphere Integrated Plan" proposed at the 18th CPC National Congress, which promotes coordinated economic, political, cultural, social and ecological advancement. The initial "Material and Spiritual Progress" has been extended to the "Material, Spiritual and Political Progress", which was put forward by the 18th CPC National Congress. The concept of "in all respects" reflects in achieving the economic, political, cultural, social and ecological progress as well as developing material, spiritual and political progress in an all-round way. The lag of development in any aspect will affect the realization of building a moderately prosperous society in all respects.

Second, completing the building of a moderately prosperous society in all respects covers more communities. Building a moderately prosperous society in all respects benefits all people in the country. It is meant to enable each and every group of the 1.3 billion population to lead a moderately prosperous life, based on achieving overall prosperity of the people in 2000. Xi Jinping stressed: Without the moderate prosperity of all people, we can't complete the building of a moderately prosperous society in all respects. In this case, by 2020, when we declare that China has built a moderately prosperous society in all respects, it means that the living standards of tens of millions of people must not be below the poverty line; otherwise, it will affect people's sense of

[1] See Xi Jinping's Speech at the Second Full Assembly of the Fifth Plenary Session of the 18th CPC Central Committee, Oct. 29, 2015.

[2] A plan to integrate economic prosperity, political democracy and advanced culture and ideology. —*Tr.*

[3] The overall arrangements for the four-in-one economic, political, cultural and social development. —*Tr.*

satisfaction and the recognition of the international community. For sure, without moderate prosperity in rural areas, particularly those impoverished areas, we can not complete the building of a moderately prosperous society in all respects, and building a moderately prosperous society in all respects must leave no ethnic group behind. In other words, no matter whether they are urban residents or rural residents, middle-income or low-income, ethnic groups with larger population or ethnic groups with less population, all of them are able to attain a common moderately prosperous life.

Third, completing the building of a moderately prosperous society in all respects covers more regions. To build a moderately prosperous society in all respects, there should be moderate prosperity for the common development in both urban and rural areas, and both economically developed and underdeveloped areas. Xi Jinping stressed: Without moderate prosperity in rural areas and underdeveloped areas, there would be no moderate prosperity in all respects in the whole country. So, when we say narrowing the development gap between urban and rural areas, it is meant to narrow not only the gaps in GDP and growth rate, but the negative gaps in the levels of residents' income, access to infrastructure, equalization access to basic public services and people's living standards. Therefore, it is an important task of building a moderately prosperous society in all respects to balance urban and rural development, coordinate regional development, promote the development of new urbanization, and speed up the process of urban-rural integration.

Fourth, completing the building of a moderately prosperous society in all respects will reach a higher level. Building a moderately prosperous society in all respects should not only cover all fields and people, but have higher goals and requirements. That is, to maintain the medium-high economic growth, achieve remarkable results in innovation-driven development, significantly enhance the coordinated development, generally improve the living standards and quality of the people, significantly level up the well-rounded development of the people and social progress, improve the quality of the ecological environment, and make the systems in all aspects more mature and better-defined. Here, the key is to "complete", which is the solemn promise by the Party to the people and the history. The difficulty of realizing a moderately prosperous society in all respects as scheduled lies in achieving the quantitative goals as well as the qualitative goals. If we unilaterally regard the limited indicators as the goal of building a moderately prosperous society in all respects, and well complete the quantifiable goals yet poorly for the non-quantifiable ones, then an embarrassing situation in which completing the goals is not in line with how the people actually feel may arise.

So, what is the core connotations of completing the building of a moderately prosperous society in all respects? It is the people-centered development. The people-centered development is for the people and by the people to share the development fruits. Along the path of building a moderately prosperous society, the people-centered development philosophy has been highlighted from stressing that some people are allowed and encouraged to get prosperity first to emphasizing the prosperity of all people. This is a major change in the development policies of the CPC and the country, adding new important connotations to building a moderately prosperous society in all respects. The philosophy of people-centered development is the core connotation and essence of building a moderately prosperous society in all respects, which reflects the fundamental purpose of the CPC to serve the people wholeheartedly, the historical materialism that the people are the fundamental force for promoting development and the goal of gradually realizing common prosperity.

1.4.2.2 New characteristics of completing the building of a moderately prosperous society in all respects

First, completing the building of a moderately prosperous society in all respects is a critical step in realizing the Chinese Dream of national rejuvenation. A moderately prosperous society has long been a beautiful dream of the Chinese people for thousands of years. To realize the Chinese Dream of national rejuvenation is the long-cherished desire of several generations of the Chinese people since modern times. Since the 18th CPC National Congress, Xi Jinping has repeatedly demonstrated the task of completing the building of a moderately prosperous society in all respects in the overall situation of realizing the Chinese Dream. It is clearly pointed out that building a moderately prosperous society in all respects and realizing the Chinese Dream are two interconnected and intergraded stages. Without realizing a moderately prosperous society, it would be impossible to realize the national rejuvenation. Building a moderately prosperous society is a critical step in realizing the Chinese Dream of national rejuvenation. It points out the historical position of building a moderately prosperous society in all respects, and reveals the significance of building a moderately prosperous society in all respects to the realization of the Chinese Dream. Now we are closer to the goal of the great rejuvenation of the Chinese nation than at any other time in history, and to meet this goal, we must go through the important foundation, the critical step and the development stage of building a moderately prosperous society in all respects. Highlighting the significance of building a moderately prosperous society in all respects will greatly mobilize the initiative and creativity of the people to devote themselves to building a moderately prosperous society in all respects, and lay solid foundation for realizing the Chinese Dream of national rejuvenation. Regarded as a phased goal of realizing the Chinese Dream, building a moderately prosperous society in all respects makes the goal of the Chinese Dream clearer, and helps to enhance people's confidence in realizing the great rejuvenation of the Chinese nation.

Second, completing the building of a moderately prosperous society in all respects occupies a leading position in the Four-pronged Comprehensive Strategy. Before the 18th CPC National Congress, the Party also attached importance to the four important issues of building a moderately prosperous society, deepening reform, upholding the rule of law and strengthening its self-discipline, but the overall efficiency of the four aspects was affected due to the lack of their effective integration and of the outstanding position of moderately prosperous development. Since the 18th CPC National Congress, the CPC Central Committee with Xi Jinping at its core has adhered to the problem-solving approach, not only placed emphasis on "in all respects", but also grasped the key points, and put forward the Four-pronged Comprehensive Strategy that highlights the leading position of building a moderately prosperous society in all respects, thus creatively integrated and coordinated the goal of building a moderately prosperous society in all respects, the driving force of comprehensively deepening reform, the significant guarantee of comprehensive rule of law, and the fundamental guarantee of strengthening its self-discipline. This injects new connotations of the times for the Party to govern the country under the new situation and uphold and develop socialism with Chinese characteristics. Both theory and practice show that the "layout" can be adjusted and supplemented with the development and changes of the situation and tasks. It is both realistic and dynamic. The Four-pronged Comprehensive Strategy is a new strategic thinking, requirement and plan formulated by Xi Jinping, based on the overall situation of upholding and developing socialism with Chinese characteristics; it is the action guideline of the Party and the country.

Third, completing the building of a moderately prosperous society in all respects is led by the philosophy of innovative, coordinated, green, open and inclusive development. Based on both domestic and foreign experience of development, the general trend of development, and the prominent contradictions and issues in China's development, the new philosophy of innovation, coordination, green, openness and inclusive development was put forward at the Fifth Plenary Session of the 18th CPC Central Committee, demonstrating the Party's growing understanding of the laws governing economic and social development. In the earlier stage, development was typically confined to the economic field, particularly emphasizing the expansion of economic aggregate. This may lead to the tendency of replacing broader development with economic growth at both theoretical and practical levels. With the continuous advancement of building a moderately prosperous society, the conditions and environment of development keep changing, and some ideas that once worked become less effective as time goes by. To realize a moderately prosperous society in all respects, China are now facing more complex issues and arduous tasks of development. It can be mainly manifested in five prominent issues: the lack of drivers of growth, the uncoordinated development, the constraints on the environment of resources, low levels of overall opening up, and insufficient joint and shared development. Thus, the philosophy of innovative, coordinated, green, open and inclusive development was put forward to resolve the prominent issues in these five aspects. As the baton and traffic lights for building a moderately prosperous society in all respects, this philosophy is rather practical.

Fourth, completing the building of a moderately prosperous society in all respects as scheduled takes the initiative in leading the new normal of economic development. China's economic development is entering a new normal. This is the inevitable consequence of the interaction between the world economy cycle and China's development stage, representing the basic nature and main characteristic of China's economic development for quite a long time in the present and future. Under the new normal, the main characteristics of China's economic development are as follows: The growth should be shifted from high speed to medium-to-high speed; the growth pattern should be transformed from large-scale and high-speed growth to high-quality and efficiency growth; the economic structure should be transformed from quantitative increase and expanding capacity to adjusting stock while optimizing increments; and the growth engines should be shifted from relying mainly on the input of factors such as resources and low-cost labor to innovation-driven ones. During the decisive period of building a moderately prosperous society in all respects, the new normal of economic development guided by building a moderately prosperous society in all respects is to more actively adapt to and grasp the major tasks of China's economic development. In view of the characteristics of China's economic development, that is, a slowdown in the rate of growth, optimization of economic structure, and shift of growth engines, China should also better leverage the subjective initiative and creative spirit, uphold the top priority of improving the quality and efficiency of development, implement an innovation-driven strategy, strengthen overall planning and coordination, and strive to promote supply-side structural reform to ensure medium-high economic growth.

Fifth, the key to completing the building of a moderately prosperous society in all respects relies on remedying deficiencies and addressing weaknesses. Currently, the issues of unbalanced, uncoordinated and unsustainable development in China remain prominent with weak links occurring nationwide. The deficiencies in economic and social development, especially the major ones, are the main factors affecting building a moderately prosperous society in all respects as scheduled, and these deficiencies have to improve as soon as possible. The weak links appear not only in specific areas like in economy, politics, culture, society and ecology, but also in every region, with the more prominent ones including poverty alleviation, the development of social undertakings, protection of the ecological environment, livelihood guarantee and so on. Therefore, the key to building a moderately prosperous society in all respects relies on remedying deficiencies and addressing weaknesses. Since the reform and opening up, China has fully leveraged the market mechanism and integrated domestic and international markets and resources, which has remedied a series of deficiencies, faced by economic development and thus created a miracle of economic growth. However, the deficiencies in some areas have not been well addressed, such as issues relating to agriculture, rural areas and rural residents, people's livelihood, ecology and so on, which are mostly caused by the inaction of the government at some levels. In the recent years, with the rapid improvement of total economic aggregate, on the one hand, the scale of China's integration of domestic and international markets and resources is getting larger, and the requirements more demanding and degree of difficulty more increasing; on the other hand, the government must play its due role in improving the major weak links when building a moderately prosperous society in all respects. Therefore, improving the weak links needs to shift from giving full play to the market mechanism to relying mainly on the "government plus market" model.

Sixth, expanding the middle-income group is the key to realizing a moderately prosperous society in all respects. It is a specific requirement for building a moderately prosperous society in all respects, an important source for effectively expanding domestic demands, a basic path to achieve common prosperity, and a significant support for realizing the transformation of an olive-shaped social structure and crossing the middle-income trap. In the past, our policies mainly encouraged some people to develop first while the policies for the development of middle-income groups were relatively vague. Since the 21st century, China has been attaching great importance to expanding middle-income groups and gradually strengthening its policies. The 18th CPC National Congress stressed: We must expand the proportion of middle-income groups. The Third Plenary Session of the 18th CPC Central Committee also proposed as follows: We must regulate income distribution by proper standards, improve the mechanism and policy system of income distribution, increase the income of low-income people, expand the proportion of middle-income people, and strive to narrow the income distribution gap between urban and rural areas, and among regions and industries, so that an olive-shaped income distribution structure can be gradually formed. We must expand the middle-income group to the track of rapid development. Under the new normal of economic development, the focus and difficulty of expanding the middle-income group is to help the low-income group develop into the middle-income ones while preventing the existing middle-income group from returning to the low-income ones for various reasons. In a sense, the expansion of the middle-income group is the only way for a country to maintain long-term stability. In fact, it is not merely the expansion of wealth, but requires a comprehensive social security system and a sound legal system to protect the rights and interests of the middle-income group as well.

1.4.3 Key and difficult issues in completing the building of a moderately prosperous society in all respects

In the Report to the 19th CPC National Congress, Xi Jinping profoundly expounded the new historical juncture in China's development, that is, as socialism with Chinese characteristics has entered a new era, and the principal contradiction facing Chinese society in the new era has evolved. What we now face is the contradiction between unbalanced and inadequate development and the people's ever-growing needs for a better life. However, the basic national condition remains unchanged that China is still at the primary stage of socialism and will remain so for a long time, and China's international status as the world's largest developing country remains unchanged. The "evolved" and "unchanged" determines that development holds the key to resolving all issues in China's development, the key to building a moderately prosperous society in all respects, and the key to building an economic powerhouse.

Since the introduction of reform and opening up in 1978, China has been focusing on development with remarkable success. Since the 18th CPC National Congress,

Xi Jinping has repeatedly stressed that the fundamental task of socialism with Chinese characteristics is to liberate and develop productive forces, and development is the golden key to solving all problems and issues facing China's development. Economic development is the foundation, without it, nothing is possible. To complete the building of a moderately prosperous society in all respects, we still need to take development as the top priority and bring it to a new level. We should adhere to the strategy that development alone can make the difference, ensuring that an effective approach is taken to development, and upholding people-centered development.

Though China has entered a new normal of economic development, and experienced an unavoidable shift in economic growth, it should be noted that the country still maintains the good momentum for development in the period of important strategic opportunity and the economic fundamentals remain favorable for long-term growth. This suggests that the sound trend of economic development we are constantly seeing can be sustained. In the meantime, it should also be noted that completing the building of a moderately prosperous society in all respects as scheduled and developing a powerful economy are also facing the arduous challenge of the transformation of principal social contradiction. Realizing a moderately prosperous society in all respects as scheduled should first advance the level of economic development, and achieve higher quality, more efficient, fairer and more sustainable development. To realize a moderately prosperous society in all respects, what is more important and difficult to achieve is the issues of "in all respects". "A moderately prosperous society" represents a certain level of development, while "in all respects" extends that level of development to one that is balanced, coordinated and sustainable. Xi Jinping pointed out that if unbalanced, uncoordinated and unsustainable development becomes a more serious problem, and areas of weakness become more prominent, we cannot truly say we have been achieved the goals even if we have accomplished the goals for GDP and growth rate by 2020. The weaknesses of completing the building of a moderately prosperous society in all respects are the key and difficult issues that we should attach importance to and strive to address.

1.4.3.1 Resolving the issue of quality and efficiency of economic development

Since the 18th CPC National Congress, the CPC Central Committee has made a major strategic judgment that China's economic development has entered a new normal. This conclusion is drawn from comprehensively analyzing the world economy cycle and China's development stage and the interaction between the two. Under the new normal, China's economic development features the changes in growth rate, growth mode, economic structure and growth engines. These changes constitute a necessary process for China's economy to evolve into a model that is more advanced, better structure and with more complicated division of labor. To promote China's economic and social development during the 13th Five-year Plan (2016-2020) period, it is necessary to adapt to, understand, and guide the new normal as the major tasks throughout the overall development and the whole process. To a great extent, this requires to improve the quality and efficiency of economic development, change the large-scale extensive growth, change the large-scale growth of wasting resources and energy, and change the high-speed growth of low-cost factors. When China enters the new era of economic development, building a prosperous society in all respects must be completed at a certain speed on condition that the green, innovative, high-quality and high-efficiency development is achieved to realize its GDP. It must be the coordinated development in accordance with the law of economy, the sustainable development in accordance with the law of nature, and the inclusive development in accordance with the law of society. As for the concrete measures, guided by the spirit of the Central Conference on Economic Work held at the end of 2017 and revolving around promoting high-quality development, the following eight tasks should be done: First, deepen the supply-side structural reform; second, energize all kinds of market entities; third, implement the strategy of rural revitalization; fourth, implement the regional coordinated development strategy; fifth, promote the formation of a new pattern of all-round opening up; sixth, improve social security and the people's livelihood; seventh, speed up the establishment of a housing system with multi-subject supply and multi-channel guarantee with both renting and purchasing being available; eighth, speed up the ecological progress.

1.4.3.2 Resolving the issues of unbalanced, uncoordinated and unsustainable development

The issues of unbalanced, uncoordinated and unsustainable development are the weaknesses of completing the building of a moderately prosperous society in all respects. At the macro level, areas of weaknesses are ubiquity, not only in the economic, political, cultural, social and ecological areas, but also in every region and even in economically developed regions. At the micro level, the types and depths of weak links are relative, diverse and different from region to region. To realize a moderately prosperous society in all respects, more efforts should be made to seek economic, political, cultural, social and ecological progress. After the economic development has entered the new normal, in order to solve many problems in China's economic and social development, it will mainly rely on promoting fairness to stimulate the innovative vitality of all people and form an inexhaustible driving force for economic growth. Therefore, in the new stage of economic development with new growth drivers replacing traditional ones, the key to addressing weaknesses is to solve the issue of inequity, extend the middle-income group. Thus, we can successfully achieve the First Centenary Goal and lay solid foundation for achieving the Second Centenary Goal. According to the requirements of realizing a moderately prosperous society in all respects during the 13th Five-year Plan period, the most prominent and common weaknesses are as follows: First, the weakness of poverty alleviation. the CPC has been placing priority to the issues of agriculture, rural areas, and rural people, and solving the problems related to them in its work agenda. Bringing about a moderately prosperous society in all respects does not necessarily follow that each and every individual is ensured the same level of moderate prosperity. But if the living standards of the currently impoverished rural population do not improved noticeably, then the realization a moderately prosperous society in all respects will lack credibility. Therefore, Xi Jinping regards poverty alleviation of the impoverished rural population in rural areas as the most arduous task and the most prominent area of weakness in realizing a moderately prosperous society in all respects.[1] Second, the weakness of people's livelihood. People's livelihood is the foundation of their happiness and social harmony. Improving people's livelihood and well-being is the essential requirement of the CPC to stick to governing the Party for the public's good and exercise the state power for the benefits of people. Xi pointed out that the starting point and focus in all of the work is to enable ordinary people to lead a good life. Third, the weakness of ecology. The relationship between man and nature is the most basic one in human society. Civilization prospers when the ecology prospers, and civilization decays when the ecology decays. The CPC has been attaching great importance to the ecological progress. After years of rapid development, China has made historic achievements in economic development, but meanwhile accumulated many ecological environment problems, which has become a prominent weakness affecting the improvement of the quality of people's life. Thus, we must spare efforts to improve the weakness in ecological progress and promote the completion of building a moderately prosperous

[1] Chen Baosheng, "Resolve the Key and Difficult Problems Hindering the Building of a Moderately Prosperous Society in all Respects", *Guangming Daily*, Jul. 23, 2016.

society in all respects.

1.4.3.3 Improving the awareness and capability of risk prevention and control

During the 13th Five-year Plan period, risks in all areas confronted by China's development continue to accumulate and even emerge in some concentrated aspects. In terms of economic risk prevention and control, with China's economic development entering the new normal, it needs time and space to cut excessive industrial capacity, and optimize and upgrade the industrial structure. The mounting downward pressure on economy will easily cause some prominent contradictions and issues: First, the risks of local government debts. The scale and speed of development in some cities exceed their financial capacity, making the local governments shoulder heavy debt burdens, thus the fiscal and financial risks continue to accumulate. Second, the financial risks. In recent years, China's macro debt level has continued to rise, and the credit risk of industries afflicted by excessive industrial capacity has gradually emerged. The financial risks of "zombie enterprises", the risks of foreign exchange market, stock market, bond market and property market under high leverage as well as the risks of abnormal cross-border capital flows have increased. Third, the industrial risks. The re-industrialization of developed countries attracts the return of domestic manufacturing industries, while emerging economies and other developing countries vigorously attract low-end industries and order transfer. In addition, the Sino-US trade friction brings many uncertainties, thus China's industries face the double challenges of enhancing competitiveness and avoiding hollowing-out. Fourth, the international trade risks. Western countries are strengthening trade protectionism. Apart from traditional means such as anti-dumping and countervailing, requirements about technical trade barriers, labor standards and green barriers become increasingly demanding in the process of market access. In particular, the new round of escalating Sino-US trade friction in early 2018 has greatly aggravated the international trade risks. Therefore, the 2018 Report on the Work of the Government emphasized that importance should be attached to win the three tough battles of risk management, poverty elimination, and pollution control to realize a moderately prosperous society in all respects. to realize a moderately prosperous society in all respects.

1.4.3.4 Avoiding simplifying the goal of building a moderately prosperous society in all respects into limited targets

From the process of putting forward the goal of building a moderately prosperous society in all respects, it is easy to see that it is a goal both quantitative and qualitative with rich connotations. Although some economic and social goals can be quantified, attention should be paid to guard against two tendencies: First, the simple treatment of quantitative goals leads to lower standards, or even deviations. For example, to achieve the goal of doubling the per capita income of urban and rural residents by 2020 compared with that of 2010, we should not just focus on the figures. The reason is that even though the per capita income doubles, the problem of large amount of poor population may arise due to the large income gap. If so, we cannot say that we have achieved the goal of "a moderately prosperous society at a higher level that benefits more than a billion people". Second, paying attention to the limited goals leads to overgeneralization. To quantify the goal of building a moderately prosperous society in all respects is to simplify and visualize the analysis, and we can only choose the important and quantifiable parts for quantification. It is impossible to comprehensively and accurately reflect and evaluate the actual progress of building a moderately prosperous society in all respects only by making a trade-off and translating the quantitative objectives into certain targets. Some targets are difficult to quantify, and no desirable results can be achieved if we force to quantify them. It should be recognized that the unquantifiable and non-quantifiable targets do not infer that they are not important. A moderately prosperous society in all respects means to promote an overall coordinated economic, political, cultural, social, and ecological advancement. The five-sphere advancements integrate with each other and support for each other. Without any of them, it is impossible to realize a moderately prosperous society in all respects.[1] Since some targets are difficult to quantify and the situation of quantifiable targets is more complex, special attention should be paid to prevent the tendency of simplifying the goal of realizing a moderately prosperous society in all respects into limited targets in practice and the misleading of realizing a moderately prosperous society in all respects. It should be also noted that the difficulty of realizing a moderately prosperous society in all respects is not to achieve the quantitative targets, but to achieve the qualitative ones. If we unilaterally regard the limited targets as the goal of realizing a moderate prosperity in all respects, and complete quantifiable targets well and non-quantifiable targets poorly, there will be embarrassment that the completion of the targets is not in line with what people actually desire.

---

[1] Zhang Zhanbin, "The Goal of Building a Moderately Prosperous Society in all Respects Cannot Be Reduced to Limited Targets", *People's Daily*, Apr. 8, 2015.

1.4.4 Strategic measures to build a moderately prosperous society in all respects

Completing the building of a moderately prosperous society in all respects is an unprecedented great leap in Chinese history, which is still facing many difficulties and challenges. To further promote the completion, special attention should be paid to the following aspects.

1.4.4.1 Accurately grasping the profound changes in the connotation of strategic opportunity for China's development

Though China has entered a new normal of economic development, and experienced an unavoidable shift in economic growth, it should be noted that China's economic fundamentals remain favorable for long-term growth and the sound trend of economic development we are constantly seeing can be sustained. China maintains great strategic opportunities to accomplish good deeds for development. At present, the world is undergoing profound changes unseen in a century, and China is turning the period of opportunities for accelerated and expanded growth into the period of opportunities for accelerated transformation of economic development mode and improvement of the quality and efficiency of development. In terms of economic aggregate, China's main economic indicators rank the top in the world, yet lagging behind in terms of per capita figures. In 2017, China's per capita GDP ranked 74th in the world. China still lags far behind the developed countries in terms of the comprehensive development, especially in innovation capability, labor productivity, social welfare and so on. In the case of such a large economy as China, we cannot expect others to help us if something goes wrong. Only by making ourselves stronger can we effectively withstand external risks with full confidence. We should aim at realizing a moderately prosperous society in all respects, constantly deepen our understanding of taking economic development as the central task, unswervingly follow the path of reform and opening up, and firmly grasp the top priority of development without neglect, distraction and laziness, and with every effort to get things done well.

1.4.4.2 Relying more on innovation to improve the quality and efficiency of economic growth

To double the GDP and per capita income of urban and rural residents by 2020 compared with that of 2010, we must maintain the economic growth at a certain rate over the next three years. During the 13th Five-year Plan period, the average annual growth of GDP should maintain a rate of more than 6.5%, and the major economic indicators should be balanced and coordinated to achieve the goal of doubling GDP and per capita income. To achieve such new requirements, we can neither rely on another massive campaign to make rapid progress nor rely on extensive mode of development to boost the growth pace through strong stimulus. What is needed is the real growth of high-quality, high-efficient development that adopts an effective approach and follows the law of economy, sustainable development in accordance with the law of nature, and inclusive development in accordance with social managements. To achieve such a development, we need to leverage the great role of innovation more than ever before. We must put innovation at the core of the overall national development, and take down-to-earth actions to enhance the independent innovation capability. We must accelerate efforts to transform from factor-driven and investment-driven development to innovation-driven development, speed up making China a country of innovators, promote the medium-high-end industrial development, and maintain the medium-high economic growth.

1.4.4.3 Staying committed to advancing the supply-side structural reform

In the decisive stage of building a moderately prosperous society in all respects, the greater the downward economic pressure, the more subjective initiative should be fully leveraged to promote the development. To stay committed to taking economic development as the central task, China must adhere to focusing on economic restructuring to promote supply-side structural reform. The 2018 Report on the Work of the Government stressed: To promote supply-side structural reform, we must continue to focus our efforts on real economies, tackle the issues of cutting overcapacity, reducing excess inventory, deleveraging, lowering costs, and strengthening areas of weakness. We must vigorously streamline administration, reduce taxes and fees, constantly optimize the business environment, further stimulate the vitality of market entities, and improve the quality of economic growth. Therefore, at present, we are promoting high-quality social development and constantly accelerating various reforms with the number and intensity of reform measures being unprecedented. We are paying attention to the top-level design, highlighting the response to building a moderately prosperous society in all respects. We are putting the philosophy of people-centered development into practice throughout the whole process of reform. Currently, what is most important is to shoulder our due responsibilities for reforms and unswervingly push forward the reforms with our political courage, and put all the supply-side structural reform measures that have been implemented in place. It is necessary to better liberate factors and productive forces, improve total factor productivity, and provide more space for the sound growth of the new economy by cutting excess capacity, reducing excess inventory, deleveraging, lowering costs, and strengthening areas of weakness. In the "Internet Plus" era, new products, new industries, new forms of business and industries, new models are bursting out vitality, and become vibrant and creative forces supporting economic growth with the new growth drivers gradually replacing the old ones.

1.4.4.4 Intensifying institutional innovation and breakthroughs to strengthen the most prominent areas of weakness

To achieve the goal of poverty alleviation, it is necessary to remedy the most prominent areas of weakness in the process of building a moderately prosperous society in all respects. The core issue is to balance the relationship between the role of government and that of the market, and to strengthen the institutional supply through institutional innovation and breakthroughs. Lifting the poor out of poverty is in essence the area where the market cannot manage. Therefore, based on the decisive role that the market plays in allocating resources, the institutional design of remedying the areas of weakness should leverage the better role of the government to address the inaction and absence of government at some levels. The absence of public services should be quickly addressed through targeted poverty alleviation and reduction, and nor should other areas of weakness through these measures. The next years will experience the continuous accumulation or even concentrated exposure of risks in all aspects facing China's development. We should remedy deficiencies through institutional innovations and breakthroughs, enhance our awareness and capability to guard against various kinds of risks, and strive to avoid or be able to withstand and survive major risks when occurred.

1.4.4.5 Removing institutional obstacles that restricts the expansion of the middle-income group

The middle-income group is the "main force" to expand domestic demands and release consumer dividends. The requirements of this group for the quality, performance and experience of product services are reversely conducive to the reform on the supply side. The larger the proportion of the middle-income group in a country, the more beneficial it is to narrow the income gap, reduce injustice and promote social harmony and stability. To expand the middle-income group, we must coordinate and plan the short-term and long-term policies. We must, in accordance with the requirements of the central government, adhere to quality and efficient development, work hard to make the "cake" of development growing larger and shared out evenly, break down various institutional obstacles that restrict the expansion of middle-income group, make development results fairer and more beneficial to all, and effectively expand the proportion of middle-income people. As an important engine for China's economic development, private capital investment has made important contributions to China's economic growth. However, we are still facing mounting downward economic pressure, and encountering many new problems and difficulties in private capital investments. Therefore, it is necessary to expand the middle-income group, vigorously promote the development of private capital investments, and work hard to overcome various difficulties encountered in private capital investments. We must take more effective measures to protect property rights, eliminate various hidden barriers, truly mobilize entrepreneurs' enthusiasm and creativity, so as to create conditions for expanding the proportion of middle-income people in all aspects. The 2018 Report on the Work of the Government clearly emphasized the need to support the development of private enterprises. We should keep committed to upholding equal rights, equal opportunities and equal rules, fully implement policies and measures to support the development of non-public sector, earnestly solve prominent problems reported by private enterprises, and resolutely break down various hidden barriers. We should form a new type of cordial and clean relationship between government and business and improve the mechanism for entrepreneurs to participate in making enterprise-related policies. We should also stimulate and protect entrepreneurial spirit, enhance their confidence, and thus help private enterprises to fully function their strengths in the tidal waves of market economy.

1.5 The new development philosophy: major compliance for developing a powerful economy

The philosophy of innovative, coordinated, green, open and sharing development was put forward in the Fifth Plenary Session of the 18th CPC Central Committee. Guided by the major practical and theoretical issues and focusing on the changing tendency and characteristics of China's economic and social development, the new development philosophy makes a comprehensive interpretation on what development to achieve and how to achieve development with Chinese consciousness and wisdom.[1] Firmly establishing and implementing the new development philosophy is a profound change related to the overall situation of China's development, a fundamental

[1] Gu Hailiang, "Discussion on Marxist Political Economy Based on the New Development Philosophy", *Marxism & Reality*, 2016 (1).

guarantee for realizing the goal of building a moderately prosperous society in all respects. It is of great and far-reaching significance for the long-term sustained and sound development of China's economy, Chinese society and building an economic powerhouse.

1.5.1 The new development philosophy breeding new development theory

Entering the decisive stage of building a moderately prosperous society in all respects, and the critical period of driving deeper reform and adjusting in-depth structure, China is now facing the acid test of getting smoothly through the "middle-income trap". In the face of new stage, situation, tasks and characteristics of China's economic development, the existing theories of economic development, especially the theories of development economics, an important branch of western economics, show their historical and theoretical limitations. They cannot deal with China's development issues, let alone solve the major theoretical and practical issues facing China's development.[1] Then, there is an urgent need to implement the new development philosophy and establish new theories of economic development.

Xi Jinping stressed that concept is the precursor of action, and is meant to make an overall, fundamental long-term arrangement and development direction. It well embodies the ideas, direction and focus of development. The new development philosophy, proposed at the Fifth Plenary Session of the 18th CPC Central Committee, profoundly reveals the path to achieving higher quality, more efficient and more equitable development during the 13th Five-year Plan period and even in a long period front from the height of overall strategy of China's economic and social development, which is bound to breed new development theories.

Since the 18th CPC National Congress, the CPC Central Committee has unswervingly upheld and developed socialism with Chinese characteristics, deepen the understanding of the law that underlie governance by the Communist Party, the development of socialism, and the evolution of human society, and formed a series of new ideas and strategies about governing the country through practice and innovation.

---

[1] Huang Taiyan, "New Development Concepts Give Birth to New Development Theories", *People's Daily*, Apr. 18, 2016.

From the Five-sphere Integrated Plan[1] to the Four-pronged Comprehensive Strategy[2], and then to the proposal of the philosophy of new development, the governance principles of the new central collective leadership is becoming clearer and more mature. In the Report to the 19th CPC National Congress, the philosophy of new development was put forward and emphasized in the essence and connotations of the "Fourteen Persistences"[3] of Xi Jinping Thought on Socialism with Chinese Characteristics for a New Era. Development is the fundamentals and key to solving all problems in China. Our development must be sound development. We must stay committed to pursuing the philosophy of innovative, coordinated, green, open and inclusive development. It can be seen that the philosophy and principle for new development profoundly reveal the new characteristics and laws governing China's economic and social development, and intensively reflect the Party's growing understanding of laws governing China's economic and social development. It is unified in the practice of realizing and developing socialism with Chinese characteristics, in the historical process of realizing the Two Centenary Goals[4] and the Chinese dream of national rejuvenation.

China's rapid economic growth in the past has created "China's miracle" in the history of world economy. At present, profound changes have taken place in the internal support conditions and external demand environment of economic development. This requires the "shift" of economic growth speed, and the "convergence" of economic growth targets within an appropriate range to make China enter a new normal in economic development. China's new normal of economy prominently manifests the comprehensive optimization and upgrading of economic structure, entailing a series of

---

[1] The Five-sphere Integrated Plan is to promote coordinated economic, political, cultural, social, and ecological advancement. —*Tr.*

[2] The Four-pronged Comprehensive Strategy is to make comprehensive moves to finish building a moderately prosperous society in all respects, deepen reform, advance law-based governance, and strengthen Party self-governance. —*Tr.*

[3] "Fourteen Persistences" is to ensure Party leadership over all work; commit to a people-centered approach; continue to comprehensively deepen reform; adopt a new vision for development; see that the people run the country; ensure every dimension of governance is law-based; uphold core socialist values; ensure and improve people's living standards through development; ensure harmony between human and nature; pursue a holistic approach to national security; uphold absolute Party leadership over the people's armed forces; uphold the principle of "one country, two systems" and promote national reunification; promote the building of a community with a shared future for mankind; exercise full and rigorous governance over the Party. —*Tr.*

[4] The Two Centenary Goals is to finish building a moderately prosperous society in all respects by the time the Communist Party of China marks its centenary and to build China into a modern socialist country that is prosperous, strong, democratic, culturally advanced, and harmonious by the time the People's Republic of China celebrates its centenary. —*Tr.*

rich connotations and characteristics, such as transforming economic growth speed, adjusting industrial structure, changing economic growth engines, transforming the mode of resource allocation, and sharing economic well-beings. This requires us to update the development vision timely and lead the new era of economic growth with the new vision.

1.5.2 The new development philosophy entailing rich connotations

Now, the environment, conditions, tasks and requirements of China's development under the new normal has changed. Based on its new trend, changes and characteristics, the new development philosophy focuses on solving the prominent weaknesses of development, emphasize the competitive strengths of deep-rooted development, clarify the targets, tasks and requirements of comprehensively completing the 13th Five-year Plan, and point out the basic thoughts and fundamental methods for securing a decisive victory in building a moderately prosperous society in all respects. Therefore, the new development philosophy possesses rich connotations.

The Report to the 19th CPC National Congress stressed that innovation is the primary driving force of development and the strategic underpinning for building a modernized economy. American economist Schumpeter once pointed out: Innovation is the driving force of economic growth and development for capitalist countries; without innovation, there will be no development for capitalist countries. Likewise, innovation is the first driving force of development under the socialist market economy. Currently, China has not resolved the traditional problem of insufficient domestic demand and the new problem of supply-side is becoming more and more serious. On the one hand, traditional industries face excess capacity, falling prices and serious losses; on the other hand, the new and old growth engines face inadequate transitions. The share of new products, new industries and new forms of business and industries is relatively low, which is inadequate to make up for the decline of traditional industries. In this severe situation, innovation is the only way to maintain the medium-high economic growth. To adhere to innovative development, we must place innovation at the core of the overall situation of national development, constantly promote innovation in theory, institution, science and technology, culture and other aspects, make innovation the dominant theme in the work of the Party and the government, and an everyday activity in society.

Coordinated development is the inherent requirement of sustained and sound development. Since the reform and opening up, China has gained remarkable results and rich experience in economic and social development, but there remain some prominent issues of development such as unbalanced, uncoordinated, non-inclusive and unsustainable development, especially the contradictions between unbalanced regional development, uncoordinated urban and rural development, unreasonable industrial structure, and unbalanced economic and social development. These issues and contradictions have revealed a series of bottlenecks and constraints in China's development, and advanced the profound transformation of development vision and growth mode. Proposed by the Fifth Plenary Session of the 18th CPC Central Committee, adhering to coordinated development is meant that during the 13th Five-year Plan period, China should pay more attention to making up for the weak links in all areas of economic and social development, seeking development potential by expanding the development capacity, and achieving all-round coordinated development through the balanced allocation of resources.

Green development is a necessary requirement for sustainable development. Lucid waters and lush mountains are invaluable assets. Since the 18th CPC National Congress, the CPC Central Committee has integrated the ecological advancement into the all aspects and whole process of economic, political, cultural and social progress, forming the Five-sphere Integrated Plan. Seeing from the process of reform and opening up, 40 years of rapid economic development has also brought about serious environmental problems such as haze pollution, river pollution, land desertification, and lake shrinking. Facing the severe situation of environmental destruction, we must correctly balance the relationship between economic development and environmental protection, focus on the long-term and comprehensive development in environmental protection, and establish the green development vision of respecting nature, following nature and protecting nature. To adhere to green development is to follow the basic national policy of enriching the country and benefiting the people through green development, advance the prosperity of the people and the country, and promote the beauty of China.

Openness is the only way to a country's prosperity and development. As a Chinese proverb says, a single flower does not make a spring, while one hundred flowers in full blossom bring spring to the garden. The development practice in China and other countries in the world has proved that openness brings progress, while self-seclusion leaves one behind. At present, China has developed into the world's second largest economy, largest exporter and second importer, largest foreign investor and third foreign investment country, as well as largest foreign exchange reserve country. It is safe to say that China is a real major economy. If we say the miracle of China's development benefits from reform and opening up, then China will open even wider under the new normal of economy without any reason to change. To adhering to open development, it is meant to enrich the connotation of opening up, improve the level of opening up, promoting strategic mutual trust, economic and trade cooperation, and people-to-people and cultural exchanges, build a new type of international relations with win-win cooperation as the core, strive to form a mutually beneficial cooperation pattern with deep integration, and create a new pattern of opening up.

Shared development is the essential requirement of socialism with Chinese characteristics. As a Chinese saying goes, "as vast as the heaven and earth may be, the people must always come first." It is the essence of socialism to improve people's livelihood, allow the people to share the fruits of development, and stay committed to pursuing the path of common prosperity. It demonstrates the superiority of socialism, and the Party's fundamental purpose of wholeheartedly serving the people. By the end of 2017, China's per capita GDP had increased to about US$9,481, and continued to reduce poverty by more than 10 million people every year. All these show our Party's governance of people-centered philosophy. The vision of development is also changing from making the country rich and strong to bringing prosperity to the people. Therefore, to adhere to shared development, our driving principle must be that development is for the people and by the people, and its benefit is shared by the people. We must make more effective institutional arrangements to make people gain a greater sense of fulfillment, and steadily lead them to common prosperity.

1.5.3 The new development philosophy showing a distinct problem orientation

The philosophy of innovative, coordinated, green, open and inclusive development was put forward in the Fifth Plenary Session of the 18th CPC Central Committee. These new development concepts did not emerge from the ether; they came from both domestic and foreign experience of development, and from a profound analysis of both domestic and foreign trends in development. They reflect our Party's growing understanding of the laws governing economic and social development based on the most prominent contradictions and issues in China's development.

China's capacity to innovate is inadequate; the overall level of science and technology is not fully developed and is unable to create momentum to support economic and social development is insufficient. Therefore, innovation makes a much lower contribution to economic growth in China than in developed countries. This is the

"Achilles' heel" for such a big economy as China. The new round of revolution in science and technology will inevitably give rise to fiercer competition. If the capacity to innovate in science and technology fails to meet the need to boost economy, it is impossible to transform the impetus for development, and we will lag behind in the global economic competition. Therefore, we must consider innovation as the primary driving force of growth and the core of the whole undertaking of national development, and human resources as the primary resource to support development. We should constantly promote innovation in theory, system, science and technology, culture and other aspects, and make innovation the dominant theme in the work of the Party and government, and an everyday activity in society.

China's uncoordinated development is a long-standing prominent issue, manifested in the relationship between different regions, between urban and rural areas, between economy and society, between material and cultural progress, and between economic development and strengthening national defense. When we lag behind in the economic development, the primary task is to speed up development, but after the period of rapid development, we need to adjust and pay attention to the overall effect. Otherwise, the "buckets effect" will show, intensifying social conflicts and contradictions. Therefore, we must hold fast to the basics of the cause of socialism with Chinese characteristics, properly handle major relationships in development and constantly enhance the harmony in development.

Green, circular, and low-carbon development, which is the most promising sector, guides the direction of current revolution in science, technology and industry. China has great potential in this regard, which can give rise to many new engines of economic growth. While we are facing ever-tighter resource constraints, serious environmental pollution and ecological degradation, as well as facing the people's growing demand for fresh air, clean drinking water, safe food and a beautiful environment. Therefore, we must uphold the basic national policy of conserving resources and protecting the environment, pursue the path of sustainable development to achieve productive development, prosperity, and a sound ecological environment, and create a society that respects resource-saving and environment-friendly principles. We must promote the Beautiful China initiative and contribute our part to global ecological security.

Now, profound changes are taking place in international economic cooperation and competition, and major adjustments are under way in the global economic governance system and rules. While the depth, breadth and pace of "bringing in" and "going global" are unprecedented, the pressure to deal with external economic risks and maintain national economic security is also unprecedented. The problem now is not whether to continue opening up, but how to improve the quality of opening up and advance the internal and external connectivity with others. As a whole, China is not opening up wide enough. We lack the strong ability to use domestic and foreign markets and resources; we are weak in dealing with international trade friction, in exerting influence on the international economy, and in applying international trade rules. We need to improve weaknesses in these areas. To this end, we must uphold the basic national policy of opening up, implement an opening-up strategy characterized by mutual benefit, strengthen cultural exchanges, and improve the layout of opening-up regions, of foreign trade, and of investment. With such efforts, we can form a new system for opening up, develop an open economy at a higher level, and drive innovation, reform and development.

Although shared development can be enjoyed by all, it is neither one-sided pursuit of average distribution of reform results, nor a gain without effort. This requires us to embody not only the relative fairness of distribution of development fruits, but that of the rights, opportunities and rules of development, so that the majority of people can maximize the sense of fulfillment. Fairness typically refers to the proper proportion of pay and return of each citizen, and so equalitarianism does not mean true fairness. As each object in the world has its own feature and cannot be completely identical, the existence of differences is objective and it is unfair to equalize differences. In the past, people failed to understand the real connotation of fairness and simply regarded it as the average between the rich and the poor. In view of Marxism, distribution is the product of production, as mode of production determines distribution. Currently, China is still in the primary stage of socialism. We have underdeveloped productive force and insufficient material wealth, and need to promote the spiritual progress to a higher level. This situation determines that the social distribution under the concept of shared development needs to unify the overall social and individual interests, and adhere to the principle of fairness and bringing benefit to all people. Therefore, in the primary stage of socialism, we must eliminate and avoid the old idea of equalitarianism, promote social equity with equity of property and income, and achieve a relative fairness corresponding to the level of economic and social development. [1]

---

[1] Fang Gao, "Sharing by all People: Unification between the Principal Status of the People and Values and Rights", *Study Times*, Feb. 15, 2017.

1.5.4 The new development philosophy guiding the building of a moderately prosperous society

We must adhere to the unified plan from both the domestic and global perspectives, take the initiative in adapting to and guide the new normal of economic development with new concept, thinking and measures, make plans from the global economic links, and attach importance to improving the capability to allocate resources on a global scale. The Fifth Plenary Session of the 18th CPC Central Committee has sounded a clarion call in building a moderately prosperous society in all respects. The 19th CPC National Congress has clarified to apply a new vision for development and develop a modernized economy. We are required to put quality first and give priority to performance, pursue supply-side structural reform as our main task, work hard for better quality, higher efficiency, and more robust drivers of economic growth through reform, and raise total factor productivity. Therefore, we must grasp the focus of development and incorporate the new development concepts into the whole process and all areas of economic and social development during the 13th Five-year Plan period.

1.5.4.1 Transforming economic growth model and improving the quality of economic growth

Economic development should maintain a certain pace, on condition that high quality and efficiency are guaranteed to realize the real growth. In general, China has enormous industrial capacity, but it is partly compromised by ineffective supply, and lacks effective supply of high quality and high level. China is a large producer and exporter, but most of products and technologies are low-end while few are high-tech, high quality and high added-value. We must not only focus on expanding demand, but improving the quality and level of supply. In the critical stage of building a moderately prosperous society in all respects, we must take firm steps in upholding the philosophy of new development to guide the practice of development, strive to transform the previous economic growth mode of high input, high consumption, high pollution and low output. We must also improve social labor productivity, enterprise and investment efficiency, and make the development reach a new level in the 13th Five-year Plan period. We must ensure that through innovation and development, the endogenous momentum for economic growth can be enhanced; through coordinated development, the overall level of economic development can be promoted; through green development, the problems of environmental pollution and unsustainable development can be solved; through open development, the capability to improve the internal and external linkage of development and to resist risks can be enhanced; and through shared development, the fruits of reform and opening up can be shared by urban and rural people.

1.5.4.2 Accelerating structural reform and fostering the driving force of economic growth

The key task of the 13th Five-year Plan is to transform the mode of economic growth and adjust the economic structure. Currently, China's economy is under significant downward pressure. This is partly due to the gross, global and periodical factors, but fundamentally caused by structural problems. For example, a major reason for the current slowdown in economic growth is that the drivers of industrial growth faces inadequacy, and the new and old industries experience uncoordinated development. Therefore, we should implement the new development vision, take the supply-side structural reform as the main line, and further strengthen the structural reform, so as to realize mutual promotion between economic growth and structural adjustment. We should implement the "Made in China 2025" plan, accelerate the "Internet Plus" plan, and further deepen the reform of systems and mechanisms based on people-centered new urbanization, and promote the optimal allocation of urban and rural resources. We should promote the vigorous development of new technologies, industries, and businesses and industries, focus on the forefront of science and technology in the world, achieve a number of major innovative fruits, promote the industrialization of scientific and technological results, turn innovative results into real economic activities, and build new product groups and industrial groups.

1.5.4.3 Promoting business startups by innovation in science and technology and creating jobs by business start ups

Business startups and innovation is not only the source of power for development, but also the way to bring prosperity to the people, to achieve fairness and to strengthen the country. It is of great significance for promoting economic structural adjustment, building a new engine for development, enhancing the new power for development and taking the road of innovation-driven development. It is an important measure to stabilize economic growth, increase employment opportunities, stimulate the wisdom and creativity of hundreds of millions of people, promote social vertical mobility, and realize fairness and justice. To adhere to the philosophy of new development, accelerated efforts should be made to implement the strategy and policy of "business startups and innovation", encourage and bring in business startups and innovation, drive the adjustment of employment structure by optimizing economic structure, guide business startups and innovation by capital chain, support the industrial chain by business startups and innovation, and drive the employment chain by industrial chain. We should consolidate the primary industry, expand the secondary industry, especially the manufacturing industry, stimulate the tertiary industry, and promote the rapid development of the service industry, especially the modern service industry, through business startups and innovation. We should further implement the strategy of giving priority to the development of talents, deepen the reform of education system and policy innovation, pay more attention to the great development of vocational education, strive to cultivate more skilled workers and engineers like Germany, and support Chinese products to seize the commanding height of international industry.

1.5.4.4 Defusing social economic risks and resolving social contradictions and issues

The 13th Five-year Plan period is a period in which risks in all areas of China's development continue to accumulate and even emerge in some concentrated areas. The major threats we may encounter include not only domestic economic, political, ideological, social risks and those from nature, but global economic, political and military risks. If major risks occur and we are not able to fight against them, our national security may face fatal problems, and the process of realizing a moderately prosperous society in all respects will probably be interrupted. Therefore, we must put the prevention of risks in a prominent position and nip risks in the bud to avoid them and improve the ability to resist risks. We must try our best to prevent any major risks, and when they occur, be able to ward them off. We must have a clear understanding of the situation. We must remain keenly alert to potential risks, firmly adhere to the new development vision, raise the awareness of hardship and risks, take precautions, and establish and improve the system and mechanism to resolve various risks. In particular, we should pay attention to handling the internal contradictions of the masses, responding to the voice and concerns of the masses, and coordinating various interest relations. We must strengthen efforts to investigate and identify various risk sources, improve the capability of dynamic monitoring and real-time alarm, and promote risk prevention and control in an effective and meticulous way. We must have a clear idea of various possible risks and their causes, suit different remedies to different risks, and adopt a holistic approach. We must make timely and effective measures to defuse risks in the bud, prevent small risks from evolving into big ones, individual ones into complex ones, local ones into regional or systematic ones, economic ones into social and political ones, and global ones into domestic ones.

1.5.4.5 Building an open economy at a higher level and a broad community of common interests

The Report to the 19th CPC National Congress pointed out: The world is undergoing major developments, transformation and adjustment, but peace and development remain the call of our day. At the critical stage of building a moderately prosperous society in all respects, the Party shoulders an extremely arduous task of development. The highly difficult reform requires a high level of opening up. There will be no way out if we do not carry out or further deepen the policy of opening up. Therefore, we must continue to maintain strategic resolve, concentrate on our own affairs, pursue the strengths and avoid the shortcomings, better utilize the international market and resources, expand opening up at a wider and deeper level, and create a new pattern of opening up. We must work to improve the level of trade investment facilitation and promote the "going global" of equipment manufacturing industries such as high-speed rail and nuclear power. We must firmly promote the vision and action of the Belt and Road Initiative, and accelerate efforts to launch a batch of achievable projects in the field of infrastructure at the early stage. We must better utilize pilot free trade zone—the innovative carrier and window, and approve the establishment of some new pilot free trade zones in an appropriate period. Meanwhile, we must work to accelerate the internationalization of renminbi. We must stay committed to pursuing the path of open development and focus on developing open economy at a higher level. We must actively participate in global economic governance and public goods supply, raise China's voice in institutional power and global economic governance, build a broad community of a shared future with common interests, and create a dynamic environment in which China and other countries in the world enjoy mutually reinforcing progress in development.

1.5.4.6 Strengthening areas of weakness in social development and winning the battle against poverty alleviation

The 13th Five-year Plan period is the final stage of building a moderately prosperous society in all respects. Seeing from the actual situation during the 12th Five-year Plan period (2011-2015), whether the goal can be completed as scheduled or not depends on the most difficult arduous tasks of building moderate prosperity in rural areas, especially in poor areas. This is the biggest weakness of building a moderately prosperous society. Without moderate prosperity in rural areas, especially in poor areas, building a moderately prosperous society in all respects will not be completed by 2020.To uphold the concept of shared development, accelerated efforts are needed to implement the strategy of targeted poverty alleviation and elimination, and we are required to take stronger determination, well-designed approaches and more effective measures to ensure that by 2020, all rural populations living under the current poverty line will have been lifted out of poverty. The 2018 Report to the Work of Government also stressed: We must strengthen targeted poverty alleviation, and by 2018, more than 10 million rural people should be reduced from poverty, including 2.8 million people relocated from inhospitable areas. We need to promote poverty alleviation through industries, education, health care, and ecological protection, strengthen weak links in infrastructure and public services, and stimulate endogenous momentum for poverty alleviation. We must strengthen the integration of funds for poverty alleviation and performance-based management, adhere to current standards of poverty alleviation, ensure the progress and quality of poverty alleviation, and that poverty alleviation gets the approval of the people and can stand the test of time.

1.6 New era embarking on a new journey to developing a powerful economy

Socialism with Chinese characteristics has crossed the threshold into a new era. This is a new historical juncture in China's development. In the Report to the 19th CPC National Congress, strategic arrangements and decisions has been made from the height of overall development of the course of the CPC and the country. That is, we must build a moderately prosperous society in all respects and achieve the First Centenary Goal, and build on this achievement to embark on a new journey toward the Second Centenary Goal of fully building a great socialist country. As a whole, the Report to the 19th CPC National Congress serves as a political manifesto and guiding principles for the CPC to step into a new era. It embarks on a new journey and open up a new chapter, directing the way forward to further developing the cause of the Party and the country. It will vigorously promote China's growth from "grown rich" to "becoming strong", and make it a modern power that stands tall and firm among the nations of the world.

1.6.1 Xi Jinping Thought on Socialism with Chinese Characteristics for a New Era guiding China's developing a powerful economy

The Report to the 19th CPC National Congress, generalizes the results of the CPC's theoretical innovation made since the 18th CPC National Congress as the Thought on

Socialism with Chinese Characteristics for a New Era. Then, the Revised Constitution of the Communist Party of China, adopted by the 19th CPC National Congress, established Xi Jinping Thought of Socialism with Chinese Characteristics for a New Era as the Party's guiding principle. This represents that the guiding ideology of the Party is keeping pace with the times. On the whole, Xi Jinping Thought on Socialism with Chinese Characteristics for a New Era, regarded as "the essence of spirit of the times", was generated in the historical juncture of China's developing from a major economy to a strong economy and the historical practice of promoting the "Four Greatness"[1]. The Thought boasts endogenous characteristics and distinctive features of the times. It is of great immediate significance and far-reaching historical significance to rally the ideological consensus and wisdom of the whole Party and Chinese people of all ethnic groups, secure a decisive victory in building a moderately prosperous society in all respects, strive for the great success of socialism with Chinese characteristics for a new era, and realize the Chinese Dream of national rejuvenation.

Xi Jinping Thought on Socialism with Chinese Characteristics for a New Era mainly includes two aspects: the basic implications ("Eight Clarifications"[2]) and basic policy ("Fourteen Persistences"). The basic connotation of the Thought is in fact about

---

1 "Four Greatness" referred to great struggle, great project, great cause, and great dream. —*Tr.*

2 The Eight Clarifications makes clear that the overarching task of upholding and developing socialism with Chinese characteristics is to realize socialist modernization and national rejuvenation, and on the basis of completing the building of a moderately prosperous society in all respects, a two-step approach should be taken to build China into a great modern socialist country that is prosperous, strong, democratic, culturally advanced, harmonious, and beautiful by the middle of the 21st century; that the principal challenge facing Chinese society in the new era is the gap between unbalanced and inadequate development and the growing expectation of the people for a better life, which requires further commitment to the people-centered philosophy of development, well-rounded human development, and common prosperity for everyone; that the overall plan for building socialism with Chinese characteristics is the Five-sphere Integrated Plan, and the overall strategy is the Four-pronged Comprehensive Strategy, with an emphasis on stronger confidence in the path, theory, system and culture of socialism with Chinese characteristics; that the overall goal of in-depth reform in every field is to improve and develop the system of socialism with Chinese characteristics and modernize China's system and capacity for governance; that the overall goal of comprehensively advancing law-based governance is to establish a system of socialist rule of law with Chinese characteristics and build a country of socialist rule of law; that the Party's goal of building a strong military in the new era is to build the armed forces of the people into world-class forces that obey the Party's command, can fight and win, and maintain excellent conduct; that major-country diplomacy with Chinese characteristics aims to foster a new type of international relations and build a global community of shared future; and that the defining feature of socialism with Chinese characteristics is the leadership of the CPC; the greatest strength of the system of socialism with Chinese characteristics is the leadership of the CPC; the Party is the highest force for political leadership, setting forth the general requirements for strengthening the Party in the new era and underlining the importance of reinforcing the Party's political foundations.—*Tr.*

upholding and developing socialism with Chinese characteristics, and theoretically answering "what is socialism with Chinese characteristics". The basic policy of the Thought is actually about how to uphold and develop socialism with Chinese characteristics, and practically answering about "what to do" in building socialism with Chinese characteristics.

Based on the historical task of China's development from being a major economy to an economic power, the "Eight Clarifications" is put forward with the internal logic as follows: Upholding and developing socialism with Chinese characteristics and achieving socialist modernization and national rejuvenation is the logical starting point of Xi Jinping Thought on Socialism with Chinese Characteristics for a New Era, as well as the fundamental theme and goal for China to develop from being a major country to a powerful one. The People-centered philosophy of development is the value orientation of the Thought, which provides value guidance to develop from being a major economy to an economic power. To develop from being a major economy to an economic power, advancing "two major layouts" is the overall strategy. Perfecting the development system and modernizing national governance is the fundamental path. Building law-based system and law-based country is the legal guarantee. Building "world-class armed forces" is the military and national defense guarantee. Building a new form of international relations and a community with a shared future for mankind will provide a favorable international environment. Strengthening the Party's building for the new era will provide a strong political guarantee. The core of "Eight Clarifications" makes it clear that how to develop from being a major economy to an economic power from the thematic goals, value orientation, overall strategy, fundamental path, guarantee of the rule of law, guarantee of national defense, international environment and political guarantee respectively.

The "Fourteen Persistences" is closely revolved around China's developing from being a major country to a powerful one. It mainly contains three underlying logics. First, it proposes to resolve the contradiction between unbalanced and inadequate development and the people's ever-growing needs for a better life, as the principal challenge facing Chinese society has evolved when socialism with Chinese characteristics entered the new era. Take for example, it is necessary to stay committed to a people-centered approach, adhere to the new development concepts, see that the people run the country, advance law-based governance in all fields, ensure and improve people's living standards through development, ensure harmony between human and nature, and pursue a holistic approach to national security. Second, it proposes to provide the basic strategy for China's developing a powerful country. Take for example, it is necessary to adopt a new vision for development, uphold absolute Party leadership over the people's armed forces, upholding the principle of "one country, two systems" and promote national reunification, and promote the building of a community with a shared future for mankind. Third, it plans to focus on the "two major layouts". Take for example, it is necessary to adopt the new vision of development, see that the people run the country, uphold core socialist values, ensure and improve people's living standards through development and uphold harmony between human and nature. Another example, it is necessary to deepen reform in all areas, advance law-based governance, and exercise full and rigorous governance over the Party.

Xi Jinping Thought on Socialism with Chinese Characteristics for a New Era builds on and further enriches Marxism-Leninism, Mao Zedong Thought, Deng Xiaoping Theory, the Theory of Three Represents, and the Scientific Outlook on Development. The Thought has systematically resolved the basic issues about overall objectives, tasks, layout, strategy, and development direction, mode, driving force, as well as strategic steps, external conditions and political guarantees for upholding and developing socialism with Chinese characteristics in the new era. It is essential to apply The Thought into the whole areas and process of modernization. In essence, Xi Jinping Thought on Socialism with Chinese Characteristics for a New Era is a theory on China's forwarding from "grown rich" to "becoming strong". The Thought also provides scientific guidance and action guideline for realizing the great rejuvenation of the Chinese nation and developing China from being a major country to a powerful one.

1.6.2 Accurately grasping the changes in the principal challenge facing Chinese society in the new era to make scientific arrangements in developing a powerful economy

The report to the 19th CPC National Congress pointed out: The principal challenge facing Chinese society has evolved. What we now face is the contradiction between unbalanced and inadequate development and the people's ever-growing needs for a better life. In essence, the transformation of China's principal challenge is a historic change that bears on the overall situation. It is a profound review of the historic achievements and changes made in China's development over the past five years, as well as a historical response to the achievements of reform and opening up over the past four decades, and even a precise positioning of China's future development direction and goals. In the future, building on continued efforts to sustain development, China must devote great energy to addressing the imbalances and inadequacies of development, and push hard to improve the quality and effect of development. By doing so, we will better meet the ever-growing economic, political, cultural, social, and ecological needs of our people, and to promote well-rounded human development and all-round social progress.

In terms of social development practice, the unbalanced development mainly involves such important areas as economy, society and institution, among which unbalanced economy is the most salient one, mainly including unbalanced industry, unbalanced region and unbalanced impetus, etc. To be specific, unbalanced industry is mainly reflected in the imbalance between some world-level Chinese industries and some low-end industries at the value chain. Unbalanced region is mainly manifested in the lack of effective strategic channels connecting the development among the eastern, northeastern, central and western regions, as well as in the gaps between urban and rural areas and between the poor and the rich areas. To address the urban-rural gaps, three major problems should be solved, that is, to grant urban residency to around 100 million with rural household registration living in urban areas and other permanent urban residents, renovate rundown urban areas and "villages" in cities involving about 100 million people, and enable around 100 million rural residents to live in local towns and cities in the near central and western regions. Unbalanced impetus is mainly reflected in the differences between innovation-driven development and the transition from the old to the new growth drivers. After China's economic development entered the new normal, it is inherent to implement the transformation of drivers of growth and accelerate the shift from the traditional factors and investment-driven to the innovation-driven track, so as to build China into a modern socialist country with strong economy.

On the whole, the problem of inadequacies mainly includes inadequacies in fairness, justice, security and environment. Among them, inadequate fairness mainly includes inadequate shared development, fair distribution, judicial justice and public services. Inadequate shared development is mainly manifested in the inadequate rights between urban and rural areas and between regions, which makes the inequality of rights salient. To some extent, it intensifies the inequality of opportunities, and the income and property gap between the rich and the poor intensifies the inequality of results. Inadequate fairness distribution is mainly reflected in the distribution by urban and rural identity and distribution by the system inside and outside. In addition, after implementing a policy of priority to efficiency together with fairness to develop economy and deal with social relations for a long period, it will be difficult to achieve equitable distribution. Inadequate judicial impartiality is mainly manifested in some judicial personnel misconduct, lack of due professional ethics, bending the law for personal gain, handling cases without integrity. Inadequate public services is mainly manifested in the big gaps between urban and rural areas and between different regions in public services such as food safety and allocating education and medical resources, where there are still deficiencies or weakness of inadequate development.

To address the unbalanced and inadequate problem, the key is to fully apply the new development concepts and develop a sound modern economic system. The Report to the 19th CPC National Congress pointed out that China's economy has been transitioning from rapid growth to high-quality development. It is in a pivotal stage for transforming its growth model, improving its economic structure, and fostering new drivers of growth, thus developing a modern economic system is both an urgent requirement for getting us smoothly through this critical transition and a strategic goal for China's development.

Since the 18th CPC National Congress, a series of new ideas, new thinking, and new strategies have been proposed by the CPC Central Committee with Xi Jinping at its core. To be specific in the economic field, it mainly includes the new normal of economic development, the new development philosophy and the supply-side structural reform. Among them, the new normal of economic development defines the development context, the new development philosophy provides the guiding principles, and the supply-side structural reform points out the direction of reform, thus forming a policy framework for developing a modernized economy. To develop a modernized economy, we must put quality first and give priority to performance; we should pursue supply-side structural reform as our main task, and work hard for better quality, higher efficiency, and more robust drivers of economic growth through reform; we need to raise total factor productivity. Developing a modernized economy is multifaceted, but the new normal of economic development, the new development philosophy, and the supply-side structural reform are what must be well done now and in the future. In developing a modernized economy, we must focus on the real economy, give priority to improving the quality of the supply system, and enhance our economy's strength in terms of quality. The supply-side structural reform has revealed the causes of the current problems in China's economy, the challenges it faces and the fundamental path to solve them. The supply-side structural reform is not a simple proposition, but a great practice of developing socialist plutonomy with Chinese characteristics in a systematical way.

1.6.3 Promoting economic development quality in an all-round way in developing a powerful economy

At the 2017 Central Conference on Economic Work, it made clear that the weighty conclusion made in the Report to the 19th CPC National Congress—China's economy has been transitioning from a phase of rapid growth to a stage of high-quality development—was the basic feature of China's economic development in the new era, and further made major decisions and plans to promote high-quality development. It is of great historical and current significance for China to move on to high-quality economic development and develop a modernized powerful economy.

From the perspective of the law of economic development, high-quality development can meet the people's ever-growing needs to live a better life. It reflects the philosophy of new development. In high-quality development, innovation is the primary driving force; coordination becomes an endogenous feature; go-green is a prevailing mode; openness is the only path; and sharing is the fundamental goal. In addition, the 2017 Central Conference on Economic Work stressed: High-quality development is an essential requirement for China to maintain sustained and sound economic development; it is an essential requirement for China to adapt to the evolution of the principle challenge facing Chinese society, and achieve a moderate prosperity and socialist modernization in all respects; it is an essential requirement for China to follow the well-established rules of economic development. We need to fully understand the "three essential requirements", and work harder to promote high-quality development with greater awareness and determination. Only by pursuing high-quality development can we lay a solid foundation for developing a powerful economy.

Now, China's economy has reached a critical stage in transforming the growth model and the traditional growth pattern is unsustainable; in the meantime, a new round of scientific and technological revolution and industrial transformation is making multiple breakthroughs all round the world. Only by promoting the high-quality development and shaping a high-quality, efficient and diversified supply system can we achieve a sustained and sound economic development through the proper balance between supply and demand at a new level. Only in this way can we accumulate new momentums for building China into an economic powerhouse. In addition, the principal challenge facing Chinese society has now evolved into the challenge between unbalanced and inadequate development and the people's ever-growing needs for a better life. This involves low-quality development as represented by unbalanced and inadequate development. From the perspective of evolutionary economics, it is necessary to win new competitiveness by relying on high-quality economic development to solve the principle challenge facing Chinese society and accelerate efforts to developing a powerful economy in China.

Indeed, the improvement in quality can be achieved by the accumulated quantity at a certain phase. This results from the law of economic development and conforms to the basic principle of materialist dialectics. According to the research of the World Bank and the Development Research Centre of the State Council of China, out of more than 100 middle-income economies after the Second World War, only 13 of them had successfully entered the high-income ranks, characterized by completing the transformation of economic growth from quantity to quality. Those countries that failed to seize the opportunity to achieve this fundamental transformation had ultimately stagnated or even withdrawn in economy. China has maintained a medium-high growth with its economic aggregate US$12 trillion, occupying 15% of the world's total. Although the quantitative development should not be neglected, more attention should be paid to quality to achieve effective growth in quantity through a substantial improvement in quality. It is the right time to shift our focus to the improvement of quality. Only through the substantial improvement of quality can the effective growth of quantity be achieved. As a strategic decision made by the CPC Central Committee with Xi Jinping at its core to assess the Chinese situation and seize the opportunity for development, promoting high-quality development vividly manifests CPC's applying the basic principle of Marxism in resolving practical problems. It is the essential requirement for China's following the well-established rules of economic development.

However, it should be also noted that with a large economic and population scale, it is not easy for China to transition from rapid growth to high-quality development in a short period. From the perspective of evolution, two pivotal stages should be crossed to get us smoothly through this critical transition: First, the unconventional stage unique to China's economic development, in particular, to take tough steps to forestall and defuse major risks, carry out targeted poverty alleviation, and prevent and control pollution. Second, the conventional and long-term stage, that is, to work hard to transform the growth model, optimize the economic structure, and transform growth drivers, in particular, to purify the market environment, improve the quality of human capital, and enhance the national governance capacity. In order to cross the two major bondages, there is an urgent need to develop a modern economic system, which is also a strategic goal for China's economic development. In accordance with the arrangements and plans made by the Report to the 19th CPC National Congress, we must firmly grasp the requirements, main line, basic path, main focus and institutional support of high-quality development, and continue to strengthen the economic innovation and competitive forces. Thus, we will be able to develop a modern economic system and constantly advance the high-quality economic development to provide vigorous support for developing a powerful economy in China.

1.6.4 Developing a modernized economy to advance a powerful economy

"Modernized economy" is a new concept and goal proposed by the Report to the 19th CPC National Congress. It is an overall plan and arrangement for economic development based on the requirements of the new development philosophy, as well as an important component of Xi Jinping Thought on Socialism with Chinese Characteristics for a New Era. As socialism with Chinese characteristics and China's economic development have now entered a new era, China has been transitioning from rapid growth to high-quality development. To promote high-quality development, we must further transform the growth model, improve our economic structure, foster new growth engines and develop a modernized economy. This is an urgent requirement for getting us smoothly through this critical transition. It is an important base for adapting to, guiding and keeping the direction of China's economic development, and an important path to build a great modern socialist country, achieve the Two Centenary Goals and realize the Chinese Dream of national rejuvenation. Developing modernized economy is closely related to the internal demand of transforming the principal challenge facing Chinese society in the new era, and implementing the socialist economy with Chinese characteristics. It is the basic path to building a moderately prosperous society in all respects, and embarking on a new journey to building a modern socialist country in all respects. It is an urgent need to transform the pattern of economic development, shift the growth drivers, and achieve comprehensive and balanced development while adapting to national economy's shifting from high-speed growth to high-quality development. It is of far-reaching and profound significance.

Xi Jinping has highly refined, summarized and sorted out the scientific connotation of modernized economy into seven aspects: First, build an innovation-driven industrial system that promotes coordinated development of the real economy with technological innovation, modern finance, and human resources, so as to make innovation in science and technology contribute more share to the development of real economy, enhance the capacity of modern financial services to the real economy and continuously optimize the role of human resources to support the real economy development. Second, establish a unified, open, competitive and orderly market system to ensure unimpeded market access, orderly market opening, full market competition, and well-regulated market order, and speed up building a modern market system, in which enterprises enjoy independent management and fair competition, consumers have free choice and make their own consumption decisions, and products and productive factors flow freely and are exchanged on an equal basis. Third, build an efficient and fair income distribution system to ensure reasonable income distribution, social fairness and justice, and common prosperity for all the people, promote equal access to basic public services, and gradually narrow the gap in income distribution. Fourth, build an urban-rural and regional development system that highlights its strengths and coordinates the development of different regions, so as to achieve good interplay between regions, integrated urban-rural development, overall coordinated land and marine development, cultivate and leverage regional comparative advantages, strengthen complementarity with each other, and shape a new pattern of coordinated development across regions. Fifth, build a green development system that is resource-saving and environmentally-friendly to promote a sound economic structure that facilitates green, low-carbon, and circular development and ensure harmony between humanity and nature, firmly uphold and practice the idea that lucid waters and lush mountains are invaluable assets, and create a new pattern of modernization featuring harmonious development between man and nature. Sixth, build a diversified, balanced, safe and efficient opening up system across the board, so as to develop an open, higher-level economy in the direction of improving its structure, expanding its depth, and promoting its performance. Seventh, promote an economic system in which the market plays its role to the full and the government better, so as to develop an economy with more effective market mechanisms, dynamic micro-entities, and sound macro-regulation.

To sum up, an innovation-driven industrial system that promotes coordinated development; a unified, open, competitive and orderly market system; an efficient and fair income distribution system; an urban-rural and regional development system that highlights its strengths and coordinates the development of different regions; a green development system that is resource-saving and environmentally-friendly; a diversified, balanced, safe and efficient opening up system across the board; a comprehensive and open system that is diversified, balanced, safe and efficient; an economic system in which the market plays its role to the full and the government better. There is no doubt that these seven aspects constitute the important components of developing a powerful economy. In short, it is the main frame of reform for developing a powerful economy in China, including the systems of growth engines, industrial support and institutional guarantee. It can be said that developing a modernized economy is the key and fundamentals for firmly advancing a powerful economy.

Chapter 2
The Index and Path of Developing a Powerful Economy

Only a nation that has created its prosperity can understand the significance of rejuvenation; only a nation that has suffered from a series of miseries can be so desperate for rejuvenation. For more than a thousand years before 1820, China had been the largest economy as well as the strongest political center all the time in the world. In the history of the modern Westphalian system, no country exemplifies the rejuvenation better than China, which revives from a long-term decline and stands tall on the world stage again.[1] After the founding of the People's Republic of China, the socialist system has been gradually established, embarking on the great journey towards national rejuvenation. Then, the launching of reform and opening up boosted China to find the correct path to the great rejuvenation of the Chinese nation, thus gaining impressive achievements. So far, China's economic power and comprehensive strength have greatly increased, and the people's living standards have dramatically improved. China is now on its way to forwarding from a major economy to a powerful economy. It is fair to say that the Chinese nation, which endured so much for so long, has achieved a tremendous transformation—it has stood up, grown rich and is becoming strong.

In the Report to the 19th CPC National Congress, the historic changes and achievements, together with the influences made since the 18th CPC National Congress, were regarded as the main basis for the entry of socialism with Chinese characteristics for a new era. Here, the connotation of "new era" has been for the first time interpreted from the following five aspects. That is, it will be an era of building on past successes to further advance our cause, and of continuing in a new historical context to strive for the success of socialism with Chinese characteristics; it will be an era of securing a decisive victory in building a moderately prosperous society in all respects, and of

[1] James Hsiung, *China into Its Second Rise*, Chinese Edition, translated by Li Fang, Wuhan: Hubei Education Press, 2016, p. 2.

moving on to all-out efforts to build a great modern socialist country; it will be an era for the Chinese people of all ethnic groups to pull together and work hard to create a better life for themselves and ultimately achieve common prosperity for all; it will be an era for the Chinese nation to strive with one heart to realize the Chinese Dream of national rejuvenation; it will be an era that sees China moving closer to the world center stage and making greater contributions to mankind. In fact, the essence of the "new era" in these five aspects is to accomplish a quantum leap forward from "grown rich" to "becoming strong", that is, from a major economy to an economic power. Now that China has reached a new historic juncture where the socialism with Chinese characteristics has crossed the threshold into a new era, it is of great significance theoretically and practically to both enhance the researches on the index system for building an economic power and analyze its development path.

2.1 Historical starting point for the Two Centenary Goals

The Two Centenary Goals, proposed at the 18th CPC National Congress in 2012, has its deep historical roots. The goal not only deposits the suffering and humiliation in the collective memory of the Chinese nation, but demonstrates the strong resolution and determination of the CPC to lead Chinese people of all ethnic groups to build a moderately prosperous society in an all-round way and bring about a great rejuvenation of the Chinese nation. Let us search horizontally and vertically for the historical starting point of the Two Centenary Goals from the historic review.

In 1750, at the peak of the High Qing (1683-1839), a period when China featured national unification, social stability, economic prosperity and strong national strength. That year, China's GDP accounted for 32% of the world's total, ranking first in the world, while the total GDP of the five European countries including the UK, France, Germany, Russia and Italy was 17%, just over half of that of China.[1] During this period, the feudal autocracy of ancient China was in its heyday when the imperial power was exercised through dictatorship and the country secluded from the outside world, while the European countries were pioneering modernization despite the fact that their economic aggregate was far lower than that of China. After the mid-18th century, the UK began its industrial revolution. With the invention of the steam engine in 1769, the UK

[1] Dai Yi, "Comparison of China's National Strength with that of Other Great Powers in the World since the Middle of 18th Century". In *Thoughts on China*, Beijing: Hongqi Press, 2010, p. 32.

spearheaded the development of industrialization in human society and then Europe took the lead in the world, while China developed slowly as an agricultural society. Hence, the High Qing era, called as the "splendor of sunset" by historians, provides us with thought-provoking lessons for reflecting on the development of modern China.[1]

In 1830, when Qing dynasty (1636-1912) was under the reign of Emperor Daoguang in his tenth year. Since the 18th century, the world pattern has undergone rapid and tremendous changes. The UK took the path of industrial revolution, France broke out capitalism revolution, and America experienced war of independence, while the prosperity of High Qing era had been bygone days. In terms of GDP, that year, China's GDP still ranked first in the world, 29% of the world's total economic aggregate, while GDP of the UK was 9.5% of the world's total. However, China's per capita GDP was far lower than that of the UK as the industrial structure in the UK was totally different from that of China. At that time, the UK was exporting steam engines and various technical equipment to Western European countries owing to its dramatic increase in steel production and rapid development of machinery manufacturing, while China's GDP mainly attributed to agricultural and handicraft products. In 1840, China was forced to open the door by the UK with gunboats brought by the industrial revolution, and gradually reduced to a semi-colonial and semi-feudal country.

In 1900, the 26th year under the reign of Emperor Guangxu in the Qing Dynasty. That year, China's GDP plummeted and its share of the world's GDP dropped to 6 percent. The Qing government carried out the Hundred Days' Reform, a political reform in 1898, but soon failed due to the obstruction of powerful feudal forces. However, Japan stepped into modernization and ranked among the world's largest economies soon after the Meiji Restoration in the second half of the 19th century. In 1900, the GDP of the seven countries including the United States, the UK, France, Germany, Russia, Italy and Japan accounted for 80.5% of the world's, 23.6%, 18.5%, 6.8%, 17.9%, 8.8%, 2.5% and 2.4% of the global economic aggregate respectively, while China's GDP was only 6% of the world's total, which suggested that China declined from a world major economy to a poor and backward country.

From the perspective of China's economic development in the modern times, at the end of the 18th century, China's arable land covered a total area of about 1.05 billion *mu* (about 70 million hectares) with the grain output of 204 billion *jin* (102 billion kilograms). As a member of Macartney Mission to visit China in 1973, Barrow

---

[1] Xu Weixin, Liu Defu, *The Splendor of Sunset*, Beijing: People's Publishing House, 2016, p. 284.

estimated that China's grain harvest rate was higher than that of the UK with the rate in China 15：1 while that in the UK 10：1 (ranking first among the European countries).[1] During the High Qing era, the handicraft industry achieved substantial development with more specific manual labor division and a more mature commodity market. Meanwhile, China's foreign trade also experienced rapid growth. Every year, the trade volume of tea purchased by the British East India Company alone valued 4 million taels of silver. Against the backdrop of this brilliant prosperity, the governors in the High Qing era arrogantly closed the door to the outside world, and in particular, put restrictions on industry and commerce, disdained science and technology, and strengthened the centralization of power and ideological shackles, which more severely impeded the economic and social development. As the old saying goes, a backward nation tends to be beaten up. The Qing Dynasty regarded itself as the "celestial empire" with abundant resources and refused revolution and opening to the outside world, which ultimately led to a recession though it experienced more than 100 years of flourishing and prosperity.

With the outbreak of Opium War in 1840, China was gradually reduced to a semi-colonial and semi-feudal society, plunging into a complete crisis in the economic and social development. All the bitter struggles, like the Taiping Heavenly Kingdom Movement, the Hundred Days' Reform, the Yihetuan Movement and the Revolution of 1911, failed to maintain China's status as a world major economy and to prevent repeated invasions by foreign economic powers. Today, reflecting on this history and summarizing its experience and lessons are of great significance to achieve the Two Centenary Goals.

First, it is necessary to seize the major opportunities for historical development. In the modern times, due to the corrupt feudalism and the arrogant rulers alongside a close-door policy, China failed to seize the available opportunity to develop in the tidal waves of industrial revolution around the world, and eventually fell behind the rapidly rising Western countries that benefited from the modern industrial revolutions, plunging into the mire of humiliation and backwardness. However, in the meantime, since the Geographical Discovery in 1500, Western countries seized every historical opportunity by reality to achieve leapfrog economic and social development. This is the case for the rising of Spain, Portugal, Netherlands and the UK. Now, summarizing the historical experience and inspired by the concept of "Important period of strategic opportunity" proposed by the 16th CPC National Congress, we must take full advantage of the new

---

[1] Zhang Zhilian et al., *Proceedings of Chengde Conference on the Bicentenary of Sino-British Relations* (1793-1993), Beijing: China Social Sciences Press, 1996, p. 188.

round of global technological and industrial revolution so as to lay the foundation for realizing the goal of making China an economic powerhouse.

Second, it is necessary to promote the national industrialization and urbanization. With the development of industrialization in the UK, France, Italy and other countries, and the outbreak of a series of bourgeois revolutions, western European countries have accordingly made dramatic revolutions, embarked on the path different from the feudal traditional development, then accelerated forward and leaped to the top of the world civilization. Take for example, according to the statistics, the UK increased its cotton-textile export from GBP6.7 million to GBP41.43 million between 1776 and 1800, up by 5.18 times in 24 years, and by 1770 its urban population had accounted for a half of the total. Driven by the industrial revolution, the UK had quickly realized the industrialization and urbanization.

Third, it is necessary to set up good mechanisms for innovations in science and technology. The British scholar Joseph Needham once mentioned that between 1st century BC and 15th century AD, Chinese outperformed Europeans in applying natural knowledge to practical needs, but why modern scientific revolution did not occur in China? This is the well-known "Joseph Needham's Question", which aroused extensive discussions through academia at home and abroad on the reason why Chinese modern science and technology fell behind. The answer goes to the law that science and technology is a primary force of productivity growth. Since the 17th century, the scientific revolution had swept across the Europe. In 1543, the European pioneer Copernicus published his *De Revolutionibus Orbium Coelestium* (*Theory of the Movement of Celestial Bodies*), in which he elaborated on the astronomical theory with the sun as the center of universe. Especially at the turn of the 17th century and the 18th century, Isaac Newton discovered three laws of motion and the law of universal gravitation. After that, the public knew more and more scientists and inventors. Then, a mechanism for innovation with science, technology and experiment as a trinity began to take shape, which dramatically boosted the productivity of western European countries. However, at that time, Chinese feudal rulers did not prioritize technological knowledge, and instead regarded the invention as "tricks", resulting in China's falling behind in the global competitive pattern of economic development.

Fourth, it is necessary to build an open economy. Marx and Engels once said in *The Communist Manifesto* that the forces of production created by the bourgeoisie during its rule of less than 100 years were more massive and colossal than that by all preceding generations.[1] The great advance of forces of production brought the western society to a higher stage of historical development, whereas China was still staggered in the shackles of Feudalism and missed the important opportunities for development. Therefore, the decline of the giant reminds us that China must develop an open economy, based on a clear understanding of the national conditions as well as the great changes, development and transitions of the current and future world, to develop and strengthen the nation through opening up.

Fifth, it is necessary to promote the forces of national reform to take shape. As for China's economic and social decline, the academia at home and abroad shares a common influential perception that China, as a continental country, had long implemented a traditional policy of advocating agriculture and restraining commerce, valuing production rather than distribution. Not only the entire agricultural field was self-sufficient, but all prefectures and counties valued the importance to plant mulberry and rice. What's more, the centralization of power and long-term imperial examination system all helped form a unique character in the Chinese society, in which all intellectuals adjusted their outlook on life according to the needs of the high-level institutions.[2] However, the rising economic powers, such as the Netherlands and the UK, all relied on the forces of national reform to achieve their goals. Take the Dutch's reform of commercial banking system and shareholding system, and the reform of political system by the Glorious Revolution in the UK for example, they all played an important role in the prosperity and development of these countries. However, the rulers of China's feudal society refused to change and even stifled the forces of reform, which eventually led to its decline and backwardness. Therefore, needless to say, the concept of "deepening reform comprehensively" and "the thought of reform as the largest dividend for China", proposed by the Third Plenary Session of the 18th CPC Central Committee, are deeply rooted in Chinese people's mind, which also represents the historical reflection and enlightenment on the decline and pain of an economic giant.

2.2 Over seventy years of struggling for making China an economic giant

In 1921, the Communist Party of China was established in the process of Marxism-

---

[1] *Selected Works of Karl Marx and Friedrich Engels* (Volume I), Beijing:People's Publishing House, 2002, p. 45.

[2] Huang Renyu, *Capitalism and 21st Century*, Beijing: SDX Joint Publishing Company, 1997, p. 26.

Leninism integrated with the Chinese workers' movement, thus embarking on a journey to China's First Centenary Goal. After the People's Republic of China was founded, in 1952 China's population accounted for 22.3% of the world's total, while its economic aggregate was only 4.6% the world's GDP. Compared with the world's per capita GDP, China's per capita GDP was only 23.8% of the world's average. Under this circumstance, China, with much to be revitalized, embarked on the Second Centenary Goal. At the beginning of the founding of the People's Republic of China, China chose the mode of Soviet Union's development. That is to say, in order to catch up with the economically developed capitalist countries in a short period, and strengthen national defense to resist military threats and aggression, China chose the strategy of prioritizing the development of heavy industry. From the perspective of economic development, at the early days of the People's Republic of China, the strategy of prioritizing the development of heavy industry enabled China to improve its national defense and military prevention capabilities in a relatively short period of time, which greatly deepened the understanding of industrialization, and laid the economic foundation for socialism construction. More importantly, since the founding of the People's Republic of China in 1949, the CPC is leading Chinese people in exploring the path of economic and social development in China. During this period, there have been triumphs as well as twists and turns. By 1978, China's population accounted for 22.3% of the world's total, and its GDP in 1978 4.9% of the world's total, up by 0.3 percentage points than that in 1952. However, in terms of per capita GDP, China's per capita GDP was only 22.1% of the world's average, down by 1.7 percentage points than that in 1952.[1] All these arduous explorations have prompted the reawakening of the members of Chinese Communist and the Chinese people.

Recovering from the Cultural Revolution, China has drawn a lesson from the bitter experience. In December 1978, in the Third Plenary Session of the 11th CPC Central Committee, the Party made the strategic deployment of "shifting the work agenda of the Party to the socialist modernization drive", proposed to reform the over-centralized economic management system and business management methods, and further develop the economic cooperation with equal and mutual benefits with other countries on the basis of self-reliance, so as to improve people's livelihood. Since then, China has embarked on a new journey of reform and opening up to realize a historic transformation

---

[1] Angus Maddison, *Chinese Economic Performance in the Long Run*, Chinese Edition, translated by Wu Xiaoying, Ma Debin, Shanghai: Shanghai People's Publishing House, 2008, p. 57.

from a weak economy to a major economy in the pursuit of the Two Centenary Goals. Over the past 40 years, China has committed to taking economic development as the central task, and actively responded to various contradictions, issues and risks on the road ahead and gained impressive achievements.

The "economic miracle", created by China since the launching of reform and opening up, has attracted many scholars to interpret and demonstrate it from different perspectives, and summarized it as a general theory on the path toward building an economic powerhouse. Chinese economist Justin Yifu Lin points out that China's economic miracle owes a lot to the full play of its resource endowment and comparative advantages, thus promoting higher international and domestic competitiveness of its products. [1] Some researchers suggest that China's reform and opening up is characterized by progressive stock adjustments and increment rise with the mode of development of "market economy plus socialism" as its core experience.[2] Some other researchers believe that the path of development created by China's "economic miracle" features social equality, meritocracy, effective system and disinterested government, which is of universal significance for the world's growth.[3]

Therefore, this book argues that the fundamental reason for China's "economic miracle" and its previous developmental path to building a major economy lies in upholding the leadership of the Communist Party of China and the market-oriented economic system restructuring. It has given full play to its comparative advantages, optimized the resource allocation, improve its competitiveness of participating in the international division of labor during the course of economic globalization, thus making the economic development access to demographic dividend, resource dividend and deposit dividend. Over 40 years of development since the reform and opening up, China has realized a major transformation from traditional planned economy to socialist market economy, with the basic socialist economic system gradually developed, and the modern market system initially taken shape. Thus, the decisive role of the market in allocating resources has been constantly strengthened. All of these led to a new pattern of mutual coordination between reform and opening up, thus promoting China to forward from a major economy to an economic power.

To be specific, over 40 years of reform and opening up has contributed a lot to

---

[1] Justin Yifu Lin, Cai Fang, and Li Zhou, *China's Miracle: Development Strategy and Economic Reform*, Shanghai: Truth & Wisdom Press, 1994, pp. 195-199.

[2] Wu Jinglian, *Selected Works of Wu Jinglian*, Taiyuan: Shanxi Economy Press, 2003, pp. 1-75.

[3] Yao Yang, *Global Implications of the Chinese Experience*, Beijing: Peking University Press, 2011, pp. 80-95.

China's striving for a powerful economy. It can mainly manifest as follows:

First, it has released the dividends of rural reform and promoted to initially resolve the issues relating to agriculture, rural areas and rural people. Resolving issues related to agriculture, rural areas and farmers is the top priority on the work agenda of the whole Party. The success of rural reform has effectively safeguarded social stability and the development of national economy. Implementing the rural household contract responsibility system took the lead in preluding China's economic restructuring, which has greatly promoted the recovery and development of productive forces of China's agriculture, brought about great changes in China's agriculture and rural areas, and greatly released the dividends of rural reform. The strategic reforms of system have been made, such as reforming the rural tax and fee system, building a new socialist countryside, coordinating urban and rural areas, and promoting integrated economic development of urban and rural areas. Meanwhile, the major decisions and plans, such as further deepening agricultural supply-side reform and implementing the strategy of rural revitalization, have been made by the CPC Central Committee. All of these have laid a solid foundation for promoting the agricultural development, rural prosperity, farmers' well-beings and the effective release of rural reform dividends. Along with the sustainable development of agriculture, the rural economy has made comprehensive progress and farmers' life has greatly improved.

Second, it has gradually improved the market-oriented pricing mechanism and strengthened the basic role of the market in allocating resources. As we know, pricing mechanism is the most effective means to regulate the allocation of resources in market economy, and the reform of price system plays a very important role in the economic restructuring. So, the price reform, proposed by the Third Plenary Session of the 12th CPC Central Committee, opened the prelude of China's reform and opening up, and then was accelerated in the late 1980s, which made beneficial explorations for actively straightening out pricing mechanism. Since then, the substantive progress has been made in the market-oriented reform of goods, services and productive factors. After the 21st century, China has emphatically promoted the process of marketization of productive factors and price system of resource products, and strengthened the price regulation of monopoly industries. These has provided strong supports for achieving the optimal allocation of resources and economic structural adjustment to establish a price system of socialist market economy, and to further release the dividends of price reform. Looking back at the early 1990s, it was found that over 80 percent of the prices of physical goods and services was liberalized and regulated by the market. Up to now, the rest have priced by the market except that the interest rate, exchange rate, oil, natural gas, electric power, land and so on adopt a price-controlled policy in a certain range. It should be said that the gradual improvement of China's market-oriented price system is of great significance for actively playing the guiding role of price signals on market entities and the decisive role of the market in allocating resources.

Third, it has constantly improved the basic economic system and promoted the common development of enterprises under diverse forms of ownership. It has been clearly stated at the Third Plenary Session of the 18th CPC Central Committee that "both public and non-public sectors of the economy are necessary for the socialist market economy and important for China's economic and social development." From the perspective of public ownership economy, after 40 years of efforts, the task of reconstructing the micro-economic foundation of state-owned enterprises has been initially completed, and the majority of state-owned enterprises have become main players in the market competition compatible with the socialist market economy. A series of reform measures, including the strategic adjustment of state-owned economic structure, system innovation of enterprises and that of state-owned assets management, has provided system safeguard for the large state-owned enterprises to grow larger and stronger, for the state assets to maintain and increase their value, for the reform of state-owned enterprises to effectively release the dividends, and for state-owned economies to play their leading roles. From the perspective of non-public economy, since the reform and opening up, China's private economy has rapidly grown stronger from scratch under the joint action of market mechanism and government support, when the number of enterprises has rapidly increased with their quality constantly improved and their vitality significantly enhanced. Thus, it has become an important part of the national economy.

Fourth, it has deepened the reform of the fiscal and taxation systems to establish a modern fiscal system. The Third Plenary Session of the 18th CPC Central Committee clearly proposed: "Finance is the foundation and an important pillar of state governance. Good fiscal and tax systems are the institutional guarantee for optimizing resources allocation, maintaining market unity, promoting social equity, and realizing enduring peace and stability." The reform of fiscal and taxation system has great impacts on a series of reforms concerning the overall economic and social issues, such as income distribution system, fiscal relationship and decision-making power between the Central and local governments. From the highly centralized fiscal and taxation system at the beginning of the founding of the People's Republic of China, to the gradual transition to unified hierarchical management under the leadership of the Central government, and then to the fiscal management system based on tax sharing, China's fiscal and tax system has provided a strong safeguard for constantly integrating with the socialist market economic system, transforming to the public financial system and releasing the dividends of fiscal and tax reform. Meanwhile, it has made great contributions for the majority of rural families and the people to share reform dividends, such as supporting SOE tax reform, rural tax and fee reform, personal income tax reform, and provided an important support for building a modern fiscal system.

Fifth, it has released huge demographic dividend and improved the efficiency of labor allocation. Based on the assessment of relevant scholars, the contribution of labor input to the economic growth reached 67.64% after 20 years of reform and opening up, which indicates that labor input is the most important factor to realize the rapid economic growth in China.[1] In terms of the absolute number of employment population, it took about 30 years for China to transform the population growth pattern from that of high birth rate, low death rate and high growth rate to that of low birth rate, low death rate and low growth rate. In the process, the number of employment grows faster than that of the total population, resulting in demographic dividend. The conception of labor market and the fundamental path of reform of labor employment system proposed by the Third Plenary Session of the 14th CPC Central Committee, well guide the direction of China's reform to release the huge demographic dividend. China's rural labor force has then constantly transferred from the inland to the eastern coastal areas. As a result, the eastern coastal enterprises have taken advantage of the comparative advantage of low labor cost to release huge demographic dividend, which has greatly improved the efficiency of labor allocation.

Sixth, it has released the dividend of investment and financing system reform and gradually strengthened capital deepening. According to the early theory of economic development, capital accumulation is the key to the success of economic development, so the fundamental difference between poor countries and developed countries lies in the different material capital per capita. In order to achieve self-sustainable economic growth, the proportion of investment in income should be increased from 5% to 12% or higher. High savings and high investments are two characteristic features of China's

[1] Cai Fang, Wang Dewen, "Sustainable Growth of Chinese Economy and Labor Contribution", *Economic Research Journal*, 1999(10), pp. 62-68.

economic growth as investment is one of the "twin engines" driving China's economic growth. In the course of reform and opening up, China has vigorously advanced the reform of investment and financing systems and mechanisms in finance, energy, railway, telecommunications and other fields, and actively promoted the continuous transfer of labor force from agriculture to industry, from rural to urban areas and from state-owned sectors to non-state-owned sectors. This is the important reason why China can keep long-term and high-speed economic growth. So, both high saving rate and high investment rate are not only the outcome of the growth pattern, but also the key reason for the continuous transfer of labor force and even the continuation of this growth pattern.

Seventh, it has deepened the system reform of opening up and released the dividends of opening up. Over the past 40 years of reform and opening up, both domestic reform and opening to the outside world have been mutually reinforced and interplayed. Opening to the outside world is a basic state policy adopted by China since 1978 as well as a major practice through drawing experience from the development of developed countries and studying the trend of world economic development. In 1979 and 1980, Shenzhen, Zhuhai, Shantou and Xiamen set up special economic zones on a pilot basis, which was the initial phase of China's releasing dividends of opening up. Since then, Dalian, Qinhuangdao, Tianjin and other 11 coastal port cities have further implemented the policy of opening up, and Nanjing, Wuhan, Chongqing and other provincial capitals along the Yangtze River, border areas or inland areas have entered the phase of all-round opening up. In November 2001, China successfully joined the World Trade Organization with its international status rapidly improved. Building the Belt and Road, setting up pilot free trade zones, planning free trade ports with Chinese characteristics, and successfully holding the First China International Import Expo, all these measures of opening up have provided a reliable institutional guarantee for deepening the reform of foreign trade system, effectively releasing the dividends of opening up, and promoting the rapid development of China's economy and society.

2.3 Transitioning from high-speed growth to medium-high growth

The "growth miracle" over the past 40 years of reform and opening up has blazed a path of development as a major country with Chinese characteristics, which enabled

China to become a real major economy. It is true that China is a major economy, yet not a powerful economy. Being a major economy does not necessarily follow that the goal of "being an economic powerhouse" will be ultimately achieved. Therefore, a profound analysis of the current phase of China's economic development is a necessary link in scientifically studying the development path to building an economic powerhouse.

After entering the 13th Five-year Plan period, different opinions arise in domestic academia on the discussions of China's economic development and growth phase. Liu Shijin believed that China's economic development will transform from high-speed growth to medium-speed growth.[1] Liu Shucheng pointed out that the world economy has entered into the deep transformation and adjustment from the rapid development before the international financial crisis, and China's economy has moved from high-speed growth to growth speed shift, or the transition period of the growth phase. Liu Shucheng concluded that China's economy has moved to a medium-high growth, as the interval of 7.5 percent to 9 percent can be called medium-high growth interval.[2]

In fact, it is a common law that a moderate slowdown in economic growth happens when an economy reaches a middle-income level. From the international perspective, after Japan, Republic of Korea, Germany and other countries, which were successful to overtake in their economic development after the Second World War, experienced rapid growth in the 1960s to 1970s, there appeared without exception the slowdown in economic growth, with an average drop of between 30% and 40%. At this phase, these countries began to transition from high-speed growth to medium-high growth, and then to medium- or even low-speed growth. As a middle-income country, China's economy has moved from high-speed growth to medium-high growth. Li Keqiang pointed out, "China needs to strike a 'golden balance' between what is necessary and what is possible, between upgrading transformation and maintaining a reasonable growth speed, to keep growth within an appropriate range and ensure relatively full employment. Meanwhile, China should speed up structural adjustment, and improve its quality and efficiency to ensure a steady and sustainable growth in China's economy." [3]

Therefore, this book argues that China's economic growth should be kept within an appropriate range to prevent it from decrease below the "minimum" in the next ten

---

[1] Liu Shijing, "Shift in China's Phase of Economic Growth and Transformation of Development Mode", *Journal of Chinese Academy of Governance*, 2012(2), pp. 10-15.

[2] Liu Shucheng, "China's Economy is in the Rapid Growth", *People's Daily*, Oct. 24, 2003.

[3] Li Keqiang, China's Development Should Seek for a "Balance" and "Golden Point", China News.com, Nov.3, 2013.

years, and that it will shift from high-speed growth to medium-high growth, which is the trend of China's economy in the new historical development phase. Here, it should be noted that "medium-speed" is relatively in terms of internal aspect and "high-speed" in terms of external aspect. "Medium-speed" refers that China's economic growth comes to the gradual slowdown between 6% and 7% on the whole after over 30 years of high-speed growth with nearly 10% per year. "High-speed" infers that China's economic growth is increasing in contrast with that of the world's. According to the statistics of IMF, the global GDP growth in 2015 was 3%, and that of the United States and the Eurozone only 2.6% and 1.6%, that of Japan as low as 0.4%. Therefore, China's growth rate between 6% and 7% is relatively high in comparison with that of other major economies. To sum up, "medium-high growth" can represent the basic features of the new stage of China's economic development. So, what is the basis for judging China's entry into the medium-high speed development? It can be analyzed from the following five aspects:

First, the profound adjustments in the global economic development pattern. Since 2011, when China's economic aggregate surpassed Japan to become the world's second largest economy, China's development has been increasingly restricted by the existing economic powers in the world, including the United States and Japan. In order to maintain their dividends of order and structure in the international economic system, developed countries frequently take all means to restrain the development of China's economy, as they are unwilling to see the rising of a strong China. Events such as "anti-dumping suits" and "interference in Chinese enterprises' overseas investment" have occurred frequently. International trade frictions are becoming more and more intense, together with a growing trend of "China threat" theory and "Trade Protectionism" theory. In particular, the escalating trade frictions between China and the US in 2018 has seriously affected China's legitimate rights and development interests. This is an unavoidable external factor that restricts China's economic development. Meanwhile, the international financial crisis has had a severe impact on the global economic development, and the global supply structure and demand structure have undergone profound changes. Both developed and developing countries are under great pressure to adjust their economic structures, which inevitably leads to the global market competition. Various forms of protectionism are rising, from trade to investment, technology, employment and other fields. The international trade system and the international financial system are undergoing profound changes, the complexity of global governance is further strengthened, the global economic pattern is experiencing profound adjustments, and the global interest pattern is reshaping. All these external environments have posed severe challenge for continuous economic development in China.

Second, the normal contraction of economic external demand. One important factor supporting the rapid economic growth in the past 40 years is that China takes the road of external-oriented economic development. That is to say, during this period, the main forces of China's economy rely on external demands to drive economic growth, and the international market to digest domestic production capacity. By doing so, it can drive the rapid economic growth. However, from the perspective of new historical stage of development, the international financial crisis since 2008 continues to extend its deep impacts. The process of world economic recovery has been seriously affected by its increasing instability and uncertainty as well as increasing downward pressure and potential risks. Meanwhile, the newly industrialized economies are unlikely to improve much in the short term. All these put forward the severe challenge for China's export scale to remain stable. Economic powers such as the US and European countries have put forward measures such as "Reindustrialization", "2020 Strategy" and "Rebirth Strategy". Developing countries are adjusting their development mode, reshape and accelerate the development of industries with comparative advantages, and seize the commanding heights of the world's industrial division of labor. As a result, the environment for China's external demand continues to shrink and slump. In this regard, Chinese government has put forward the strategic policy of "building a robust long-term mechanism for expanding domestic demand and promoting to shift the economic growth to relying on consumption, investment and export in a coordinated manner". Therefore, the normal contraction of economic external demand is an important factor for China's economy to enter the medium-high growth.

Third, the constrains and bottlenecks of the environment of energy and resources. Over the past 40 years of reform and opening up, China's economy has grown at an average annual rate of 9.5%, much higher than that of the world economy, 2.9%, in the same period. It is a miracle by China as well as by the world. However, at this phase, if it continues to rely more on investment and high consumption of energy and resources, environmental constraints will become more and more obvious, and high-speed growth relying on high investment and high-energy consumption will be difficult to sustain. According to the data of the National Bureau of Statistics of China, the foreign dependence of China's oil and iron ore reached 56.4% and 56.7% respectively in 2011, the foreign trade dependence of China's iron ore 80% in 2015, that of China's oil over 65% in 2016, and that of China's oil 67.4% in 2017. It is obvious that the bottleneck factors of energy and resources are gradually becoming prominent. The supply constraints of important resources, such as crude oil, raw coal, natural gas and iron ore, have been increasing as China's economic development has been for years developed with high input, high consumption, high pollution and low output. Although China's energy consumption per unit of GDP fell by 3.7% in 2017 compared with the previous year, China still has a long way to go in terms of energy consumption per unit of output, exhaust gas emissions and wastewater treatment compared with other economic powers in the world. To sum up, China still has a long way to go in terms of the development of low-carbon economy, circular economy and green economy. Meanwhile, China's environmental pressure is increasing. This is a prominent manifestation of the worsening constraints on energy and resources environment. Therefore, through initially adjusting the economic growth speed, China gradually slow down the pace of economic growth, so that it can adapt to the characteristics of China's resource endowment and break through the constraints of energy and resources environment. This is one important internal factor of China's economy from high-speed to medium-high growth.

Fourth, the gradual narrowing of traditional demographic dividend. The "Lewis turning point" is approaching. The shortage of labor supply is more obvious in the developed region of eastern China, and many enterprises reflect that the rapid rise in labor costs in recent years put them under great pressure. Thus, China's traditional demographic dividend is gradually decreasing. Statistics show that in 2012, the labor force aged between 15 and 59 in China was 937 million, 3.45 million less than that in 2011, accounting for 69.2% of the total population, 0.6 percentage points lower than that at the end of 2011. By 2015, the total labor force aged between 15 and 59 in China will reduce to 928 million, and by 2020 approximately to 916 million.[1] Meanwhile, the trend of aging population in China is gradually intensifying. The pace of aging population has noticeably accelerated, since China entered the aging society in 2000. China's elderly population has exceeded 200 million and is expected to account for about one third of the total population by the middle of the 21st century. Compared with that of the current world economic powers, China's aging population is facing more serious situations, more complex problems and more difficulties. Objectively speaking,

[1] China Center for International Economic Exchanges, *Upgrade the Chinese Economy*, Beijing: People's Publishing House, 2013, p. 150.

China's rapid economic growth model supported by the "demographic dividend" with abundant labor resources and low labor costs is no longer sustainable.

Fifth, the consequent reflection of economic structural contradictions. In terms of the development structure, China's structural contradictions accumulated over the years have gradually become prominent with the imbalances in the structure of domestic demand, industrial structure, urban and rural structure, regional structure and income distribution structure. It is fair to say that in the coming period of development, China must fully implement the strategy of "reinvigorating China through education", of "making China a country of innovators", and of "strengthening China through human resources development", and vigorously build systems and mechanisms conducive to economic restructuring. This requires China to take the initiative to lower the growth rate and leave time and space for economic structural adjustment. If we continue to pursue an excessive high growth rate, it will not only run counter to the law of economic development, but also aggravate existing structural problems and undermine the sustainability of China's economic development. Therefore, from the perspective of economic development structure, timely and initially adjusting the economic growth expectation and growth rate is also one important factor for China's economy to shift from high-speed to medium-high growth.

However, given China's basic national conditions and the gap between urban and rural areas and between different regions as well as the relative lag in urbanization, there is much space to extend and expand in China's economic development and to unleash the dividend of a major country. This can guarantee healthy economic development in China. According to our preliminary research, China's economic growth adjustment can be divided into three phases. The first is from 2013 to 2020, during which China's economy shifts from high-speed growth to medium-high growth with a growth rate of 6% to 7%. This is a period of strategic opportunity for China's First Centenary Goal and such a growth rate will provide a strong guarantee for completing the building of a moderately prosperous society in all respects. The second is from 2020 to 2035, during which China's economy will shift from a medium-high growth to a medium-speed growth, with the overall growth rate of 5% to 6%. This is an important period for China to basically realize socialist modernization. The third is from 2035 to 2050, during which China's economy will maintain medium-speed growth with the overall growth rate of 4% to 5% to ensure that China will ultimately realize the great goal of being an economic powerhouse.

2.4 How far to develop from a major economy to a powerful economy

The academia generally counts on five comprehensive indexes to characterize and quantify the basic connotation of an economic power, namely the share of global GDP, the index of innovation level in science and technology, the share of output value of service industry, the urbanization rate and the share of international reserve currency. Here, our research refers to the relevant research results by the academia and adopts the approach of "expert investigation" to determine the theoretical threshold for a country to become an economic power. In our opinion, there are five indexes for a country to become an economic power. First, its GDP should account for at least 6% of the world's total. Second, the index of its innovation capability in science and technology should rank the world's top five. Third, the output value of service industry should reach more than 70%. Fourth, the urbanization rate should be more than 70%. Fifth, the proportion of international reserve currency should exceed 4%.[1]

It should be noted that it does not necessarily require a country to pass all these five theoretical thresholds to determine whether it is an economic power or not. Through the approach of "expert investigation", further conclusion is obtained that any country that meets at least four out of the five indexes at the theoretical threshold can be called an economic power. According to the statistics in 2012, the United States exceeded the theoretical threshold on all these five indexes; Japan missed only 0.1 percentage points to meet the requirement of passing 4 percent of the index of "international reserve currency share"; and Germany missed only 1 percent to meet the requirement of passing 6 percent in the index of "world share of GDP"; whereas the other countries failed to meet at least two or more indexes among the five indexes at the theoretical threshold. Therefore, it can be said that the United States, Japan and Germany are the real economic powers in the world today.

First, in terms of the world share of GDP, China has already stepped across the threshold of being an economic power. Economic scale is an important prerequisite to measure whether a country is an economic power or not, which means being an economic power should, first of all, be a country with large economic aggregate. In 1978,

[1] See Zhang Zhanbin, *China's Dream to Be Economic Powerhouse*, Shijiazhuang: Hebei People's Publishing House, 2014; Wei Liqun, Lin Zhaomu, Zhang Zhanbin et al., *From Large Economy to Economic Powerhouse*, Beijing: People's Publishing House, 2015; Zhang Zhanbin, Zhou Yuehui, *The Economic Aspects of Great Power Under The New Normal*, Changsha: Hunan People's Publishing House, 2015.

China's economic aggregate ranked 11th in the world, and then it caught up with and overtook other major economies all the way. In 2010, China surpassed Japan to become the world's second largest economy. Since then, China has remained the world's second largest and China's share in the world economy has been increasing year by year. In 2017, according to the International Monetary Fund (IMF) data, China's GDP reached US$12 trillion, 13.2 percentage points higher than that of 1978 (see Table 2-1), accounting for 15% of the world's total and equaling the total GDP of Japan, Germany and the UK, which ranked the third, fourth and fifth respectively in the world. Judging from this index, China has already met the threshold requirement of economic aggregate for becoming an economic power, which is necessary but insufficient for becoming an economic power.

Table 2-1 GDP of major countries and the world share

Country	1978			2017		
	Ranking	GDP (US$100 million)	World share (%)	Ranking	GDP (US$100 million)	World share (%)
The world total		85,429			798,655	
the US	1	23,566	27.6	1	193,906	24.3
China	11	1,495	1.8	2	120,146	15.0
Japan	2	10,084	11.8	3	48,721	6.1
Germany	3	7,377	8.6	4	36,848	4.6
the UK	5	3,359	3.9	5	26,245	3.3
India	12	1,355	1.6	6	26,110	3.3
France	4	5,082	5.9	7	25,836	3.2
Brazil	8	2,008	2.4	8	20,550	2.6
Italy	6	3,140	3.7	9	19,379	2.4
Canada	7	2,186	2.6	10	16,524	2.1

Source: Statistics in 1978: WDI database; Statistics in 2017: predicted by WEO database of IMF.

Second, according to the index of innovation capability in science and technology, China still has a long way to meet the threshold requirement of being an economic powerhouse. Having strong innovation capability in science and technology is the core competitiveness of the world economic powers. It can be measured by four secondary indexes, that is, the number of scientists engaging in research and development, the number of invention patents, the number of papers published the journals of science and technology and the total R&D expenditures. Statistics in 2012 show that the top five countries in the index of innovation capability in science and technology are the United

States, Japan, Germany, Republic of Korea and the United Kingdom, while China ranked only 14th although the year of 2015 and 2016 had witnessed China's further progress in the innovation capability in science and technology. There remained a long way to go before becoming an economic power supported by the strong innovation capability in science and technology. In October 2017, the report to the 19th CPC National Congress put forward such important decisions as "making China a country of innovators" and "innovation is the primary driving force behind development; it is the strategic underpinning for building a modernized economy". Obviously, it is important and urgent to continue to adhere to the innovation-driven development strategy in the New Era.

Third, in terms of the share of output value of service industry, China's industrial restructuring should go further. Today's world economic powers have all completed the process of industrialization with typically high-end structure, which is generally represented by the "proportion of output value of service industry" by economic theorists. According to the statistics of the World Bank, the service output value accounted for 78.6%, 71.4%, 71.1%, 77.7% and 79.8% of GDP in the United States, Japan, Germany, the United Kingdom and France respectively in 2012, while it was 51.6% of China's GDP in 2016 as well as in 2017. From the analysis of this economic index, China still needs to move forward before achieving the industrial structure standards that an economic power should possess.

Fourth, in terms of urbanization rate, China's urbanization leaves much space to improve. Urbanization is an important part of a state's modernization and high rate of urbanization is a must for becoming an economic power. According to the statistics of the World Bank, the urbanization rate of the United States, Japan and Germany in 2012 was 82.6%, 91.7% and 74.1% respectively. By contrast, the rate in China was only 58.52% by the end of 2017, and the urbanization rate of registered population only 42.35%, much lower than 70%, the urbanization rate commonly exceeded by developed countries. According to this standard, China's urbanization rate needs to further improve with the gap of nearly 30%. In addition, China lacks urban agglomerations with international influence, which is another important gap between China and the world's economic powers.

Fifth, in terms of the share of international reserve currency, China needs to go further before meeting its requirement of being an economic power. Typically, powerful economies possess the developed and stable financial systems, and their currencies are used by other countries in the world for circulation, valuation and calculation, especially as the reserve currency. By the general measuring standard, a state's currency can be considered as an international currency when it accounts for 4 percent of the world's reserve currency. The International Monetary Fund announced that since October 1, 2016, the renminbi has been recognized as the world's freely usable currency and as a fifth currency, together with the US dollar, the European dollar, the Japanese yen and the British pound, to constitute the Special Drawing Rights (SDR) currency basket. Although the renminbi has historically become the world's reserve currency, the proportion of renminbi in the international reserve currency is far behind that of the US dollar and the European dollar. In December 2017, the Chinese economist Yi Gang said at the China Financial Forty Forum that there remained a gap for the renminbi to be the truly first-class reserve currency, which meant its currency in credit cards, third-party payment, payment clearing system, custody system and market openness needed to be improved. In this light, it remains an arduous task for China to become an economic power supported by the financial power.

2.5 Choice of path to developing from a major economy to a powerful economy

As Xi Jinping pointed out, "Today, we are closer, more confident, and more capable than ever before of making the goal of national rejuvenation a reality." [1] Xi also stressed that "A major country like China cannot afford any disruptive mistake on fundamental issues."[1] To realize the historic transformation of building a moderately prosperous society in all respects from a major economy to a strong economy at the node of "two strategies" (i.e., strategies of building China into a modern and powerful socialist country), China needs to follow the strategic arrangement and the fundamental direction made by the Third Plenary Session of the 18th CPC Central Committee and the 19th CPC National Congress.

First, strengthen and improve the basic economic system and promote the modernization of the national economic governance system and governance capacity. The economic system with the public ownership playing a dominant role with diverse forms of economic ownership developing side by side, is the basic economic system of

[1] Literature Research Office of the CPC Central Committee, Central Literature Press, *Selected Important Works of Xi Jinping*. Beijing: Party Reading Books Publishing House, 2016, p. 18, 102.

China's socialist market economy as well as an important pillar of the socialist system with Chinese characteristics. As the Third Plenary Session of the 18th CPC Central Committee pointed out, the state protects the property rights and legitimate interests of economic entities under all forms of ownership, ensures that all of them have equal access to productive factors according to law, participate in market competition in an open, fair and just environment and are equally protected by law, and supervise various ownership economies according to the law. To achieve the Two Centenary Goals and the historic transformation from a major economy to a powerful economy, China must give full play to the comparative advantage of economic entities under all forms of ownership, to the potentials of all labor, knowledge, technology, management and capital as well as to the enthusiasm, initiative and creativity of all main bodies that create social wealth. Therefore, firmly developing mixed ownership economy is an important focus to strengthen and enhance China's basic economic system in the future. The mixed ownership economy should be constantly enhanced in which state capital, collective and non-public capital have cross shareholdings and integrate with each other. The property rights of economic entities under all forms of ownership should be equally protected, which means the property rights of both public and non-public sectors of the economy are inviolable since the two ownership economies are mutually dependent, coordinated and supportive rather than mutually exclusive. Equal right to use various productive factors should be given to economic entities under all forms of ownership, which means to fully mobilize the enthusiasm of all sectors of society to participate in the national economic governance through marketization, promote the modernization of national economic governance system and governance capacity, and truly stimulate the vitality and creativity of economic entities under all forms of ownership. By doing so, it can provide the fundamental institutional guarantee for realizing the dream of becoming an economic power.

Second, step up and accelerate the improvement of modern market system, and fully leverage the decisive role of the market in resource allocation. As the Third Plenary Session of the 18th CPC Central Committee pointed out, "the key to comprehensively deepening reform lies in the reform of economic system. The underlying issue is how to strike a balance between the role of the government and that of the market, and let the market play the decisive role in allocating resources and the government better fulfill its functions." It is a major theoretical innovation as well as a major breakthrough in the ideological emancipation made by the plenary session to let the market play the decisive role in resource allocation. This is of great significance to further straighten out the relationship between the government and the market, accelerate the transformation of government functions, stimulate the market dynamism, and realize the Two Centenary Goals. Generally speaking, a perfect modern market system has three basic characteristics. That is, enterprises can operate independently and compete fairly; consumers can choose freely and consume independently, and commodities and factors can flow freely and exchange equally. To advance the modern market system, efforts should be made on the following four aspects: The first is efforts to gradually establish fair, open and transparent market rules, improve the pricing mechanism mainly determined by the market, and give full play to the role of the market in price formation. The second is efforts to remove market barriers, improve the efficiency and fairness of resource allocation, abolish regulations and practices that impede the unified national market and fair competition, and oppose local protectionism and unfair competition. The third is efforts to advance the financial market system, improve the market-based mechanism for renminbi exchange rate regime, and implement financial regulatory reform measures and stable and sustainable standards. The fourth is efforts to accelerate the transformation of government functions, improve the national macro-control system, and fully and correctly perform government functions. These four aspects are important for China to achieve the Two Centenary Goals and move forward from a major economy to a powerful economy.

Third, keep the economic growth rate within an appropriate range, and strive to improve the economy quality and efficiency. The Third Plenary Session of the 18th CPC Central Committee stressed that "China should adhere to the major strategic judgment that development is still the key to solving all problems in China", and called for "promoting sustained and sound economic and social development". Although China has passed the threshold of being an economic power in terms of economic aggregate, China's GDP does not meet the quality demands. In the future development, China must firmly keep economic development as the central task and unswervingly continue to expand economic aggregate, and meanwhile improve economic quality and economic efficiency. This is not only an important condition for China to achieve the Two Centenary Goals, but a requisite for increasing social wealth, improving people's livelihood and promoting social progress. Therefore, we must stick to the principle of expanding domestic demand, strive to increase the proportion of consumption and promote a virtuous cycle of economic development. We must accelerate industrialization, IT application, urbanization, and agricultural modernization, and promote the coordinated development and sound interplay of the four modernizations. We must actively yet prudently carry forward urbanization, improve the systems and mechanisms for its healthy development, strive to improve the quality of urbanization, and gradually form a number of city clusters with international influence, so that they can act as the engines for driving regional and national economic growth, and provide impetus and space for China's sustained, sound and steady economic development. We must promote the revolution of production and consumption of energy resources, strive to improve the efficiency and effectiveness of resource utilization, control and reduce the total consumption of energy resources, make economic development more driven by energy resources conservation and circular economy, and promote green and sustainable economic development.

Fourth, attach more importance to industrial support and development, and promote the transformation and upgrading of industrial structure. Looking back on the rising course of economic giants and economic powers, it is found that the top economic aggregate is only necessary for moving towards an economic power, yet the key lies in the strong economic structure. With the Opium War in 1840, China was weakening though its GDP was much higher than that of the United Kingdom at that time, while the United Kingdom was an economic power. The most important reason was that the old China remained at the low end of the industrial structure. Therefore, China should persist on solving problems related to agriculture and rural areas and farmers as the top priority in our national economic work. To promote the modernization with a population of 1.4 billion in China, the top priority highly valued is to accelerate the development of modern agriculture, increase overall agricultural production capacity and ensure China's food security and effective supply of important agricultural products. Meanwhile, China must work actively to promote the coordinated development of the primary, secondary and tertiary industries to build a new system of modern industrial development by strengthening demand orientation, persisting in vigorously developing manufacturing industries, especially advanced manufacturing industries, speeding up the transformation and upgrading of traditional industries, seizing the opportunity of developing emerging industries and adhering to the rational layout and construction of infrastructure and basic industries. It is necessary to intensify efforts to promote and expand the service industry, especially modern service industry, and make the service industry a new engine for sustainable economic and social development. It is necessary to give full play to the dominant role of industry in the real economy to promote China's transformation from a industrial major to an industrial power. It is necessary to strengthen the coordination and cooperation between fiscal, taxation, financial and investment policies and industrial policies, and let policies play the guiding role. China must continue to take ecological progress as the basic requirement for optimizing industrial structure, so that the economic development depends more on modern service industries and emerging industries as drivers of growth, and more on energy and resources conservation and developing circular economy to advance.

Fifth, deepen the system reform of science and technology and enhance self-innovation capacity. The economist Schumpeter first put forward the "innovation theory", which triggered a long-term discussion in the economic circle and promoted the publicity and development of innovative ideas. Since the founding of the People's Republic of China in 1949, historic breakthroughs have been made in the areas such as "two bombs and one satellite" (including atomic bomb and hydrogen bomb and the satellite), manned spaceflight, lunar exploration projects, and high-speed railways, all of which are innovation results in science and technology. Since the reform and opening up in 1978, China's total factor productivity (TFP) has been significantly in an upward trend, indicating that technological changes and other factors play an important role in the economic growth. Relevant research further shows that there are obvious misplaced factor resources among enterprises in China, and unreasonable allocation of factor resources in state-owned enterprises and collective enterprises. Strong innovation capacity in science and technology and transformation capacity in application are the strategic underpinning for China to become an economic powerhouse, which must be placed at the core of realizing the Two Centenary Goals and the goal of becoming an economic power. In order to achieve this, firstly, it is necessary to adhere to the path of independent innovation with Chinese characteristics, plan and promote innovation from a global perspective, improve the capacity for original innovation, integrated innovation and reinnovation through introduction, digestion and absorption, and place greater emphasis on collaborative innovation; secondly, it is necessary to deepen the system reform of science, technology and education to speed up developing a market-oriented system for technological innovation, in which enterprises are the main players, and synergy is created through the joint efforts of enterprises, universities, and research institutes; thirdly, it is necessary to improve the knowledge innovation system, strengthen basic research, cutting-edge technology research, and technology research of social welfare, raise the level of scientific research and the ability to commercialize research results, and seize the commanding heights of scientific and technological development strategy; fourthly, it is necessary to improve the evaluation criteria, incentive mechanism and transformation mechanism for innovation in science and technology. Further improvement should be made to improve the policies of innovation in science and technology, including implementing the intellectual property strategy in depth, strengthening intellectual property protection and exploring the establishment of intellectual property courts. In the meantime, it is necessary to constantly improve the legal environment for innovation and promote the efficient allocation and comprehensive integration of innovation resources.

Sixth, implement the strategy of making China rich in human resources, and strive to unleash new demographic dividends. With the advent of global economic integration and the arrival of knowledge economy, the significance of human capital has been increasingly recognized and accepted. Human capital has increasingly become the core competitiveness of a country, playing a crucial role in the development politics, economy, society, culture and ecology, and being an important supporting force for a country to move from a major economy to a powerful economy. China is a populous country, but not strong in human resource power. To achieve the Two Centenary Goals and the goal of becoming an economic power, China must speed up implementing the strategy of strengthening China through human resources. From the practical perspective, firstly, it is necessary to gradually carry forward the implementation of the strategy of rejuvenating the country through science and education, deepen comprehensive education reform, innovate the system and mechanism of training talented personnel in universities and research institutes, and vigorously promote education equality and universal education; secondly, it is necessary to adjust and improve the birth policy to ensure long-term balanced population growth, a high-quality population base should be provided for the accumulation of human resources by promoting long-term balanced population development, further studying preventive eugenics and progressive eugenics, and strengthening services such as genetic counseling, examination, screening and diagnosis; thirdly, it is necessary to further enhance medical and health care treatment in China, promote the vertical flow of high-quality medical resources, strengthen the integration of regional resources of public health services, gradually standardize pharmaceutical pricing, improve the nutritional supply for our people, and provide medical and health supports for the high-quality labor force; fourthly, it is necessary to strengthen vocational training for rural migrant workers to greatly improve their technical quality, and deepen the reform of education system for the children of migrant workers, so as to create conditions for creating new demographic dividends;[1] fifthly, it is necessary to take active measures to respond to the aging trend, speed up the establishment of social pension service system and develop the elderly service industry. The system of postponing retirement age should be further studied and prudently treated to tap the potential of labor resources of the early elderly.

Seventh, comprehensively deepen reform and opening up, and develop new systems and mechanisms. The core theme of the Third Plenary Session of the 18th CPC National Congress is to study the system and mechanism of comprehensively deepening reform. Therefore, it is an important and urgent task for China to break the institutions that impede further economic development and promote institutional innovation, so as to achieve the Two Centenary Goals and step forward from a major economy to a powerful economy. In the process of deepening the economic system reform, efforts should be made to advance the reform and innovation of political system, social system and cultural system. Only when an economy boosts a good system and mechanism can it ensure orderly market competition, and that all factors of production participate in market exchanges equally, stimulate the vitality of market entities to the maximum extent, and better mobilize the initiative, enthusiasm and creativity of officials and the general public in starting businesses. Consequently, in accordance with the decisions and arrangements made at the Third Plenary Session of the 18th CPC Central Committee, China will further deepen reforms in the fiscal and taxation systems, financial system, urban-rural integration system and mechanism, and building an open economy. Following the 19th CPC National Congress, we must uphold and improve the system of socialism with Chinese characteristics and continue to modernize China's system and capacity for governance. We must have the determination to get rid of all outdated thinking and ideas and all institutional ailments, and to break through the blockades of vested interests. We should draw on the results of other civilizations, develop a set of institutions that are well conceived, fully built, procedure based, and efficiently functioning, and do full justice to the strengths of China's socialist system. This objectively requires China to pursue reform in a more systematic, holistic and coordinated way, dare to take on tough problems, navigate poential dangers, and actively build systems and mechanisms conducive to realizing the dream of becoming an economic power.

Eighth, develop the maritime economy and work quickly to build China into a

---

[1] Chen Siwei, Li Yining, Wu Jinglian et al., *Reform is the Biggest Dividend for China*, Beijing: People's Publishing House, 2013, p. 28.

maritime power. The Eighth Collective Study of the Political Bureau of the CPC Central Committee conducted a special study and research on the theme of "building China into a strong maritime country". Xi Jinping made the judgment that "an advanced maritime economy is an important support for building China into a strong maritime country". China boasts a vast maritime territory, thus implementing the strategy of maritime power is an important factor for the country to break through resource and market constraints. Building a maritime power can not only help the rational development of marine resources, but help the homeland national security and sustainable economic and social development in China. According to the Statistical Bulletin of China's Maritime Economy released by the State Oceanic Administration of China in 2017, the national maritime production value totalled RMB7,761.1 billion, up by 6.9%, and accounted for 9.4% of GDP. Among them, the added value of its primary industry was RMB360 billion, that of secondary industry RMB3,009.2 billion, and the tertiary industry RMB4,391.9 billion, accounting for 4.6%, 38.8% and 56.6% of the marine GDP respectively. It was estimated that there were 36.57 million sea-related employments in China in 2017. According to the statistics, China has become an open economy highly dependent on the ocean, and the safety of maritime transport channels is directly related to the lifeblood of the country. To fully implement the strategy of making China a maritime power, the following points should be strengthened. Firstly, improve the capacity for developing marine resources and maritime economy. Secondly, resolutely protect the marine ecological environment and ensure the sustainable utilization of its resources, as it is an indispensable part of China's ecological progress. Thirdly, improve the capability to enforce maritime rights and resolutely safeguard national maritime rights and interests. The coordinated mechanism of maritime rights protection and law enforcement should be strengthened, the strength of maritime military should be enhanced, and the maritime rights and interests of our country should be defended. Fourthly, make solid efforts to develop and strengthen the maritime administrative management system and maritime law enforcement system. Through the reform and innovation of relevant system and mechanism, it can provide a vigorous support for building China into a strong maritime country.

Ninth, build an open economy based on new systems and further liberalize the economy. To achieve the Two Centenary Goals and become a powerful economy, China must adapt to the new trend of economic globalization, promote domestic reform and opening up, better integrate "bringing in" with "going global", and foster new advantages in leading international economic cooperation and competition at a faster pace. Firstly, we will make innovations in the mode of opening up, encourage coastal, inland and border areas to draw on strengths in opening up between each other, and create a new regional opening mode with division of labor, cooperation, complementary advantages and balanced coordination. Secondly, we will pay equal attention to both export and import, develop new strengths in export competition with technology, brand, quality and service as the core, speed up the transformation and upgrading of processing trade, and promote the gradual expansion of processing trade from assembly to the high-end industrial chain such as R&D and design. Thirdly, we will improve the comprehensive strengths and overall benefits of utilizing foreign capitals, broaden the channels of utilizing foreign capital, optimize the structure, and strengthen the macro-management of utilizing foreign capital. Fourthly, we will accelerate the pace of "going global", actively expand the intensity of foreign investment, rationally utilize the country's foreign exchange reserves, give full play to China's comparative advantages in light textile and garment industries and other industries, and encourage enterprises to invest and set up factories overseas. Fifthly, we will take steps to innovate the cooperation mode with developed countries, strengthen cooperation with developing countries and their neighboring countries, improve cooperation mechanisms, expand cooperation fields, develop new foreign aid methods, continue to pursue the Silk Road Economic Belt and the 21st Century Maritime Silk Road initiatives, develop the free trade zone strategy at a faster pace, and build the Shanghai Free Trade Zone as an innovative supporter to help realizing the Two Centenary Goals and the dream of becoming an economic powerhouse.

Chapter 3
The Strategy and Impetus for Developing a Powerful Economy

3.1 Promoting supply-side structural reform under the new normal of economy

The new normal in economic development is a major strategic judgment, made by the CPC Central Committee since the 18th CPC National Congress, to comprehensively analyze the world economy cycle and various development stages in China and the interaction between them. Supply-side structural reform is an initiative governance strategy adopted by the CPC Central Committee to adapt to, grasp and guide a new normal in economic development. Both the new normal in economic development and supply-side structural reform profoundly embody Xi Jinping's thoughts on governance in the new era, and act as the important milestone of the development of socialist political economy with Chinese characteristics. It plays an important guiding role in developing a powerful economy.

3.1.1 Background of the new normal of economy and supply-side structural reform

At the Central Conference on Economic Work held in December 2013, the vision of new normal of economy was put forward by Xi Jinping. The term "new normal" then gained ground in China when Xi had his inspection tour in Henan Province in May 2014, and it was reported to the whole society for the first time by Xinhua News Agency. In November 2015, the supply-side structural reform was put forward by Xi at the Eleventh Conference of the Central Leading Group of Finance and Economy. These expositions about China's economic development and structural reform have its profound historical and realistic backgrounds.

3.1.1.1 Background of the new normal in economic development from historical periods

In January 2016, at the seminar for provincial and ministerial leading cadres held to implement the spirit of the Fifth Plenary Session of the 18th CPC Central Committee, General Secretary Xi Jinping pointed out: "Historically, new situations, patterns and phases have constantly emerged in China's economic development, and the new normal is just one more stage in a long historical process."[1] From the perspective of epistemology, the new normal in economic development is a long-term phenomenon at a certain stage of economic development, which is determined by the objective law governing economic development. Therefore, we are required to observe and analyze the new normal in economic development with a broad outlook and long time span, and even from the research results of economic history.

From the global perspective, the world is in the era of industrialization, which lasts more than 200 years. During this period, several industrial revolutions took place, while most of countries have not completed industrialization yet. Since the 18th century, the industrial revolutions have boosted each and every economy to grow at a much higher speed than ever before with its unique driving force one wave after another. From the history of human development, high-speed economic growth can be regarded as a special historical phenomenon in the period of industrialization, or a characteristic normal different from other periods of industrialization. Before the industrial revolution, the economic growth was extremely slow, while after the completion of industrialization, the high-speed growth will recede. That is to say, it is a normal regular phenomenon that China's current economic growth falls to a certain extent under the new normal.[2]

On the whole, China is now in the middle-to-late stage of industrialization. The new normal in economic development proposed by Xi Jinping has arrived, and the economic growth has shifted from high speed to medium-high speed. From the actual situation in recent years, China's economic growth has fallen from two digital rate to below 7%. While China's economic aggregate constantly expands, it is a common law that the economic growth will slow down when it reaches medium-high speed. With the development of economy, the growth rate may further decrease in the future. Nevertheless, the decline of China's economic growth rate is much smaller than that of Republic of Korea and Japan. Both researches at home and abroad show that the

[1] Xi Jinping, *The Governance of China* (Volume Ⅱ), Beijing: Foreign Language Press, 2017, pp. 245-246.

[2] Jing Bei, "Study on the New Normal of Chinese Economic Development", *China Industrial Economics*, 2015(1).

potential growth rate of China's economy tends to decline significantly. According to a research by Chinese Academy of Social Sciences, the structural slowdown has become the main feature of China's new normal in economic development. The research also predicts that China's potential growth rate will range from 7.8% to 8.7%, 5.7% to 6.6% and 5.4% to 6.3% respectively in 2011 to 2015, 2016 to 2020, and 2021 to 2030.[1]

Every stage of development in human society has its own distinctive features, which are prominently manifested in two aspects: First, various constraints of development. This includes external and internal factors, material and non-material factors, explicit and implicit institutional factors, etc. Second, dynamic structure, mode, method, and basic situation of economic operation, which are compatible with various development constraints. This is because every stage of development will face new contradictions, although the main challenges in the previous stage are resolved. On the one hand, the evolution of history has continuity and inheritance, that is to say, the normality of each stage is the continuation of previous stage. On the other hand, the historical evolution follows a spiral upward law, that is, a law of difference. The normality of different stages significantly differentiates from the previous one, and presents new historical features in different time and space, and a series of characteristics.

The new normal in economic development is a new cycle of economic development, which can be reviewed by China's several major historical stages of development—from wax to wane and then to wax again, especially by the evolution and development of modern industry. China's industrialization lasted for more than 100 years, and its economic cycle, for better narration, regarded as the same to political cycle, can be roughly divided into four stages: the germinated stage of industrialization (1912-1949), the early stage of industrialization (1950s-1970s), the accelerated stage of industrialization (1980s-2012) and the deepening stage of industrialization (2013-the mid-twentieth century). The duration of each historical stage is about 30 years. Compared with the previous stage, each historical stage is an obvious "new normal". According to this rule, the deepening stage of industrialization coincides with the new normal in economic development put forward by Xi Jinping. That is to say, China's new normal in economic development may last for about 30 years. The deepening stage of China's industrialization started in 2013, and will last until the middle of the 21st century. For sure, this is an era of striving to modernize national governance system through

[1] Li Yang, Zhang Xiaojing, "On the New Normal of China", Research Reports Series of Institution of Economics, Chinese Academy of Social Sciences, 2014.

deepening reform; this is an era of building a moderately prosperous society in all respects and realizing the Chinese dream of the great rejuvenation of the Chinese nation. This is the background of the new normal in economic development that we are discussing.

3.1.1.2 Background of the new normal in economic development from 40 years of reform and opening up

The new normal in China's economic development does not emerge from the other. It is an achievement of economic growth through over 40 years of reform and opening up. Therefore, we should understand the new normal of economic development from a strategic perspective and avoid taking it as a policy excuse for China's economic downward pressure, which will weaken the guiding significance of the new normal to China's economic policies and strategies.

With 40 years of rapid development, remarkable achievements have been made in China's economic development, while some problems in structure, institutions and quality have long been accumulated. The past 40 years has witnessed the glorious era of reform and opening up. Development is the absolute principle, which not only reflects the driving force of economic development in that era, but marks the source of impetus for reform and opening up. Under such a dynamic mechanism, reform and opening up is in full swing and has made great achievements, whereas many contradictions and issues arose. This is the precondition to adapt ourselves to the new normal, grasp and guide the new normal in economic development. The new normal in economic development is an objective, internal, inevitable state of development mode we have chosen. Turning a blind eye to the new normal can only further distort China's economy, and it will not take long before we pay more costs.

(1) *Domestic factors*

First, the high rate of economic growth is unsustainable. Since the launching of reform and opening up, China has maintained a high growth rate in economy for more than 30 years. From 1978 to 2012, it maintained an average annual growth of 9.8 %, and from 2003 to 2007, that of 11.6%, which effectively supported the building of a moderately prosperous society and national modernization. After years of rapid growth, China's economy is bound to enter a period of adjustment. In the future period to come, the potential growth rate will decline. With the decline of labor force supply, the rise of environmental governance costs, and the inclination of consumption to service goods, the potential of China's economic growth will decline, thus the growth rate of GDP will decline as well and it is impossible to maintain high-speed growth. Second, the mode of economic development is unsustainable. The extensive economic growth used to play a great role in China, but now it is unsustainable to follow this mode, because it cannot win the approval from both domestic and international conditions. We must be soberly aware that the problems of unbalanced, uncoordinated and unsustainable development are still prominent. Third, the industrial structure is at the middle or low level of global value chain. The important reason is that the development of modern industry lags behind, and backward traditional agriculture and low-end industries widely exist. Fourth, the economic growth is mainly driven by factors and investments. Since 40 years of reform and opening up, China's economic growth mainly depends on the input of labor force, capital and land, which is a typical factor-driven economy. From the current situation, these three factors are confronted with many bottlenecks and constraints, and they are not likely to support the sustainable development of China's economy. Fifth, the market economic system is not sound. Currently, it still has many problems, such as the non-unified market rules, the unfairness of competition, the under developed factors, and the dislocated, offside and absent government functions.

(2) *Foreign factors*

The international financial crisis has destroyed the driving force of world economic growth, while the new independent driving force has not been formed; therefore, the world economy is likely to maintain a period of slow growth. In the meantime, developed countries are generally aware of the harm of industrial hollowing-out, and take preferential measures to attract investment and develop the real economy; therefore, some multinational companies withdraw from their own countries, which results in more sluggish growth of international trade. In recent years, the growth rate of international trade is even lower than that of the world economy. All these have created obstacles for China to use world economic growth and international market expansion to promote domestic economic growth.

3.1.1.3 Background of the new normal in economic development from the 12th Five-year Plan period

After China's economy surpassed Japan to become the world's second largest economy in 2010, China's economic growth rate continued to decline. The contradictions and risks accumulated in the past years of rapid growth have become prominent, and the economy presents characteristics different from the past. However, there has been a great debate in the theoretical field over a period of time on whether the decline of China's economy is affected by external factors, or it means that China's economy has entered a new stage. This kind of debate is not only theoretical, but more importantly, the macro policy orientation will be different. If the slowdown of China's economy is caused by external factors, it means that the current economic growth is lower than the potential growth rate; therefore, China will adopt the stimulus policy. If China's economic slowdown is caused by internal factors, it means that the cause of economic slowdown is the decline of potential growth rate. Macro policy must be adopted to restrain the economic slowdown, and at the same time, we must make up our mind to solve the problems faced by China's sustained economic growth through reform. According to the new development stage and the reality of China's economic development, Xi Jinping has made a series of elaboration on the new normal economic development, and the effect is convincing. China's economy has entered a completely different stage from the past. We must think about China's economy with new thoughts and grasp the general direction of economy with new policy means. The correct understanding of China's new economic cycle has laid a foundation for implementing supply-side structural reform.

Since the 12th Five-year Plan (2011-2015), the economic growth has significantly declined. The obvious reason is insufficient demand, while it is in fact due to supply failure caused by the disconnection between supply structure and market demand. On the one hand, some industries, such as steel and coal, have serious overcapacity and inefficient resource allocation. On the other hand, the effective demand of residents is restricted by the supply side, and the disconnection between domestic consumption and production is becoming obvious. If the problem of supply failure cannot be effectively resolved, then the policy of simply expanding domestic demand will inevitably aggravate the difficulty of long-term structural adjustments.

In December 2014, the Central Conference on Economic Work comprehensively summarized the characteristics of China's economic development stage to grasp the new normal in economic development. First, from consumption demand. Consumption in China used to flow in waves. Now, the stage of consumption in waves has ended. Second, from investment demand. Through more than 30 years of high-intensity and large-scale development, traditional industries and real estate has reached capacity. Third, from the export and balance of payments. Now, global aggregate demand is sluggish, and China's low-cost comparative advantage is receding. Fourth, from the production capacity and the industrial structure. China used to have insufficient supply for a long time, but now the supply capacity of traditional industries has greatly exceeded demand. Fifth, from the comparative advantages of production factors. Low labor cost was the biggest advantage in the past, but now the aging population is increasing, and the rural surplus labor is decreasing. Sixth, from the market competition. Increase in quantity and price competition used to dominate, but now it is gradually turning to competition in quality and product differentiation. Seventh, from the resource and environment constraints. China used to have sufficient energy resources and extensive eco-space, but now the carrying capacity of its environment is approaching or has reached the upper limit. Eighth, from the accumulation and defusing of economic risks. Hidden risks are gradually becoming evident as the economic growth slows down. Ninth, from the resource allocation mode and the means of macro-economic control, the marginal effects of comprehensive stimulus policies are obviously decreasing.

These problems are not cyclical, but mainly structural. Currently, a number of China's productive capacity is formed in the golden period of world economic growth for external demand and domestic high-speed growth. In response to the impact of the international financial crisis, some productive capacities have expanded. In the case of the slowdown of international market, it is difficult to solve the problem of overcapacity only by stimulating domestic demand. This is like the situation that a table of guests can not eat up two tables of prepared dinner. Not only China, but also other countries have encountered this problem.[1] Therefore, the supply side structural reform is the main line of economic work under the new normal.

3.1.2 Significance of practical guidance of the new normal of economy and supply-side structural reform

Based on both domestic and foreign trends of economic development and China's basic situations, a series of expositions of China's economic development has been made by the CPC Central Committee with Xi Jinping at its core since the 18th CPC National Congress, and they gave shape to many important thoughts. Among them, the new normal of economic development and the supply-side structural reform are particularly rich in connotations, focusing on the characteristics of China's economic development. It is of great significance to guide the practice.

[1] Seven Questions for Supply-side Structural Reform: Authorities' Views on Current Chinese Economy, *People's Daily*, Jan. 4, 2016.

3.1.2.1 The new normal as main features of China's medium- to long-term economic development

The new normal in economic development has exerted both domestic and foreign impacts. It represents that we have entered a medium- to long-term historical stage featuring a new normal in economic development, and it will serve as the basic essence and main feature of China's economic development for quite a long time in the future.

The new normal in economic development is closely related to the development stage of China's economic transformation and upgrading, and the sustained and sound economic development. The domestic and foreign concept of new normal is relatively independent of each other. Comparatively speaking, the new normal in China boasts richer connotations, and the practice is much more complicated than that in foreign countries. The foreign concept of new normal is at least resigned, if not pessimistic, while it is totally different concept of new normal in China. The new normal of China's economy declares a higher stage in economic development. It not only analyzes the essentials of transforming and upgrading economy, but its direction and power structure of transformation in China.

Xi Jinping pointed out: "the new normal is not a basket that can hold everything. It is mainly economic. It should not be misused as a concept. Further, negative phenomena should not be denounced as the new normal. The new normal is not a shield or an excuse for not resolving difficult problems. Instead, it means promoting development with more subjective initiatives and more creativity."

The new normal in economic development entails specific connotations and features. During the inspection tour in Henan province in May 2014, Xi Jinping pointed out: "China maintains its important strategic opportunities for development. We must strengthen confidence to adapt ourselves to the new normal and keep the strategic thoughts in place, based on the current characteristics of economic developments in China". In an opening speech at the APEC CEO Summit in November 2014, Xi elaborated the characteristics of the new normal in China's economic development—a slowdown in the rate of growth, optimization of economic structure, and shift of growth engines, and pointed out that the new normal has brought the new development opportunities for China. At the Central Conference on Economic Work held in December 2014, Xi analyzed the trends brought by the new normal in detail and pointed out: "Entering the new normal manifests the inevitable periodic characteristics of China's economic development. Understanding, adapting to and guiding the new normal are the major tasks in the present and future stage of our economic development". At the seminar for provincial and ministerial-level leading cadres to learn and implement the spirit of the Fifth Plenary Session of the 18th CPC Central Committee in November 2015, Xi systematically demonstrated the main characteristics of China's economic development under the new normal. These characteristics are more prominent and more perfect in system, compared with his previous view at the 2014 APEC CEO Summit. He pointed out: "Our economic growth should be transitioned from high speed to medium-high speed. The growth mode should be transforming from large-scale and high-speed growth to high-quality and high-efficient growth. The economic structure should be transitioned from quantitative increase and expanding capacity to adjusting stock while optimizing increment. Growth engines should be turned from relying more on the input of factors such as resources and low-cost labor forces to innovation-driven development". Xi's expositions on the new normal of China's economic development are profound in thinking and rich in connotations. It is a new important strategic thought for CPC's governance.

Currently, China's economic growth rate has declined, compared with that of previous years, which is a normal phenomenon under the new normal of economic development. Since the 18th CPC National Congress, Xi Jinping repeatedly stressed that economic development should maintain a certain pace, on condition that high-quality, high-efficient and sustainable development is pursued, rather than a simple pursuit of growth rate. At the symposium of the Boao Forum for Asia in April 2013, Xi pointed out: "China will remain in a rising period of development for quite a long time in the future, in which industrialization, informatization, urbanization, and agricultural modernization will bring broad space for domestic market with a solid foundation of social productive forces, obvious comprehensive advantages of productive factors, and the improving system and mechanism. It is quite possible for us to maintain the economic growth at a relatively high level", and "it is not that we cannot promote the economic growth at a faster speed, but that we won't do so". In July 2014, shortly after Xi put forward the new normal of economic development, the Working Conference of the Political Bureau of the CPC Central Committee stressed: "China's development must be kept at a certain speed; otherwise, it will be difficult to resolve many related problems. Meanwhile, development must be the development that follows the economic laws, the sustainable development that follows the natural laws, and the inclusive development that follows the social rules." These are several important statements made by Xi Jinping about economic development under the new normal, playing an important role in helping us gain a thorough understanding of the new normal.

Then, how to understand the new normal in economic development and interpret the decline of economic growth rate under the new normal in China? Since the international financial crisis, both developed and emerging economies have experienced economic deceleration of varying degrees, and China is no exception. However, China's economic slowdown is related to not only international factors and external shocks, but even structural factors. Recently, Xi Jinping has repeatedly stressed: "Now and in the future, China's economic development is facing and will encounter the problems on both the supply side and the demand side, but the major problem lies in the former."[1] Here, the supply-side aspect refers to the structural problem.

While the global new normal is mainly described as a "new mediocrity" or long-term stagnation, the main characteristics of China's new normal of economy in growth is structural deceleration. We can see that China's economic growth is shifting from high speed to medium-high speed caused by the structural change. However, in the meantime, such deceleration results in improving the overall quality and efficiency of our economy at the middle-to-high-end level. In general, if the global new normal represents a pessimistic interpretation of the future trend of the world economy, then China's new normal contains the positive content of the economy toward evolving into a model that is more advanced, and with more complicated division of labor and reasonable structure.

The decline of potential growth rate in China is mainly caused by the relative scarcity of productive factors on the supply side and the changes of total factor productivity. Since the 12th Five-year Plan period, there have been two main reasons for China's economic slowdown. First, the growth rate of the supply of factors and resources has slowed down. The gradual disappearance of demographic dividend means the weakening of the traditional drivers for rapid growth, leading to a decline in the potential growth rate. In the meantime, the growth rate of urbanization slows down, showing a trend of deceleration. Second, the industrial structure is changing. Industrialization made resources and labor force flow from agriculture to the secondary industry. Now, China's industrialization has entered the late stage, and resources and labor force have begun to flow to the tertiary industry. The growth rate of investment in the tertiary industry began to exceed that of the secondary industry.

So, the decline of potential growth rate caused by demographic dividend reduction and other factors is an irreversible trend. In the meantime, there remain some institutional factors that increase the institutional transaction fees and production costs

[1] Xi Jinping, *The Governance of China* (Volume Ⅱ), Beijing: Foreign Language Press, 2017, p.253.

of economic activities on the supply side, which can be remedied by reform. Under the joint impact of these variable and immutable factors, China's economy will experience a process of downturn as it enters different stages of development, then gains new growth momentum through reforms to contain the downturn, and then enters a new development cycle.

The driving force of economic growth is an important issue under the new normal of economic development. The new normal of economic development means a transition from investment-driven and export-driven to innovation-driven growth mode. We must constantly improve the quality of factors, rely more on the quality of human capital and technological progress to make innovation a new driving force to boost development. In this regard, Xi Jinping has made many expositions. When attending the deliberation of the Shanghai delegation to the Third Session of the 12th National People's Congress in March 2015, Xi pointed out: "Innovation is the first driving force that guides development. Innovation is development. Innovation is the future. The key to adapting to and leading the new normal of China's economic development is to prioritize innovation in science and technology to transform the driving force for development." In his speech at the 18th Academician Conference of the Chinese Academy of Sciences and at the 13th Academician Conference of the Chinese Academy of Engineering in May 2016, Xi pointed out: "Implementing the strategy of innovation-driven development is the sure way to cope with the changes of development environment, grasp the autonomy of development, improve the core competitiveness, accelerate the transformation of economic development, solve the deep-rooted contradictions and issues in economic development, and better lead the new normal of China's economic development and maintain the sustained and sound development of China's economy." The series of speeches made by Xi Jinping highlights the driving forces of the new normal of economic development from many perspectives, and is of great significance in guiding the current work.

As China's economic development enters the new normal, it must be made clear that China is still in the period of strategic opportunity during which the development keeps promising, and whose connotations and conditions have been changed. Therefore, we must have accurate, deep, and full grasp of the changes in the conditions for development, take advantage of the situation, and more consciously adhere to improving the quality and efficiency of economic development as the central task, so as to vigorously promote the strategic readjustment of the economic structure. The key to achieving these targets, as Xi Jinping said, lies in comprehensively deepening reform, implementing the innovation-driven development strategy, and solving problems facing the development.

Since China stepped into the late stage of industrialization, its economic and social development has entered the new normal, facing the new requirements of changing the economic structure and transforming the driving forces. In terms of supply of factors, the contribution of labor force and capital accumulation to growth has significantly decreased and will be further reduced. The new driving force of growth improves productivity mainly through the improvement of factor quality and the optimization of allocation. In terms of total social demands, since entering the late stage of industrialization, it has been hard to keep the contribution of investment and exports to growth at a high level, and the new driving force of growth mainly lies in innovation.

China's modernization is very different from that of developed countries in the West. The western developed countries went through a "cascaded" process of development with industrialization, urbanization, agricultural modernization and informatization being carried out in sequence, which took more than 200 years to reach the current level. China, as the latecomer in developing, should prevail by making up for "the lost 200 years", which means to go through a "paralleled" process of development with industrialization, informatization, urbanization, and agricultural modernization developing side by side. [1] Thus, the new normal of economic development in this state needs to leverage the role of science and technology to promote the simultaneous development of industrialization, informatization, urbanization and agricultural modernization. Currently, innovation is the core of promoting supply-side structural reform, and the business start-ups and innovation has provided new driving forces for reform and development. Promoting employment through business start-ups can hedge the employment risks caused by the economic downturn, and improving quality and efficiency through innovation can promote the industrial upgrading and innovation. Through the business start-ups and innovation, we can create new demands, provide new supplies, cultivate new technologies, new industries, new forms of business and new models, and promote the economic growth to transform from the traditional factor-driven and investment-driven development to innovation-driven development. In order to promote the supply-side structural reform, we must first stimulate the enthusiasm and creativity of the "three major entities", namely, the entrepreneurs (the

[1] *Extracts of Xi Jinping's Statements on Technological Innovation*, Beijing: Central Party Literature Press, 2016, pp. 24-25.

market entity), the researchers (the innovation entity), and the government officials (the reform entity), to apply reform activities into practice. Besides, it is necessary to promote the innovation of modes and the integration of elements for innovation.

Then, where does the new driving force of economic growth generate from under the new normal? In general, it generates from three aspects: First, improve the quality of human capital and gradually replace introduction and imitation of technologies with independent innovation to provide inexhaustible power for economic growth. Second, constantly create new productive factors, such as information, knowledge, creative ideas and systems, to give more new impetus to economic growth. Third, eliminate the distorted factor allocation and improve total factor productivity to stimulate the internal driving force of economic growth through the supply-side structural reform. The driving force in the first aspect generates from the innovation in science and technology, and the second and third generate from the institutional innovations and the system innovations. It can be seen that innovation provides the core driving force for economic growth under the new normal. Thus, supporting, encouraging and guiding innovation is the key to promoting the development and charting the course for the future.

Implementing innovation-driven development and developing national innovation system should be based on market mechanism and led by enterprises. Anyway, it does not mean that the government can stand by and neglect its due role. In fact, the role of government in innovation-driven development is often irreplaceable. Under the market economic system, the government is expected to create and maintain a social and economic environment conducive to enterprise innovation. Besides, it should play a leading role in developing the innovative public goods and in regulating industries with externality and monopoly. Here, it needs to be emphasized that the government should not excessively intervene enterprises in choosing industries and technologies, and should avoid its direct participation as a market entity. If necessary to implement industrial policies, the government should play its due role to distinguish between preferential industrial policies and functional ones, and between directly-intervened ones and indirectly-intervened ones. This is the core essence of innovation development.

3.1.2.2 Supply-side structural reform as major innovation to adapt to and guide the new normal

In the fifth chapter "Main Line of Development" of the Outline of the 13th Five-year Plan for National Economic and Social Development of the People's Republic of China, it points out: To fully implement the Philosophy of New Development, and adapt to, grasp, and guide the new normal of economic development, we must strive to promote the supply-side structural reform while moderately expand aggregate demand, so that supply capacity can meet people's ever-growing, upgrading and personalized needs for a better material, cultural and ecological environment.

Supply-side structural reform is a new economic term as well as a major innovation made by the CPC Central Committee. To better study the supply-side structural reform, we need to find its theoretical source in economics. For sure, the classical liberal economics advocated by the French economist Jean-Baptiste Say at the beginning of the 19th century that is the most important ideological source of the supply-side economics. The Say's Law of Market holds that supply creates its own demand, which is the most important prescription between supply and demand in classical economics. The economic policy advocated by Say's Law basically features laissez-faire and non-intervention, emphasizing the absolute dominant position of the market. Since then, the supply-side economics has experienced a spiral development for more than 200 years. In the 1930s, the state interventionism advocated by John Maynard Keynes overturned the trend of liberalism, but the supply-side economics came back after the stagflation crisis in the 1970s. The supply-side economics emphasizes that supply creates its own demand, supply is the key to promoting economic development, and tax cuts are a must to improve people's savings, investment capability and initiative.

The economic liberalism advocated by classical economics is deeply imprinted in various logical frameworks which is put forward by many economists of the supply-side management school. For example, the economist Milton Friedman represented by the supply-side economics was a typical libertarian, who opposed the government intervention in the economy through monetary policies and advocated implementing the single currency rules to control inflation. Another example is Arthur Betz Laffer, the representative of the supply-side economics, who stressed the view to reduce the burden of enterprises through tax cuts, so that enterprises can develop and the government can be guaranteed long-term tax revenue when the burdens that are shouldered by enterprises become lighter.

The theoretical foundation of China's supply-side structural reform is socialist political economy with Chinese characteristics. The supply-side structural reform has the obvious characteristics of the primary stage of socialism and economic transformation. The key to China's supply-side structural reform is to release and develop social productive forces, promote structural adjustment through reform, and reduce ineffective and low-end supply while expanding effective and medium-and high-end supply, so as to make the supply structure more adaptive and flexible to changes in demand, and improve total factor productivity. This is not only about taxation and tax rates, but a strategy to resolve China's supply-side economic problem through a series of policy measures, especially those to promote innovation in science and technology, develop the real economy, guarantee and improve people's living standards.

From the perspective of socialist political economy with Chinese characteristics, the supply-side structural reform aims to improve China's supply capacity to better meet people's ever-growing, upgrading and personalized needs for a better material, cultural and ecological environment, thus achieving the goal of socialist production. The supply-side structural reform emphasizes both supply and demand, stresses both developing social productive forces and improving relations of production, allows the market to play its decisive role in allocating resources and the government to fulfill its better roles, and looks to both present and future.

Now, the global value chain is being reshaped. China has formed its own characteristics in participating in the constant dynamic adjustment of the global value chain, although it has lost some advantages of traditional industries. Chinese people are firm in their determination and demonstrate great courage in carrying out the supply-side structural reform. If the reform can proceed successfully, needless to say, it is of significance to the global value chain and China's development itself.

In this sense, both short-term tasks and long-term strategies must be included in China's supply-side structural reform. Preparations should be made for taking long-term strategies while completing short-terms tasks in key areas. In the short term, it is necessary to complete the five major strategic tasks of cutting overcapacity, reducing excess inventory, deleveraging, lowering costs, and strengthening areas of weakness. In the long run, the supply-side structural reform should aim at transforming the mode of economic growth, especially the philosophy of development to implement the innovative, coordinated, green, open, and inclusive development.

After a synthetic judgment, the CPC Central Committee believed that to address China's deep-rooted economic problems, it should be determined to redouble efforts in promoting economic structural reform, so as to make the supply system more adaptive to the changes in the demand structure. Now and in the future, China's economic development is facing and will encounter the problems on both the supply side and the demand side, but the major problem lies in the former. So, as an important task in the future, the supply-side structural reform should be promoted mainly through defusing overcapacity, transforming and upgrading traditional industries, and supporting and cultivating emerging industries.

The central government pointed out that promoting the supply-side structural reform is the main line of China's economic work now and in a period to come. To promote the supply-side structural reform, we must uphold the strategy of making progress while maintaining steady growth, with an appropriate pace and intensity. Besides, we should effectively manage and control the various financial risks by completing the five major tasks of cutting overcapacity, reducing excess inventory, deleveraging, lowering costs, and strengthening areas of weakness.

Since the international financial crisis in 2008, more and more countries have realized that the structural reform is the fundamental way out of the predicament, but it comes at a price. The 24th Conference of the Central Leading Group for Comprehensively Continuing Reform held in May 2016 stressed: "Promoting supply-side structural reform is a vital test of our determination to comprehensively deepen reform. We should be aware that reform comes with labor pains, while failure to take reforms will bring long-term pains. We should know well various contradictions, keep focus on reform, seize every available opportunity for reform, and aim at the reform for success." At this conference, Xi Jinping pointed out: "Supply-side structural reform is in essence a reform, and structural adjustment should be promoted through reform to stimulate the internal momentum and create an external environment for improving the quality of supply. All regions and sectors should place priority on promoting supply-side structural reform through comprehensively deepening reform, strengthen their determination to reform, highlight problem orientation, enhance targeted guidance, focus on targeted policies, improve reform effects, and maximize institutional strengths." As reform and development integrated with each other, every step forward in development requires a step forward in reform, and the continuous progress of reform can provide a strong driving force for development. Xi defined supply-side structural reform as "reform", which means that supply-side structural reform should be promoted in accordance with the law of reform. So, we should strengthen structural reform, relocate misplaced factors of production, increase effective supply, make the supply structure more adaptive and flexible, and improve total factor productivity.

Supply and demand are the two fundamentals of the internal relationship of market economy, which are both opposite and unified. Without demand, supply cannot be realized, while without supply, demand cannot be met. New demand generates new supply while new supply creates new demand. In January 2016, At a study session of provincial and ministerial-level officials on implementing the spirit of the Fifth Plenary Session of the 18th CPC Central Committee, Xi Jinping stressed that: "Supply-side and demand-side are the two basic means of economic management and macro-control. Demand-side management addresses economic aggregate problems, focuses on short-term macro-control, and propels economic growth mainly by adjusting taxation, fiscal expenditure, currencies and credits to stimulate or restrain demand. Supply-side management tackles structural problems, creates the driving force of economic growth, and boosts economic growth mainly by optimizing the allocation of productive factors and adjusting the productive structure to improve the quality and efficiency of the supply system." In delivering the Report on the Work of Government in March 2018, Li Keqiang stressed that it is necessary to step up supply-side structural reform, focus on the real economy in economic development, and continue to cut overcapacity, reduce excess inventory, deleverage, lower costs, and strengthen areas of weakness. It is also necessary to take big steps to streamline administration and cut taxes and fees, keep improving the business environment, and further energize market entities, so as to increase the quality of economic growth.

Since the proposal of supply-side reform, there has been a misunderstanding that emphasizing the supply-side reform seems to give up the demand side. In fact, China's economic growth under the new normal involves both supply and demand. While promoting supply-side reform, we cannot ignore the demand side and give up its expansion. It is necessary to integrate supply-side reform with demand-side expansion with more focus on the former.

Under the new normal in economic development, the problems facing the economic growth come from both supply side and demand side, and the key lies in the former. Due to the insufficient role of consumption in the demand side, the growth is only driven by the factor of investment, which makes the economic development trapped in the investment-driven mode and scale expansion, and hard to be transformed to the efficiency-driven mode. The problem of supply, that is, the problem of production, as the key in the new normal in the economic development, are manifested as that of supply structure, supply efficiency, insufficient innovation capability and so on. Therefore, the economic development under the new normal should be promoted not only by supply-side reform, but by expanding demand. We should adjust the economic structure, cut overcapacity, promote the development of service industry through supply-side reform, and address the employment problems through the demand-side expansion.

Promoting the supply-side structural reform does not mean abandoning the demand-side management. It is meant to implement the regulation and control of aggregate demand, keep economic performance within an appropriate range, and create a macro environment conducive to structural reform. However, implementing the demand-side management does not mean taking measures through massive stimulus. It is meant to tap the potentials of domestic effective demand, and open up more space for development to create stable and lasting domestic demand support for the economic growth. It is necessary to strengthen the basic role of consumption in driving the economic growth, adapt to the trend of consumption upgrading, remove policy barriers, optimize the consumption environment, and safeguard consumers' rights and interests. It is necessary to fully leverage the effective investment in stabilizing the growth and adjusting the structure, focus on strengthening areas of weakness in China's infrastructure facilities and people's livelihood, transform and upgrade traditional industries, further promote new urbanization and activate its greatest potentials of domestic demand and growth drivers. It is necessary to optimize the regional development pattern and promote further implementation of the Belt and Road Initiative, the coordinated development of Beijing-Tianjin-Hebei region, and the development of the Yangtze River Economic Belt.

3.1.2.3 Achievements in promoting supply-side structural reform

Currently, positive progress has been made in China's supply-side structural reform, with an obvious effect of the five priority tasks of cutting overcapacity, reducing excess inventory, deleveraging, lowering costs, and strengthening areas of weakness. In terms of cutting overcapacity, key industries such as iron and steel and coal overfulfilled their annual planning tasks in 2016. In terms of reducing excess inventory, the area of commercial housing for sale has significantly declined, with 695.39 million square meters for sale in 2016, down by 3.2% compared with that in 2015. In terms of deleveraging, the debt ratio of enterprise sectors has steadily declined, and the trend of funds flowing from the real economy to the virtual economy has been contained, which is conducive to better serve the real economy. In terms of lowering costs, the enterprises' costs of taxes, labor, energy, land, logistics, and finance and institutional transactions have all decreased in varying degrees. In terms of strengthening areas of weakness, by increasing investments in weak links such as ecological protection, environmental governance, infrastructure facilities, innovation in science and technology, people's livelihood, water conservancy management and primary industry, the areas of weakness in economic and social development have effectively improved.[1] On the whole, various measures for the supply-side structural reform have been gradually implemented, and the economic policy framework that adapts to the new normal has been gradually formed. The problems of economic development and structural imbalance have been constantly resolved through the reform. Thus, China is showing a steady and positive momentum in developing economy. The Report on the Work of the Government 2018 stressed: Over the past five years, building on work to cut backward production capacity in the cement, plate glass, and other industries, we have intensified efforts to cut overcapacity, prioritizing industries such as steel and coal; and a RMB100 billion fund for rewards and subsidies has been put in place by the central government to support the relocation of employees. We have cut steel production capacity by more than 170 million metric tons and that of coal by 800 million metric tons, and over 1.1 million employees have been assisted and relocated. We must actively remove barriers to market-based allocation of productive factors and reducing government-imposed transaction costs. According to statistics, the central government-priced items have been cut back by 80%, and local government-priced ones down by over 50%. Comprehensive reforms have swept the business system, including registering industry, commerce and capitals, and shortening the time it takes to start a business by more than one third. It is safe to say that China has scored significant achievements in promoting the supply-side structural reform. The business environment has consistently improved, the market is more energized, and people can access government services more easily. However, in general, the structural problems of unbalanced and uncoordinated economic supply and demand in China are still prominent. Thus, based on the existing achievements, efforts should be made to address new problems, improve policies and measures and avoid the short-sighted vision and old ways, so as to ensure the achievements of supply-side structural reform for a long period.

3.1.3 Deepening supply-side structural reform under the new normal in economic development

The Central Conference on Economic Work held in December 2017 pointed out that it was necessary to complete eight key tasks with focus on promoting high-quality development, one of which was to deepen the supply-side structural reform. To do so,

[1] Gao Peiyong, "Winning the Tough Battle of Supply-Side Structural Reform is the Key to Comprehensively Deepen Reform", *Qiushi*, 2017(9).

efforts should be made to promote the transformation from "made in China" to "created in China", from China speed to China quality, and from a large manufacturing country to a manufacturing power. To deepen the reform of market-oriented allocation of factors of production, efforts should be made to vigorously eliminate invalid supply, prioritize the disposal of "zombie enterprises", and cut overcapacity. Efforts should be made to vigorously cultivate new driving forces, strengthen innovation in science and technology, promote the optimization and upgrading of traditional industries, and foster a number of pioneering enterprises with innovative capability. Currently, since socialism with Chinese characteristics has entered a new era, at this new historical starting point, we should firmly grasp and properly balance the following three relationships while deepening the supply-side structural reform under the new normal of economic development.

3.1.3.1 Striking a balance between the role of government and that of market

The role of government and that of market is an important theoretical issue in cultivating and developing the system of socialist market economy, as well as the core issue in the process of reform and opening up in the long run. Through the long-term exploration and experience summarization, the Third Plenary Session of the 18th CPC Central Committee clearly put forward the judgment of "letting the market play the decisive role in resource allocation and the government play its functions better", which is also a major principle of promoting supply-side structural reform under the new normal of economic development. Under the new normal, the economic development has shifted from a single pursuit of speed growth to a priority to coordinated development of speed and quality, and the driving force has shifted from factor-input focus to innovation-driven technology. These shifts need to be supported by a more balanced relationship between the role of government and that of market. On the one hand, the government should fully create conditions for the market to take reforms itself. On the other hand, we should resolutely avoid the claim by western supply-side economics that the reform should exclude the function of government's macro-control, emphasize the role of market's regulation and correct the government's "distorting" the market. For sure, China's supply-side structural reform gives priority to both the role of government and that of the market. Taking overcapacity as an example. Some scholars believe that overcapacity is a common phenomenon in market economy, thus there is no need for the government to take measures to deal with it. However, it should be noted that in China overcapacity resulted not only from the market, but from government's regulation and control to some extent. To address this problem, the government must intervene. It requires the government to play a role in promoting the supply-side structural reform in varying degrees, and it will be difficult to complete the task of supply-side structural reform by relying solely on the market mechanism.

3.1.3.2 Striking a balance between short-term goals and long-term goals

Striking a balance between short-term goals and long-term ones is an important relationship in reform. In terms of supply-side structural reform, in our opinion, the general principle currently is to accelerate the reform when the two goals are in consistency, and the short-term goals should give way to long-term ones when they are inconsistent. For example, some regions have cut overcapacity, which may have a certain impact on economic development in the short term, but will bring opportunities for industrial upgrading in the long run. Therefore, we should be firm in our determination and demonstrate great courage in cutting overcapacity and cleaning up "zombie enterprises" to boost long-term economic development. In terms of medium-long-term goals, we should complete the short-term and long-term goals coordinately, for the reason that focusing on one side will lead to new market distortions and inappropriate market expectations, thus weakening the potential for long-term growth. Therefore, currently we should take a far view of the issues of real estate and avoid the phenomenon of marked ups and downs of housing prices caused by excessive policies. In the meantime, we should aim at transforming the growth model and improving the sustainability of growth, strengthen policy coordination, and improve the overall effect of supply-side structural reform.

3.1.3.3 Striking a balance between supply and demand

Supply and demand are the two fundamentals of the internal relationships of market economy, while supply-side and demand-side are the two basic means of economic management and macro-control. The relationship between supply and demand determines the price change, which is the objective law of market economy. Since the launching of reform and opening up, with the rapid expansion of consumer and investment demands, China has been unable to meet the supply-side needs in economic development for a long time. It is imperative to solve the problems of vitality and driving force in the development of social productive forces. Therefore, the focus of the reform is to delegate powers and surrender part of the profits, and further enhance the vitality and momentum of the economy. In the reform of power delegation and profit surrender, the relevant systems and mechanisms, which support enterprises to produce more and faster, have been quickly established while those that constrain enterprises to produce or manufacture well quite slowly. When the market demand for the quality of supply keeps growing, the problem of insufficient supporting measures on "responsibilities, power and interests" in the economic system will be highlighted. The reason is that when the efficiency of capacity utilization has been at a very low level for a long time, the enterprises will suffer losses for a long time. In this case, some enterprises need to reduce production and cut overcapacity, and some with poor management and low production will go bankrupt and recede from the market. The economic policy with focus on whether supply-side or demand-side reform should be determined by the macro-economic situation, so as to maintain the cooperation, coordination and unity between them. To push forward the supply-side structural reform, we must not only firmly grasp the main direction of improving supply quality, but fully utilize the important tools of demand-side management. Thus, we can achieve a dynamic balance between supply-side reform and demand-side management and create conditions for the supply-side structural reform.

3.2 Innovation-driven: core strategy for developing a powerful economy

With the advent of the Third Industrial Revolution and the Sixth Technological Revolution, the world has entered an innovation-intensive era with knowledge creation and technology innovation significantly accelerated and major innovation results flourished. Many countries are giving top priority to innovation as the national development strategy in an endeavor to enhance their international competitiveness. To this end, China must catch up to seize the windows of opportunity offered by a new round of technological revolution and industrial transformation, and accelerate efforts to implement the innovation-driven development strategy so as to obtain the leading position in science, technology and industry, improve the quality of economic growth and build China from a major economy to a strong economy.

3.2.1 Innovation is a growth mode at a higher level

The innovation-driven approach can create a new combination of intangible factors including knowledge, human resources and innovation-motivated systems, bringing about new growth drivers. It can not only increase the diminishing marginal returns and mitigate the constraints of rare resources in the long-term development, but provide opportunities for sustained, stable economic growth. Moreover, innovation enables countries to gain strengths in the increasingly fierce global competition and avoid trading disputes coming with traditional growth patterns. Compared with the intensive growth, the innovation-driven economic growth is more advanced and at a higher level.

Michael E. Porter, a US scholar specializing in management and strategy, suggests that economic development exhibits four progressive stages: factor-driven, investment-driven, innovation-driven and wealth-driven stages.

The initial stage is factor-driven stage where the economy is mainly boosted by basic factors of production such as land, capital and labor force. In other words, economic advancements in this stage show high dependence on healthy and inexpensive workforce, favorable conditions for crop growing, and natural resources. In this stage, the dominant and competitive industry is resource-intensive or labor-intensive industries such as mining and oil industries. That is, the factor-driven economy is characterized by extensive growth.

The second stage is investment-driven stage where the economic growth is based on large-scale investment. Enterprises acquire advanced technology through investments and engage in high value-added industries, thus their competitiveness is enhanced. Besides, they show better capabilities in assimilating and improving technology than that of the innovation-driven stage. In this stage, heavy and chemical industries like steel production and machinery manufacturing dominates in the economy and holds competitive strengths. It is a transitional stage where the economy is moving forward from extensive to intensive growth, with massive investment of productive factors and increased total factor productivity.

The third stage is innovation-driven stage where the creation and application of knowledge enable enterprises to improve their independent capacity to innovate, thus ensuring sustained and stable economic development. The innovation-driven economy rests on the higher level of national education, increased investment of human capitals, efficient markets of goods and factors, and a favorable ecosystem and culture to innovate. In addition to the technology domains, innovation also takes place in institutions, systems, organizations, environments and so on. By virtue of independent innovation, enterprises differentiate their technologies and products and obtain competitive advantages in the world market. Technology-intensive industries such as IT, new energy and biomedicine become the predominant industries. In this stage, innovation supplants the investment of factors as the main impetus for economic growth characterized by a typical mode of intensive growth.

The fourth stage is wealth-driven stage where the industries are evolved to a relatively higher level. Sectors such as finance and real estate occupy a large share of social wealth and business costs surge significantly while the investments in real assets and innovative activities are undervalued. Enterprises prefer to reduce competitiveness to increase the stability of the businesses by capital operations, which undermines their capacities to innovate and fails to increase their competitive strengths fundamentally. When a state moves to the wealth-driven stage, its industrial competitiveness begins to fall and then ebb.

According to the basic principle of economics and the practices of countries earlier in developing, the economic growth is propelled by different driving forces in different stages. As shown in Table 3-1, in the factor-driven stage, the factor contributions are up to 60 percent, while the innovation contributions are only 5 percent. In the innovation-driven stage, the innovation contributions rise to 30 percent while the factor contributions fall to 20 percent. Among the four stages, the first three stages, particularly the innovation-driven stage, are essential drivers to maintain a nation's competitive edges. Generally speaking, the longer innovation-driven stage is, the longer economic prosperity lasts.

Table 3-1 GDP of major countries and the world share Unit: %

Stage	Factor contributions	Efficiency contributions	Innovation contributions
Factor-driven stage	60	35	5
Investment-driven stage	40	50	10
Innovation-driven stage	20	50	30

Source: *The Global Competitiveness Report*, 2013. *World Economic Forum*.

So, more and more countries have attached importance to innovation in contributing to economic growth and increasing national strengths. In recent years, particularly, many countries have employed innovation strategies to boost their national competitiveness with the deepening of economic globalization, intensified international competition and emerging Internet.

To be specific, China's innovation-driven strategy aims to achieve growth through advancements in science and technology, rather than through the primary factors such as land, resources and labor force. Characterized by resource conservation and environmental friendliness, the strategy fully utilizes knowledge and talent, takes innovation as the main driving force, focuses on developing products and technologies with independent intellectual property rights and fosters enterprises to innovate. The innovation-driven approach features reduced material consumption, high-quality economic growth, the green ecological environment and strong sustainability.

3.2.2 Innovation is an important engine for China to build an economic powerhouse

Innovation-driven is the most fundamental and critical force to promote economic transformation and upgrading, and to realize the strategic goal of national development. It can take the initiative in leading China from a major economy to an economic power house.

3.2.2.1 In a critical period of transforming and upgrading economy from factor-driven and investment-driven to innovation-driven approach

Over the years, China's rapid growth is based on inexpensive labor, cheap land and other essential resources under the guidance of the so-called comparative advantage theory. However, after entering the medium-high growth, the endowment factors that originally supported China's rapid economic growth no longer exist, the low-cost competitive advantage is gradually weakening. China's economic growth is facing increasingly tight development bottlenecks, which requires the growth momentum to switch from factor-driven growth to innovation-driven growth. As mentioned above, instead of relying mainly on the expansion of initial factors such as land, resources and labor, innovation-driven mode mainly relies on advanced factors such as knowledge, technology, improvement of workers' quality and management innovation. Its essence is to rely on independent innovation, give full play to the supporting and leading role of science and technology, embark on the path of endogenous growth, and realize the scientific, comprehensive, coordinated and sustainable development.

3.2.2.2 Innovation-driven conducive to improve quality of economic growth

Currently, China's economic output ranks second in the world, but the fact is that its overall quality is not high. In many industries, China's output ranks first in the world, but the gap between China and developed countries is also obvious in the top-end industries. For example, China's integrated circuits dependency on foreign countries is as high as 85%. In the contest between major economies, "quality" is far more important than "quantity". Before the Opium War, China's economy accounted for nearly one third of the world's total economic output, far exceeding that of the UK. However, the "qualitative" gap between the two was extremely wide. Therefore, China was at a disadvantage when competing with the UK. The Sino-US trade friction also exposed the obvious areas of weakness in China's science and technology and industries. In short, the gaps between China and the world economic powers come down to innovation capability. Thus, innovation-driven approach is adopted to promote the industrial structural adjustment and enhance China's status in the global value chain, and to constantly improve the quality and efficiency of China's economy.

3.2.2.3 Innovation-driven approach conducive to promote industrial transformation and upgrading

Through the innovation in science and technology, it can promote the informatization of traditional agriculture and establish a modern agricultural system to push forward agricultural modernization. Through the extensive utilization of high-tech and advanced information technology, it can promote the equipment and technology level of traditional industries as well as the integration of informatization and industrialization, speed up improving the traditional industries with high-tech and advanced applicable technologies to provide effective technical supports for upgrading traditional industries, so that it can realize the transformation from "made in China" to "created in China". Adapting to the general trend of global industrial development and through the innovation-driven approach, China will vigorously promote technological innovation in production services, develop emerging services such as the Internet and e-commerce, and improve the international competitiveness of industries.

3.2.2.4 Innovation-driven approach conducive to relieve pressure of ecological environment

Undoubtedly, the cost of China's economic growth includes not only economic cost, but social and ecological environment costs. As mentioned above, China's economic achievements have been made at the expense of the ecological environment to a large extent, which manifests the unbalanced relationship between man and nature, and between man and society. China are now facing more severe ecological and environmental challenges than ever before—the negative impacts of haze, soil, water and acid rain are emerging. Through the innovation-driven approach, it can improve China's innovation capability in science and technology and the efficiency of resource utilization, promote the transformation from extensive utilization of resources to intensive utilization of resources, reduce resource consumption and pollution emissions, and promote resource conservation and optimal allocation. By doing so, it can help realize the synchronous improvement of economic development and ecological environment. This is the Chinese dream that the people are pursuing.

3.2.2.5 Innovation-driven approach conducive to improve China's international competitiveness

Some American scholars like Kissinger and Brzezinski believe that China is a major economy but not an economic powerhouse. The competition in today's world is to a large extent the competition of innovation capability, and a country's capability for innovation determines its future and development. Innovation-driven is not only the key strategy for countries to maintain economic growth and constantly enhance national competitiveness, but the core measure to achieve economic recovery after the financial crisis and face the challenges of the Third Industrial Revolution. In the coming world competition pattern, it has become the consensus of developed countries that innovation wins and gains an upper hand in the future competition.

3.2.3 Primary basis for China's innovation-driven development

The past years have witnessed the rapid growth of China's science and technology, among which some significant areas have leaped into the front of the world, and have made China an influential leader in science and technology. China has already boasted a relatively good basis for further innovation-driven development.

3.2.3.1 Substantial improvement of economic strength

With 40 years of reform and opening up, China has significantly raised its overall economic competitiveness with an annual growth of more than 9%, exceeding that of several superpowers and ranking second in economic aggregate worldwide, next only to the United States. Per Capita GDP of China has risen from US$155 in 1978, among the bottom of the list, to US$8,836 in 2017, ranking the middle-income countries and reaching 74th in the world. In 1978, China had only US$167 million of foreign reserves, ranking 38th in the world, and only US$0.17 per capita; whereas in 2017, China held US$3.13 trillion of foreign reserves, up by US$129.4 billion compared with that in 2016. It can be concluded that China has financial basis for the innovation-driven development with affluent capitals and significant improvement in material conditions.

3.2.3.2 A rather comprehensive industrial system

China has long been fully leveraging its comparative advantages, such as abundant labor resources and complete industrial categories, proactively utilizing global resources and undertaking international industrial transfer to develop and expand labor-intensive industries. Light, textile and electronic industries have boasted competitiveness all over the world. China has now become the major manufacturing country with over 225 products' output leading the world and rather comprehensive industrial sectors. The scale and overall capability of China's manufacturing industry have reached such a stage that it can reverse engineering and assist mass production with new product lines within a few months. All of these benefit from the research and development (hereinafter referred to as R&D) as well as manufacturing capability of China's leading industrial centers, which have laid a solid foundation for a vibrant innovation system.[1]

3.2.3.3 Increasing investments in research and development

The R&D investments have been increasing as the economy grows. Since 2006, China's R&D investments has shown stable and strong growing momentum. And the state financial allocation for science and technology plays a leverage role to effectively leverage social funds to increase investments in science and technology. According to statistics, China's R&D investments achieved RMB11,900 trillion in 2013, up to 2.09% of its GDP. However, China's R&D investments in 2017 totalled RMB17,500 trillion, accounting for 2.12% of its GDP. From a vertical view, in 2017 the total amount of R&D investments have increased by 11.6% and the growth rate increased by 1 percentage point compared with that in the previous year. From a horizontal view, China's R&D total investments now rank second, next only to that of the United States. Undoubtedly, the development of science and technology supported by the increasing R&D input is effectively promoting China's innovation-driven strategy, supply-side structural reform and economic transformation and upgrading.

3.2.3.4 Revealing strengths of human resources

Up to September 2014, the number of China's technical professionals has reached over 55.5 million, representing 45.6% of the total talents nationwide. The proportions of high, medium and junior technical professionals are 11 : 36 : 53, among which talents with a college degree or above account for 68.6%, and the structure is constantly optimizing. In particular, the past five years witnessed a growth of 8.6 million technical professionals, nearly 60,000 post-doctoral researchers, 1.0557 million returned overseas talents and 9.4515 million people with qualification certificate of technical skills. The development of technical professionals has continued to be strengthened.[2] Currently,

---

[1] World Bank, Development Research Center of the State Council, *China* 2030: *Building a Modern, Harmonious, and Creative High-Income Society*, Beijing: China Financial & Economic Publishing House, 2013, pp.191-192.

[2] Sheng Ruowei, "Technical Professionals of China are expanding", *People's Daily*, Sep. 22, 2014.

China boasts about 3.6 million R&D professionals each year, surpassing that of the United States, 1.93 million each year, ranking the top in the world. According to statistics, from 2007 to 2017 (up to December 2017), the international papers issued by China's technical professionals were quoted for more than 19.35 million times, up by 29.9 percent compared with that in 2016, which ranked second by overleaping that of the UK and Germany. On the whole, the quantity of China's papers in science and technology is rapidly growing with its quality significantly improving.

3.2.3.5 A huge domestic market

The huge domestic market of more than 1.4 billion people enables China to attract multinational companies and a large number of innovators. China has embedded its own industrial system into the global chain. Local enterprises can utilize both domestic and foreign markets to gain the effects of scale economies, form clusters and enhance competitiveness. Moreover, China is following a strategy of new urbanization, which will help develop innovation in urban planning, public transportation, and green technology. What comes with it is the upgrading of consumption and industrial structures, infrastructure projects, development of social programs, and ecological and environmental protection, which all contain huge market demand and space for future development. This represents China's potential strengths as well.

3.2.4 Challenges facing China's innovation-driven development

China is neither a resource-dependent country, nor can it follow the path of external dependence. For sure, China must pursue the innovation-driven development. On the whole, China's innovation capacity falls behind the world advanced levels. According to the global innovation index 2023, co-authored by Cornell University, European Institute of Business Administration (INSEAD) and the World Intellectual Property Organization (WIPO), Switzerland, Sweden, the US and the UK are among the most innovative countries in the world.

3.2.4.1 Insufficient innovation capacity of enterprises

Chinese enterprises neglect the importance of innovation and have low input on innovation. Some enterprises lack motivation and are unwilling to innovate; some have weak innovation capacity and are unable to innovate; and still some worry about the risk of innovation and do not dare to innovate. Only 25% of industrial enterprises with an annual revenue of RMB20 million or more from their main business operations have R&D institutions and their R&D investments in sales volume is only 0.78%, while the corresponding data in developed countries is 80% and above 5%. Most enterprises do not invest in innovation sustainability, have weak secondary innovation capacity, less IP production and low new product contribution.

3.2.4.2 Inadequate enterprise patents and ignorance of digestion and absorption

According to World Intellectual Property Organization, in 2016, the number of international patent applications in China reached 43,000, up by 44.7%, ranking third in the world. However, according to a report conducted by Zentrum für Europäische Wirtschaftsforschung (ZEW) in 2016, although the number of international patent applications in China has grown rapidly in recent years, the quality of its patents has not been able to keep up with the level of leading technological powers. In the meantime, China has not digested and absorbed enough after its technological import. The science and technology department once calculated that for each US dollar spent by Japan and Republic of Korea on technological introduction, it would cost seven US dollars for digestion, absorption and secondary innovation. The cost of digestion and absorption in China is only 7% of its introduction cost, which is far from that of Japan and Republic of Korea.

3.2.4.3 Relatively insufficient R&D investment

Compared with the status quo of R&D investment of global enterprises, the overall R&D investment of Chinese enterprises is insufficient. According to the 2016 EU Industrial R&D Investment Scoreboard, Volkswagen in Germany ranked first and Huawei in China ranked eighth. The R&D investment of the world's top 100 R&D companies accounted for 53.1% of the top 2,500 companies' R&D investment, and the top 50 companies accounted for 40%. U.S. companies accounted for 38.6% of the global R&D investment, followed by Japan, Germany and China. The investment of Chinese companies soared up by 24.7%, and its global share increased from the previous year's 5.9% to 7.2%. The industries with the largest R&D growth are ICT (information and communications technology), health and automotive. On the whole, China's R&D investment has rapidly increased, but it has a large gap with that of developed countries such as the US and Japan. Thus, it is necessary to further guide enterprises' R&D investment.

3.2.4.4 High foreign dependence ratio of technology and low application rate of research results

Currently, China's dependence on foreign technology is 10.4%, while that of the US and Japan is around 5%. The application rate of China's scientific research achievements is relatively low, and the actual industrialization is less than 5%, while the number of developed countries is as high as 40% to 50%. A classic example is synthetic insulin. As early as the 1960s, China took the lead in realizing synthetic insulin. This result was recognized by the international counterparts to have reached the Nobel Prize level. Unfortunately, it has not been transformed into an industry. More than 95% of China's annual insulin market with over RMB25 billion is monopolized by foreign companies.[1]

3.2.4.5 Unreasonable allocation of scientific and technological resources

For a long time, the phenomenon of closed, repeated and scattered government financial resources in science and technology has been more prominent. Some scientific technical programs, special projects, and funds have not been clearly positioned, and the arrangement of scientific research projects has been "small, scattered, and partial". The management of different types of scientific research projects is "one size fits all" with serious phenomena of "offside", "absence" and "dislocation" of government functions. The establishment of scientific research projects is not open and transparent enough, the procedures are complicated, the projects are packaged and assigned to the wrong person, and its check before acceptance is more of a formality. The capability to apply the scientific and technological achievements into actual productive forces is relatively weak, and in particular the scientific and technological fruits of universities and academies cannot effectively joint with the market. The efficiency of utilizing scientific research funds needs to be improved, as some violations of regulations and disciplines and corruption have even occurred.

3.2.5 Direction and path of implementing innovation-driven development strategy

To implement the innovation-driven development strategy, the most urgent issue now is to further free our mind, remove spiritual and institutional barriers that restrict innovation in driving development, and unleash all potential driving forces of innovation, so as to create a strong new impetus towards building an economic powerhouse.

3.2.5.1 Giving initiative role to enterprises in innovation-driven development

The Third Plenary Session of the 18th CPC Central Committee pointed out that we

[1] Luo Yongzhang, "The Urgent Need of Technological-transformed Innovative Talents", *Guangming Daily*, Aug. 2, 2014.

must strengthen the principal position of enterprises in technological innovation, give play to the key role of large enterprises in innovation, and stimulate the innovation vitality of small and medium-sized enterprises. Efforts should be made to promote the reform of applied R&D facilities to be marketed and enterprise-modeled. It should be noted that strong enterprises can help build strong sci-tech strengths, develop strong industries, promote strong economy and make a country more powerful. The innovation-driven enterprises are the main players in the innovation-driven development, and important foundation for strengthening national competitiveness. Hence, more endeavors should be made to energize the internal innovative drive of enterprises, so that the enterprises can really play the principle role in decision-making, R&D input, scientific and technological institutions, and the application of scientific and technological advances. By doing so, the scientific and technological advances can be applied into actual productive forces at a faster pace.

First, strengthen the original supports for technological innovation of enterprises. It is necessary to encourage enterprises to establish their own R&D institutions to meet the needs of market, and guide them to increase the R&D inputs, improve the mechanism of technological development, product innovation and commercialization of scientific and technological advances. It is necessary to strengthen the ties between innovation and market, support enterprises to speed up applying the major scientific and technological advances to industries, and energetically foster small and medium-sized sci-tech enterprises. To guide the technological innovation and upgrading of these enterprises, the government can take measures such as setting up special funds for small and medium-sized enterprises.

Second, promote the strategic transformation and upgrading of technological innovations of enterprises. It is necessary to encourage enterprises to choose a path of independent innovation that is reflective of their own comparative advantages, leverage the role of sci-tech personnel in developing new products, introducing new technologies and applying new techniques. It is necessary to boost the productive factors, such as capital, management and technology, to participate in the distribution. It is necessary to stimulate the vitality of scientific and technological talents to innovate and start businesses, strengthen theoretical research on cutting-edge areas of technological innovation of enterprises, and improve technological innovation of enterprises with an aim to increase the core competitiveness of enterprises in market competition.

Third, advance open innovation. Now, the global innovation and production tend to feature diversification and decentralization. The value chains originally restricted in certain regions are expanding to different countries, thus forming the global value chain. Therefore, competing behind closed doors instead of in an open environment would only reduce a state's innovation capacity and place it in the low-end of the global value chain. In the new global competition, Chinese enterprises must have a global vision in developing and driving innovation, learn to integrate global resources, and enhance their own innovation capabilities by learning from and competing with excellent foreign enterprises. It is necessary to establish a strategic alliance for technological innovation in industry, strengthen innovation in technology, commercial mode and management, and improve cooperation in technological innovation of enterprises.

3.2.5.2 Establishing a sound institutional system for innovation-driven development

The path to innovation-driven development is inseparable from the corresponding institutional strategy, whose rationality will directly influence the ultimate effects of innovation-driven development and economic transformation and upgrading. Hence, it is imperative to resolutely remove institutional obstacles to improving innovation capability in science and technology, and strongly open up the channel for the transfer and transformation between technology and economy. Thus, an effective institutional guarantee can be provided for the innovation-driven development.

First, establish intellectual property system. Intellectual property is of great value to encourage innovation, prevent infringement, promote competition, ensure sufficient supply of creative inventions, and stimulate sustainable and extensive economic growth. An effective intellectual property system serves as the basis of guaranteeing economic benefits for innovators. Patent system, as the core of intellectual property system, is particularly important to innovation. In the view of Americans, it provides benefits as fuel to keep the flame of genius' inspiration. The constant innovation of America and other developed countries is closely related to the design of intellectual property systems which are mainly based on patent system. Therefore, at the Third Plenary Session of the 18th CPC Central Committee, it proposed to strengthen the application and protection of intellectual property, improve the incentive mechanism for technological innovation, and explore the establishment of intellectual property court. These proposals offer important supports for innovation-driven development. By strengthening the application and protection of intellectual property, we can guide various subjects involved in the application of scientific and technological advances to establish a mechanism for intellectual property where benefits and risks are shared.

Second, improve fiscal and finance system. Innovation-driven development does not mean reduction in capital investment; instead, more financial supports are required for sci-tech innovation. It is necessary to increase financial investments on science and technology, adjust the structure of investment, and improve related tax policies and government procurement policies that support innovation and give priority to it. For instance, tax incentives for high and new tech enterprises and sci-tech business incubators, as well as additional tax deductions for R&D expenses of enterprises, should be fully implemented to give full play to the financial funds. Meanwhile, innovation in science and technology and financial innovation should be promoted by increasing financing supports for enterprises' sci-tech innovation, encouraging financial institutions to develop related loan models, products and services, and guiding more social capitals into the innovation area. Besides, it is necessary to construct an equity investment system with venture capital as the core and improve the multi-level "pyramid-shaped" capital market, in order to support technological innovation with financial innovation. Furthermore, a new investment and financing platform for sci-tech innovation should be set up to provide diversified related services for sci-tech enterprises at different stages of development. It is necessary to make innovation on new sci-tech financial products, organizations and service models in line with the growth law and characteristics of small and medium-sized sci-tech enterprises.

Third, establish system for collaborative innovation. Collaborative innovation refers to the effective aggregation and deep cooperation of innovation resources and elements by removing the barriers among innovation subjects and fully stimulating the vitality of innovation factors such as talent, capital, information and technology to achieve deep cooperation. So, it is necessary to develop the mode of collaborative innovation featured non-linearity, networking and openness and based on mutual association and collaborative interaction among multiple subjects. From another perspective, collaborative innovation is to bridge the gaps among enterprises, government, universities, scientific research departments and financial institutions, and to create open, collaborative and efficient innovation ecology, with focus on designing innovation chain based on industrial chain and improving capital chain based on innovation chain. Specifically, enterprises put forward industrial demands, and then the government guides universities and scientific research departments to collaboratively conduct related researches and strive for technological breakthroughs. By doing so, we can promote the seamless connection between research capabilities and industrial demands. Thus, it is necessary to further deepen the reform of scientific research institutes and the research system in universities, and facilitate the establishment of industry-university-research cooperation mechanism, where they have clearly defined rights and responsibilities, complement each other's strengths, as well as share benefits and risks.

Fourth, establish evaluation and assessment system. Research evaluation is to researchers what college entrance examination is to students, serving as a baton that directly affects their behavioral orientation. Influenced by the social environment, researchers tend to struggle for "GDP of scientific research". Some of them devote more energy to negotiating projects and dealing with inspection and review, lacking sufficient efforts in research activities, which causes negative style of study and academic misconducts. Thus, the current evaluation system for scientific research needs to improve through shifting its value from quantity to quality instead of the pursuit of the publications. More attention should be paid to the creativeness of scientific and technological advances and their contributions to the society. It is necessary to decrease the utilitarianism in the assessment of scientific research and encourage researchers to create original research results.

3.2.5.3 Cultivating talents for innovation-driven development

In essence, innovation-driven can be explained as talent-driven. Without a strong foundation of talented personnel, self-innovation is like water without a source or a tree without roots. Since the second half of the 20th century, as the impact of science and technology grows increasingly stronger, high-level and innovative talents have become a significant mark for national core competitiveness. Therefore, the innovation-driven development strategy should be well implemented to form a group of innovative talents who are large in scale, rich in innovative spirit, and dare to take risks. We must discover, nurture and retain talents throughout the whole process of innovation, so as to turn China from a country with a large population into one with a large pool of talents and human resources.

First, develop high-caliber personnel. We will strive to strengthen training high-caliber personnel and labor workers. With focus on producing innovative scientists and engineers, we aim to develop a group of leading talents in science and technology and innovative research teams, leading them to become the core forces in innovation-driven development. We will continue to improve the technological, management and labor skills of general workers and enhance their quality through training. We will work to foster an environment where talents will stand out and knowledge, labor, and creativity will be fully respected, so that innovation will continue to be inspired throughout the society. The implementation of innovation-driven strategy needs not only talents and scientists for research and development, but high-quality administrative talents and other types of personnel. It should be seen that China still lacks highly-skilled personnel, such as advanced technicians. To some extent, this has become one of weak links in the innovation-driven strategy. Therefore, we will continue to strengthen personnel training, such as school education, on-the-job training, and self-studying, to promote training for technical talents in a large scale.

Second, improve the talent evaluation index system. Talents should be evaluated largely through the indicators of innovation performance, peer review and market assessment, rather than the approval ratings from leaders or interpersonal relationships. The system for evaluating talented personnel should be constantly improved to reflect innovation results and form an advanced talent evaluation institution.

Third, vigorously attract and select talents. A large number of globalized talents are required for designing and improving innovation under a global view. As mentioned above, a secret why America becomes the world top powerhouse in science and technology is that it has attracted a large number of top-level scientists and engineers from all over the world. According to statistics, 40% of global skilled immigrants gather in the US, where foreign scientists and engineers account for about 20% of the total number of its sci-tech personnel. Although China ranks front in the world scale of sci-tech human resources, it suffers from a critical shortage of top talents and leading scientists. Therefore, efforts should be made to introduce high-level talents, innovative teams, and leading scholars in various fields from domestic and overseas, so that high-level innovation can be led by high-level talents. The third-party power should be utilized in assessing and selecting innovative talents, and more efforts should be made to constantly encourage and support high-level technical experts and innovative and entrepreneurial personnel. Institutional obstacles should be removed for talent mobility and utilization, so as to promote the flow of innovative talents from colleges and research institutions to enterprises. Innovative talents should be encouraged to gather in enterprises, and entrepreneurs should be given the opportunity to reach full potentials in innovation. That is, we must strive to build a platform for activities of multilevel workforce and promote the flow of talents in inter-sector and interdisciplinary fields.

Fourth, create a good environment for talent development. Efforts should be strengthened to support innovative personnel to start their own businesses. It is necessary to raise the payment of scientific researchers and lay a solid talent foundation for the innovation-driven development. The polices of encouraging the technical factors to participate in the distribution of income will be further improved, and the salary motivation mechanism of emphasizing real performance and contributions will be established. The wrong concept that boasts the so-called "low labor cost" as comparative advantage has to be abandoned in China. As is known to all, low salary only attracts low-quality labors. To become a country of independent innovators, China must boast a large number of high-end professionals with high salary and high-level skills, so that innovation can be further improved and China's competitive strength can be enhanced. Young talents in science and technology should be valued, as they are most creative and crucial for a country to sustain innovative development. However, frankly speaking, currently the growth and career environment for young talents is not good enough in China. Burdened by low titles, relatively low income and strong pressure of promotion, most of them find it hard to focus on innovative activities, which has become a prevalent symptom in universities and scientific and research institutions. Moreover, "Matthew Effect" exists in the current management system and distribution of expenditures in scientific researches, where young researchers are not in favorable condition in competing for programs and supporting funds.

3.2.5.4 Improving governance capacity for innovation-driven development

To implement the innovation-driven development strategy and promote the integration of scientific and technological innovation and economic and social development, the key is to balance the relationship between the role of government and that of market. Through deepening reform, we will further open up the channel between scientific technology and economic social development, so that the market can truly play the decisive role in allocating resources of innovation.

First, striking a balance between the role of government and that of market in the innovation-driven development. Striking a balance between the role of government and that of market has been the key to deepening the economic system and implementing the innovation-driven development. To fully leverage the decisive role of the market, the government should first shift from economic-oriented to public service-oriented one. Based on the proposals by the Third Plenary Session of the 18th CPC Central Committee, the functions of government are positioned in five aspects: macro-control, market supervision, social management, public services and environmental protection. That is, the government should further streamline administration and delegate power to the lower levels, cancel unnecessary administrative review and approval items, reduce the distorted market signals caused by government intervention in micro-economic activities and stimulate the vitality of enterprises to the maximum extent. The government should establish fair rules for market access, and remove various hidden restrictions and hindrances for private enterprises to promote fair competition. The government should have trust in and respect the market, and leave the market and enterprises to play their due roles to further stimulate innovation. The government should accelerate efforts to reform the resource price and tax system, establish a resource price system and tax policies that reflect the scarcity of resources and environmental impacts, and leverage the market mechanisms to promote and guide enterprise innovations.

Second, give full play to the government's public service duties. For sure, emphasizing the role of the market does not mean that the government does nothing. Due to the strong externalities of science and technology, it is a common problem that the failure of innovation in science and technology exists in both developed countries and emerging countries. Thus, in the process of innovation-driven development, when leveraging the role of the market, the government should play its due role in the areas where enterprises are unwilling or unable to invest, serving as a guidance and complement to the market. As the provider of public goods, the government should focus on supporting cutting-edge and major common technologies, and technologies for the public as well as other products and services with "public goods" attributes and externalities. The government should promote the integration of sci-tech innovation policies and industrial ones, gain an upper hand and inject new impetus for innovation in science and technology.

Third, create a healthy innovation ecosystem. Innovation has its law, and supporting innovation means to respect the law of innovation. As mentioned above, innovation, different from invention and creation, is a process of transforming new technologies into new products and industries. In this process, innovation activities are innovation chains which are composed of a series of links, including incubators, public research and development platforms, venture investments, industrial chains based on innovation, property rights transactions, legal services, logistics platforms etc. So, one of the government's responsibilities is to create a healthy innovation ecosystem based on the innovation chain. By eliminating the obstacles in the innovation chain, the government should reduce the cost of innovation to the maximum for enterprises, and improve the innovation efficiency.

3.2.5.5 Cultivating culture conducive to innovation-driven development

Innovation-driven development requires not only the norms and guidance of formal institutions, but incentives of informal institutions. A culture of innovation is necessary to innovation-driven development and economic transformation and upgrading.

First, develop a social atmosphere that advocates science, pursues excellence and respects talents. Importance should be attached to publicizing knowledge, methods and spirits of science, so as to improve the public's understandings and appreciation of science and culture, and develop a good atmosphere of innovation in the whole society. Spirit of science should be advocated in the area of scientific research, which features seeking truth, being pragmatic, honest, fair, skeptical, critical, cooperative and open. The principle must be adhered to respect labors, knowledge, talents and creations. It is necessary to change the old practices in the current evaluation system of scientific research, which only focuses on quantity instead of quality, and does not evaluate the innovation and contribution of scientific and technological advances. It is also necessary to vigorously publicize scientists and engineers who have made great contributions and devoted themselves to scientific and technological undertakings, as well as entrepreneurs who have successfully transformed scientific and technological advances.

Second, advocate the spirit of innovation that encourages competition and risks, and tolerates failures. It is necessary to overcome the mentality of being eager for quick success and instant benefits, to remove the consciousness of power orientation and small-scale farm that stifles the innovation spirits, to promote the consciousness, spirit and vitality to innovate, to develop atmosphere for innovation, and to protect innovation results.

Third, fully draw on the fruits of human civilizations. Fostering a culture of innovation does not mean to reject changes. In this process, we should not only vigorously inherit and carry forward the fine traditions of Chinese culture, but absorb the beneficial results of foreign cultures. We should plan and promote innovation with a global vision, which is also a part of culture to innovate.

Fourth, provide institutional supports to cultivate a culture to innovate. A culture to innovate does not naturally take shape, as the institutional arrangements are indispensable. For example, it is necessary to cultivate the consciousness of young people to innovate, and improve their practical capabilities through improving educational institutions. Another example, it is necessary to further improve the public sharing of scientific and technological resources by accelerating efforts to develop and improve the national reporting system, management information system and innovative investigation system of science and technology, which are conducive to develop a culture to innovate.

3.3 New urbanization: sustainable impetus for developing a powerful economy

Urbanization is a natural historical process in which non-agricultural industries and rural population are concentrated in cities and towns accompanied by the development of industrialization. Urbanization is the only way to achieve modernization, a powerful engine for maintaining sustained and sound economic development, and an essential requirement to promote social progress in an all-round way.[1] Since the reform and opening up in 1978, China's urbanization has constantly developed and made remarkable achievements, which has effectively boosted China's developing a powerful economy. However, some issues arose, such as population urbanization lagging behind land urbanization, prominent semi-urbanization problems, and various prominent "urban diseases". This has seriously restricted sound development of urbanization. Under such circumstances, it is necessary to take a path of new urbanization according to the requirements of the central government.

3.3.1 Why taking a path of new urbanization

Now, China's urbanization is at the critical stage of accelerated development. By effectively promoting new urbanization with Chinese characteristics, it can create new space for China to gain comparative advantages and the latecomer's strengths in developing. As a great strategy in the process of developing modernization, new urbanization has become an important engine for promoting sustained and sound economic development in China. By fully recognizing the strategic significance of new urbanization, it can make the key task of developing new urbanization clear at the new phase of China's development. Thus, it can help seize the opportunity to promote the

[1] *Major Monographic Study on the 13th Five-Year Plan Proposal* (Second Edition), Beijing: China Market Press, 2016, p.89.

reform with resolve and courage, improve the system and institution for advancing the development of urbanization, properly address various issues in the process of urbanization, and promote sound development of urbanization and economic society.

3.3.1.1 Urbanization as a general law and an important symbol of modernization

Urbanization has become an important engine for developing modernization in a country. Seen from the process of urbanization in different countries around the world, it can be generally classified into three stages: the initial stage when urbanization rate is less than 30%; the middle stage when urbanization rate reaches 30% to 70%; and the later stage when urbanization rate amounts to over 70%. In the initial stage, agricultural economy plays the dominant role and the urbanization speed is relatively slow. In the middle stage, the foundation of modern industry is established, and urbanization enters a period of accelerated development. In the later stage, the urbanization speed slows down and stays stable, and the phenomenon of "adverse urbanization" appears in some countries. Urbanization has brought about transferred and concentrated population, industrial agglomeration and urban expansion, transformed social structure, and changing lifestyle. The process how developed countries become powerful countries can thus be regarded as the process how they gradually improve their urbanization rate. Currently, there are about 3.6 billion urban residents in the world, and 70% to 80% urban population in developed countries. The urbanization rate in developed countries is mostly from 70% to 80%, with only a few from 80% to 90%, and few up to 100%. When it comes to the development of urbanization in countries around the world, it cannot be simply regarded as a gathering of population, but as the transformation of basic form of the whole society from an agricultural society to an urban society. It is a "barometer" of industrial development, economic growth and social progress. Actually, it is due to its special significance that there is reason to regard urbanization as a historical task of China's modernization.

Urbanization develops when industrialization develops, and urbanization provides internal forces for industrialization. There is a mutualistic relation ship between the two, with industrialization being the engine for urbanization and urbanization being the accelerator of industrialization. On the one hand, industrialization needs the concentration of factors of production, as its cluster effect and economies of scale are formed by concentrating production activities to reduce the cost of industrial production. On the other hand, urbanization creates favorable conditions for industrialization, as it can gather more factors of production in a relatively concentrated area, and produce benefits of scale and benefits of division of labor and cooperation. In this sense, urbanization is an inevitable trend of industrialization; meanwhile it can greatly promote the continuous improvement of industrialization and achieve better development with the progress of service industry and science and technology.

Urbanization has become an important carrier for both the government and the market to play a role together. The reason is that urbanization requires both the government and the market to play their roles and leverage their comparative advantages respectively, which will be conducive to sound development of urbanization; otherwise, "urban diseases" is likely to occur. The UK, the cradle of industrial revolution, had gradually formed a public intervention policy with urban and rural planning as main body when encountering some serious problems in the process of urbanization. The US had paid a huge price in terms of resources and environment due to excessive dependence on market demand in the process of urbanization. Some Latin American countries had put overemphasis on market mechanism in the process of urbanization, and then a large number of farmers flooded into cities, leading to excessive urbanization and "urban diseases". However, the Japanese government had played an active role in intervening industrialization and urbanization according to its national conditions with large population, scarce land and insufficient resources, thus achieving a higher speed of economic development at a lower social and environmental cost. Here, important experience can be drawn from the urbanization in different countries around the world, that is, both the government and the market must play their due roles.

3.3.1.2 New urbanization as the "trump card" for China's sustained and sound economic development

In terms of China's medium- and long-term development, the biggest national reality is to advance urbanization and modernization on the basis of being a large agricultural country. It is of vital importance to advance urbanization actively yet prudently to address the issues relating to agriculture, rural areas and rural people, complete the building of a moderately prosperous society in all respects, and push forward China's modernization in an overall situation. Urbanization can generally act as a "trump card" to bring strengths to promote China's sustained and sound economic development, and realize the scientific development that puts the people first.

New urbanization is conducive to coordinate urban and rural development. In terms of realizing China's modernization, the key and difficulty lies in addressing the issues relating to agriculture, rural areas and rural people, and the fundamental solution lies in promoting urbanization, industrialization, IT application and agricultural modernization. Agriculture strengthens when industry develops, and farmers can become rich with the decreasing number of farmers. On the one hand, urbanization is linked to both industrialization and modernization in agricultural and rural areas. By actively yet prudently advancing urbanization, it cannot only effectively promote industrialization and strengthen economic strengths in cities, but also create conditions for industry to feed back agriculture and cities to support rural areas, transfer and absorb rural labor force, promote agricultural scale operation, increase rural income, and fundamentally address the issues relating to agriculture, rural areas and rural people. On the other hand, IT application can greatly contribute to industrialization and serve the whole society.

New urbanization is conducive to coordinate regional development. Since modern times, a general law governing economic development in various countries is that the economic development in coastal countries mostly starts from that in coastal areas and then extends inland along the inland rivers. China has experienced such similar situation. Since the reform and opening up in 1978, the regions around Bohai Sea, the Yangtze River Delta and Pearl River Delta have taken the lead in opening up and developing. It has formed an export-oriented economic pattern and city clusters with a high degree of urban population and economic agglomeration, which has effectively driven the rapid development in the eastern coastal areas. With the industrial transfer in the eastern region and the development strategy of the central and western regions, the central and western regions have accelerated the development of urbanization. From a long-term perspective, the development of urbanization in the central and western regions can create more space for China's economic development.

New urbanization is conducive to balance the economic and social development. The history of development at home and abroad shows that the process of promoting urbanization means to constantly promote balanced economic and social development. Theoretically, the development of urbanization is not merely the spatial transfer of population, but more importantly, the transformation of social structure, and the major reform of political system and economic system triggered by it. As far as a region is concerned, cities and towns mean not only economic centers, but also centers of education, culture, science, arts and talents. Urbanization can create favorable conditions for balanced economic and social development. Therefore, the process of urbanization should be coordinated in the context of balanced economic and social development.

New urbanization is conducive to the harmonious development between man and nature. Due to its large population, weak economic foundation and uneven development, China is facing many issues and contradictions in advancing urbanization, such as large population, scarce resources and fragile environment. In recent years, regional resources, energy and environment have shown increasingly obvious constraints in the process of promoting urbanization. This requires China to focus on resolving the contradictions between the people's ever-growing demand and the limited supply capacity of nature, balance the relationship between urbanization process and resource development and environmental protection, and the relationship between immediate benefits and long-term benefits, promote the harmonious development between man and nature, and realize the goal of developing a beautiful China.

New urbanization is conductive to balancing domestic and foreign development. Unbalanced and rebalanced world economy have posed great challenges for China's foreign trade and export. As it is difficult to maintain the traditional trade pattern of large-scale importing and exporting, expanding domestic demand will become a national strategy for China's sustained economic growth in the future. Through the large-scale urbanization of rural population, it can resolve income distribution gap between rural and urban areas, improve residents' income level and consumption capacity, cultivate and expand middle-income group, and then release huge consumption demand. This is the objective requirement of China's economic transformation during the new period. It will provide powerful and everlasting impetus for expanding domestic demand. In the meantime, it will provide impetus and space for rebalancing world economy.

3.3.1.3 New urbanization can provide impetus and space for creating huge domestic investment

Industrialization creates supply and urbanization stimulates demand. New urbanization will generate the largest domestic demand and investment as well as the most important comparative advantage for China's future development.

New urbanization will stimulate demand and raise household consumption effectively. Currently, per capita living expenditure of urban residents is 3.6 times that of rural residents. If urbanization rate increases by one percentage point every year in next 20 years, another 300 million rural residents will have become urban residents up to 2030. Consequently, it will generate huge demand and investment. With a large number of rural population flooding into cities and towns, it is bound to generate new demands for urban housing, water supply, power supply, gas supply, transportation and other infrastructure construction, thus creating a huge investment market. Meanwhile, it has transformed rural consumption into urban consumption, and raised new demands for education, culture, sports and public services, thus creating new engines for economic growth and investment. That is, reducing rural population can make rural residents become rich. Due to the development of urbanization, it can accelerate the transfer of rural surplus labor force, and gradually turn rural population into urban residents. This helps to promote the moderate scale of agricultural operations, improve labor productivity, and brings obvious effects on increasing rural income and improving rural consumption, thus making potential consumption demand in rural areas into reality.

New urbanization is conducive to promote the development of service sectors and service quality. On the one hand, as an important carrier for developing service industry, new urbanization can not only promote the public services, such as education, health care, social security and employment, but also promote the consumer services, such as commerce and trade, catering and tourism, as well as the development of productive service industry, such as finance, insurance, logistics etc. All this will create huge sustainable demand for labor force. On the other hand, the lag of urbanization has led to the low proportion of tertiary industry in national economy. By promoting urbanization, a large number of rural people can quit their agricultural posts every year to become practitioners of non-agricultural industry. This will help realize population concentration in cities and towns, promote the service industry, change the current situation that urban development relies much on increasing the consumption of material resources. Thus, it can help realize the transformation of development mode.

New urbanization is conducive to expand and create more employment for rural workforce. To further develop rural economy and promote modernization, it needs to transfer a large number of surplus labor force stranded in rural areas to second and tertiary industries in cities. By doing so, it can get rid of serious unbalanced population distribution pattern between urban and rural areas, which restricts sustained and sound development of national economy. Therefore, it is necessary to advance urbanization actively yet prudently through the development of urban economy. It can create new employment areas and labor demand, and improve capacity for absorbing surplus rural labor. Meanwhile it can promote the development of second and tertiary industries in rural areas and expand employment space in rural areas.

3.3.1.4 New urbanization is conductive to improving the quality of urbanization and better people's livelihood

Since the reform and opening up in 1978, China's urbanization has made remarkable achievements. However, some issues emerge that urbanization still lags behind the development of industrialization. It is urgent to address the issue of urban pathology, and new urbanization can help improve the quality of urbanization and better improve people's livelihood.

It is an urgent requirement to promote new urbanization actively yet prudently for changing lagged urbanization in China as soon as possible. From the relationship between urbanization and industrialization and economic development, or from the international perspective, China's urbanization still lags behind. Lagged urbanization will affect the agglomeration economy and the exertion of urban functions. It will restrict the flow of agricultural surplus labor force and hinder the process of agricultural modernization and unified urban-rural dual structure. It will restrain both consumption growth and investment growth, resulting in insufficient domestic demand. It will hinder the development of tertiary industry and the adjustment of industrial structure. It will aggravate the destruction of resources and environmental pollution. These are not conducive to promote sustained development. Therefore, to avoid negative effects by lagged urbanization, it is necessary to promote new urbanization actively yet prudently for changing the lagging state.

It is an urgent requirement to promote new urbanization actively yet prudently for realizing population urbanization and land urbanization synchronously. In essence, new urbanization is a simultaneous process of population urbanization and land urbanization. However, in the process of developing China's urbanization, a phenomenon arose that land urbanization was faster than that of population, that is, the non-agricultural development of land did not go hand in hand with that of population. Driven by making interests from land, some local governments blindly expanded urban construction, arbitrarily occupied land, and made extensive use of land by expanding urban areas and increasing development zones. Some local governments had artificially integrated non-urban areas into cities and towns, and rural population into urban population, resulting in a rapid increase in urban population in the short term. In particular, in name of collectively owned rural land, some local governments forcibly and arbitrarily occupied contracted rural land without negotiating with farmers, thus harming their legitimate rights and interests. All these contradictions and issues need to be resolved urgently.

It is an urgent requirement to promote new urbanization actively yet prudently for coordinating development among large, medium and small cities. Due to the influence of economic resource endowment structure and the difference of economic development stage, the development of China's urbanization is unreasonable and uncoordinated at both national and regional levels. On the one hand, due to unbalanced regional development, China's urban population is more concentrated in the eastern regions and big cities, with obviously low urbanization in the central and western regions. This widens the gaps between regional developments. On the other hand, the layout of large, medium and small cities within a region is unreasonable with low population density in small and medium cities, which aggravates the unbalanced development of large, medium and small cities.

It is an urgent requirement to promote new urbanization actively yet prudently for ensuring and improving people's livelihood. Under the current public finance system, new urban residents have different social welfare due to different status and time of urban residence. Some of them are excluded from the social welfare under the current urban social security system. Take for example, although 160 million rural people have transferred as regular residents in cities and towns with their identity from farmers to practitioners and main forces of second and tertiary industries, they cannot get the same national treatment as that of urban residents. That is, their production and lives remain in a town-marginalized state, facing a series of problems such as household registration, housing, medical care, social security and children's enrollment. Such phenomenon of "dual structure" in cities and towns deserves our great attention. Therefore, it is urgent to address the issue between urban and rural areas and within cities and towns through promoting new urbanization for ensuring and improving people's livelihood.

3.3.2 New characteristics of new urbanization

In view of various problems in the process of urbanization, the 18th CPC National Congress proposed that urbanization must develop together with new industrialization, IT application and agricultural modernization. In 2012, the Central Economic Work Conference proposed that urbanization should follow a new path to intensive, intelligent, green and low-carbon development. This set new requirements for China's urbanization in the future. In general, China's new urbanization mainly manifests as follows: new core, new concept, new driving force, new mode, new pattern and new focus. The 2016 Central Economic Work Conference stressed that continuous efforts should be made to promote the "people-centered" new urbanization and the migrant workers citizenship. The 2017 Central Economic Work Conference stressed that more efforts should be made to improve the quality of urban agglomeration, promote the networking construction of large, medium and small cities to make them more attractive and capable to accommodate rural migrant population, and accelerate the pace of implementing the reform of household registration system.

3.3.2.1 New core: developing with a people-centered approach

Here, new urbanization stays focused on a people-centered approach. During the process, it not only transfers labor force from agricultural to non-agricultural industry and rural population to urban population in cities and towns, but also progresses urban production mode and life style in rural areas. In essence, it means to allow rural people to move into cities and towns to enjoy modern production mode and life style, and share fruits of modernization. Therefore, its core is to put the people first, and make better jobs and lives for both urban and rural residents. More advanced and prosperous cities need to be developed with a people-centered approach instead of launching a movement of building construction to make a mere economic pursuit.

Due to the lack of a people-centered approach, the original urbanization was inclined to separate land urbanization from population urbanization. Experts from the National Development and Reform Commission estimated that since the 21st century the built-up area of cities has expanded by 50% with urban population only up by 26% in China. That is, the speed of land urbanization is nearly twice as that of population urbanization. Cities are growing increasingly larger and more rural people flooding into cities, however, the increase of people who really enjoy fruits of urban development is very small. In 2016, China's urbanization rate was 57.35%. Among them, it included 792.98 million regular urban population, up by 21.82 million over the previous year, and 589.73 million regular rural population, down by 13.73 million. Statistics show that the total growth rate of migrant workers was down year by year from 2011 to 2015, that is, 4.4%, 3.9%, 2.4%, 1.9% and 1.3% respectively. However, according to the data in 2017, the urban population accounted for 58.52% in the total population (urbanization rate), up by 1.17 percentage points than that of the previous year. In 2017, the urbanization rate of registered population was 42.35%, up by 1.15 percentage points than that of the previous year. Seen from the above figures, hundreds of millions of people have gradually transferred to the non-agricultural production mode with their way of life urbanized. In contrast, they stay in a semi-rural and semi-urban state with agricultural identity for a long period. Therefore, new urbanization aims to fundamentally change the deficiencies that the previous development prioritized constructing buildings instead of putting the people first. It stays focused on developing with a people-centered approach and firmly adheres to the people-oriented concept. Here, the term "people" refers to both urban migrant workers and rural residents and those who used to work and live in cities. First, lower the threshold of urban access to promote the migrant workers' citizenship and better integrate themselves into urban society as soon as possible; meanwhile resolve the problems concerning the identity and treatment of urban migrant workers to help them truly gain a foothold in cities and become regular urban residents in the long run. Second, reduce rural population through urbanization to create favorable conditions for those who stay in rural areas to live a better life and become rich, and meanwhile promote the rural development through the fruits of urban development to improve farmers' lives. Finally, coordinate the interests between original urban residents and new arrivals, and achieve win-win results through development without harming the interests of original urban residents for the sake of new arrivals.

3.3.2.2 New concept: more emphasis on inclusive development to ensure all the people share fruits of urbanization

Here, more emphasis on inclusive development means that the urbanization development should benefit all the people, especially vulnerable groups. Continuous efforts should be made to break urban-rural dual system and the inequity of opportunities and rights caused by the institutions in cities and towns, provide equal opportunities and rights for urban and rural residents, and change the status of different identity, treatment and rights between urban and rural residents.

First, balance the urban and rural development. The original urbanization put more emphasis on urban development rather than rural development, and even at the cost of the interests of rural areas and farmers. This resulted in the coexistence of the prosperity of cities and the depression of villages. Therefore, without sacrificing the interests of rural areas and farmers, new urbanization aims to balance the development between urban and rural areas, abolish the urban-rural dualism, promote the integrated development of urban and rural areas, and form new relations between urban and rural areas in which industry promotes agriculture, urban areas support rural development, and agriculture and industry benefit each other. Second, break the current social management system in which household registration integrate with social welfare, and gradually provide urban financial expenditure and public goods that cover all the residents with no differences. It is necessary to ensure that urban migrant workers enjoy equal treatment as that of urban residents and rights in terms of children's education, social security, housing, elderly care services and social management, and make the second generation of urban migrant workers better integrate into lives in cities and towns. Third, gradually improve the carrying capacity of cities and towns to provide more opportunities and better environment for urban migrant workers. It is necessary to improve the functions of cities and towns, the living environment, infrastructure and public services, and better the livable living standard. It is also necessary to stimulate the vitality of small and medium cities and towns, focus on industrial development and increase employment. In the meantime, it is necessary to improve urban management, address traffic congestion, housing shortage, environmental degradation and other "urban diseases", and continue to improve carrying capacity of cities to ensure that more people can enjoy the fruits of new urbanization.

3.3.2.3 New driving force: coordinated advancement of "Four Modernizations" to form a synergy for urbanization development

New urbanization should follow the path of coordinated interaction and synchronous advancement of "Four Modernizations", namely, new industrialization, IT application, urbanization and modern agriculture. It is necessary to promote the deep integration of IT application and industrialization, positive interaction between industrialization and urbanization, mutual coordination between urbanization and agricultural modernization, and the synchronous development of industrialization, IT application, urbanization and agricultural modernization.

First, from the perspective of international experience and China's actual situation, agricultural modernization lays a basis for urbanization development, while urbanization is a prerequisite for realizing and driving the development of agricultural modernization. To advance urbanization, it needs to strengthen the foundation for agriculture, rural areas and rural people. If the development of agricultural modernization lags behind that of urbanization, it not only affects the sustainable development of rural economy, but also weakens the foundation for further development of urbanization. Thus, the primary goal of agricultural modernization is to ensure national food security. Second, industrialization drives urbanization while urbanization accelerates industrialization. Urbanization needs the supports by industry and market. In a sense, urbanization and industrialization are the two sides of the same coin. Led by industrialization, they develop with strong synchronicity and generally with urbanization rate and industrialization rate positively correlated. Thus, it is necessary to balance the development between urbanization and industrialization. If industrialization develops rapidly and urbanization lags behind, then no market and conditions are accessible to industrial development, which makes it impossible to realize advanced industrialization. If urbanization develops rapidly and industrialization lags behind, the phenomenon of "excessive urbanization" will emerge, which brings about serious "urban diseases". Third, urbanization is the main carrier of IT application while IT application serves as the hoister of urbanization. Urbanization helps promote the development of IT application, and IT application has an effect on driving urbanization. Urbanization can provide space for IT application as well as demand for IT industry, and make IT application play its role in cities and towns. IT application can enhance and integrate urban functions, further optimize urban functions and industrial structure, and promote urbanization at a higher level.

3.3.2.4 New mode: integrating ecological progress to build a beautiful China in harmony with man and nature

New urbanization integrates ecological progress during the whole process to realize the coordination among population, economy, resources and environment, build a beautiful China and achieve sustainable development of the Chinese nation. Here, it underlies three aspects. First, new urbanization must develop and integrate with the concept of ecological progress. Second, the process of new urbanization must meet the requirements and index of ecological progress. Third, the development of new urbanization that integrates with ecological progress must be a sustainable development in harmony with man and nature.

First, whether in overall planning of urbanization development or in the layout of large, medium and small cities (towns), industries, and energy structures, the concept of ecological progress must be implanted. That is, the top-level design should take into consideration the harmonious development between man and nature, man and society, and man and man. Second, the process of urbanization development should integrate with indicators of ecological progress. To adapt to the requirements of green, resource-saving, environment-friendly, sustainable development with low-carbon and circular economy, it is necessary to stay intensive, intelligent, green and low carbon, and build "livable cities" with beautiful environment, sound public services, pleasant cultural atmosphere, social harmony and stability, and convenient and comfortable life. Third, new urbanization aims to develop cities and towns with ecological progress and build a beautiful China. It will change the serious situation of unsustainable land, space, energy, water resources and environment facing many cities, as well as serious pollution. It will turn lucid waters and lush mountains into invaluable assets, and meet the needs of the current generation without affecting that of future generations.

3.3.2.5 New pattern: shaping new cities and towns guided by main functional zones planning

Guided by main functional zones planning, the layout of new urbanization should be carried out nationwide to change the previous disorderly urban development and form a new pattern of cities and towns across the country. Despite the fact that China has a vast territory, its natural environment and resource conditions vary greatly among different regions. Some regions are suitable for urban development with relatively good foundation and livable human habitations, whereas some other regions are not suitable for urban development with poor natural environment and weak carrying capacity of water and soil resources. Judging from the current layout of urban development, some regions developed with relative imbalance between production and living land, which has seriously affected the quality of people's lives. In addition, the proportion of industrial land in urban areas reached 26 percent and even over 50 percent in some cities. The trend is continuing. Thus, the unified planning and layout should be carried out. Here, main functional zones refer to a spatial unit that determines a specific orientation of main functions based on the carrying capacity for resources and environment, existing development density and development potential in different areas. Based on the overall national territory development planning and specific conditions of various regions, China's land space can be classified into areas for optimal development, areas for key development, areas for limited development and areas for non- development. Guided by main functional zones planning, new urban layout is conducive to adjust and optimize the spatial pattern of urban clusters, and coordinate population distribution, economic layout, and resources and environment. First, in terms of spatial layout, urban clusters should be the main form with large, medium and small cities developing with small towns in a coordinated way. Urban clusters should be taken as the main form in the spatial layout to highlight its radiative and driving role. Second, large, medium and small cities and small towns should focus on the coordinated development in accordance with local conditions. Third, the carrying capacity of cities should be enhanced with focus on its comprehensive capacity.

3.3.2.6 New focus: more prominent importance on developing sound systems to release the dividends of reform

Urbanization is not only a process of urban construction and development, but also a complex system engineering, which will bring about profound economic and social changes. The previous urbanization focused more on building construction and building roads, and less on people-centered development, which led to many problems in urban construction. On the contrary, new urbanization adheres to a people-centered approach to solve actual problems, with its focus and center gradually shifting from infrastructure construction to software construction and reforms such as systems and institutions etc. To promote new urbanization, more emphasis should be put on the driving force of reform. To unleash the huge potential of domestic demand generated by new urbanization and provide everlasting impetus for China's economic and social development, it is necessary to accelerate efforts to remove institutional obstacles restricting sound development of urbanization. It is necessary to strengthen the top-level design of systems, make overall planning, and vigorously promote the reforms in household registration system, land system, social security, fiscal, taxation, and administrative divisions so on. It is necessary to gradually remove welfare benefits attached to household registration, and better population management system that links household registration system with residence permit system. It is necessary to explore and implement the policy that links the increase in the scale of urban construction land with the number of agricultural transfer population settled in cities. It is necessary to establish a sustainable urban public finance system and investment and financing mechanism to provide financial guarantee for the realization of basic urban public services, full coverage of permanent resident population, and urban infrastructure construction. It is necessary to form fund guarantee mechanism and effective incentive mechanism that help promote the sound development of urbanization through the reform of fiscal, taxation and financial systems.

3.3.3 Orientations for advancing new urbanization

The orientations of advancing new urbanization are mainly as follows.

3.3.3.1 Accelerating efforts to grant urban residency to agricultural transfer population settled in cities

China is now at a crucial stage of rapid urbanization. In 2017, the ratio of permanent urban residents in total population was 58.52%, up by 1.17 percentage points over the previous year, and that of registered population 42.35%, up by 1.15 percentage points over the previous year. However, amidst the remarkable achievements in granting urban residency to agricultural transfer population settled in cities, the process of settling urban migrant workers is not fast enough. There remains a large gap between the urbanization rate of registered households and that of permanent resident population with failure to meet the governmental requirements by the year of 2020. The main reasons are as follows. First, due to the imperfect mechanism for solving the costs for agricultural transfer population settled in cities, local governments have not great enthusiasm for absorbing agricultural transfer population, especially granting cross-provincial urban residency in the eastern regions. Second, part of agricultural transfer population has not great enthusiasm to settle down in cities, as they are worried that it is difficult to safeguard their "three rights"[1] and hard to fully enjoy their urban welfare benefits after settling down in cities.

3.3.3.2 Optimizing the layout and form of urbanization

With the continuous and in-depth development of urbanization, China's urban layout has been constantly optimized and urban system constantly improved. The regional layout is more reasonable and appropriate, and the urbanization process in the central and western regions has been significantly accelerated. In the process of promoting new urbanization, more emphasis has been put on guiding the development of urban clusters to form a new pattern of coordinated development among large, medium and small cities through strictly controlling mega-cities, rationally developing large cities and actively developing small cities. In 2016, the State Council approved of and implemented the development planning for five urban clusters, which includes the Yangtze River Delta, the middle reaches of the Yangtze River and the Central Plains, and defines a number of new national center cities such as Chengdu, Wuhan and Zhengzhou. Then, the Beijing-Tianjin-Hebei region, the Yangtze River Delta region and the Pearl River Delta region have gathered 18% of the total population with a land area of 2.8% of the total, and created 36% of GDP in China. They have played an important role in supporting and leading the national economic development.

Since the 13th Five-year Plan period, China's urban spatial layout and scale structure have been greatly optimized. However, there remains a certain gap to meet the requirements of making a scientific and reasonable urbanization layout. It mainly manifests as follows: First, it is difficult to remove the gaps between regional urbanization developments in a short period of time, though it has been gradually narrowed in the process. Urban clusters are mainly distributed in the eastern regions, and those in the central and western regions mostly stay in the initial stage. Second, the division of labor and coordination within urban clusters is insufficient and the cluster

---

[1] Here, it refers to rural land contracting and management rights, rural residential land use rights, and rural collective income distribution rights.

efficiency not high. The contradictions between the population of some megacities and its comprehensive carrying capacity are intensified. The potential of small and medium cities to gather industries and population has not been brought into full play to realize the integrated and efficient development. Third, the overall number of cities is small, especially that of small and medium cities. At present, China has reached an urban population of 771 million and only has 653 cities, while Japan has 115 million urban population and 787 cities, and the United States has 258 million urban population and 10,158 cities. Apart from the inadequate number of small and medium cities, the development of a large number of county towns and administrative towns remains insufficient, mainly due to the lack of construction land indicators, capitals, talents and other important resources. Consequently, it resulted in the weak attraction of small and medium cities.

3.3.3.3 Building a harmonious and livable city

Since the 13th Five-year Plan period, the city infrastructure such as water, electricity, road, air, and information network has significantly improved in China. The development of affordable housing projects, underground comprehensive pipe racks and sponge cities have been accelerated. The public services such as education, health care, culture, sports and social security have notably improved. Positive results have been achieved in developing green cities, smart cities and innovative cities and cultural cities. However, urban planning, urban construction and management have not reached a high level, and the issue of "urban diseases" is becoming increasingly prominent. This is mainly reflected in the disorderly development of some urban space, excessive concentration of population, low management efficiency, lack of characteristics in design, insufficient supply capacity of public services and so on.

So, accelerated efforts should be made to develop new urbanization. It is necessary to develop green cities by adjusting the city scale according to the carrying capacity for resources and environment, implementing green planning, design and construction standards, and carrying out ecological corridor construction and ecosystem restoration projects. It is necessary to develop smart cities by strengthening modern information infrastructure, improving the speed and cost reduction of broadband networks, and promoting the development of big data and logistics internet. It is necessary to develop innovative cities by leveraging their strengths in intensive innovation resources, and building a paradise for business startups and a cradle of innovation. It is necessary to develop cultural cities by improving their openness and inclusiveness and strengthening the protection of cultural and natural heritages to extend historical cultures. It is necessary to develop compact cities by strengthening the regulation of the development and utilization of urban space, promoting the sound development of new state-level urban regions, transforming qualified development zones into functional urban ones, and guiding the standardized development of industrial clusters.

Efforts should be made to improve urban governance. It is necessary to develop new ways of urban governance, reform the urban management and law enforcement system, and promote the urban management in a fine, full-cycle and cooperative way. It is necessary to develop new concepts and methods of urban planning, rationally define urban scale, development boundary, development intensity and protective space, and strengthen urban space planning from its three-dimensional nature, plane coordination, style integrity and context continuity. It is necessary to comprehensively promote urban design, urban organic renewal and urban renovation. It is necessary to develop applicable, economical, green and beautiful buildings, improve the technology, safety standards and project quality of construction, and promote the industrialization of construction and steel structure buildings.

3.3.3.4 Improving the housing supply system

The issue of housing has a bearing on the overall situation of the people's living and economic development. Since the reform and opening up in 1978, China's urban housing market has constantly developed with housing security system gradually improved, total housing volume significantly increased, and per capita housing area of urban residents raising from 18.7 square meters in 1998 to 36.6 square meters in 2016. During the 12th Five-year Plan period, local governments had vigorously promoted the affordable housing projects and accelerated the renovation of rundown urban areas. Up to the end of 2015, 26.81 million housing units in rundown urban areas had been renovated. The housing issue of low- and middle-income urban families has been effectively addressed, and the real estate sector has played an important role in sustainable and rapid economic growth.

In the meantime, there is still structural imbalance between supply and demand in the real estate market to a certain extent. On the one hand, the inventory of commercial housing, especially in the third- and fourth-tier cities, has continued to increase. By the end of 2015, the completed area for sale has reached 719 million square meters, and the growth rate of national real estate development and investment continued to decline. On the other hand, the housing issue of non-registered urban population is still prominent, urban housing supply and security system is not perfect, and housing rental system has not yet taken shape.

3.3.3.5 Promoting the coordinated development between urban and rural areas

During the 13th Five-year Plan period, the living standards of urban residents in China have comprehensively improved, and new urbanization and rural construction developed in a coordinated way. The annual growth rate of rural per capita net income or disposable income was faster than that of urban per capita disposable income in the same period. According to the data by the National Statistics Bureau, the per capita consumption expenditure reached RMB18,322 in 2017, up by 7.1% in nominal terms or 5.4% in real terms after deducting price factors. Of this, the per capita consumption expenditure of urban residents was RMB24,445, up by 5.9% over the previous year, or 4.1% in real terms after deducting price factors. The per capita consumption expenditure of rural residents was RMB10,955, up by 8.1% over the previous year, or 6.8% in real terms after deducting price factors. In the meantime, due to the relatively weak foundation for development, and the unbalanced and uncoordinated development between urban and rural areas, the per capita consumption expenditure of urban residents was 2.23 times that of rural residents in 2017. There is a large gap between urban and rural infrastructure and public service resources, the systems and institutions for urban-rural integrated development are not sound enough, and the capacity of county economies to support and radiate needs to be strengthened.

Efforts should be made to develop county economy with characteristics. It is necessary to foster and upgrade a vigorous, distinctive and specialized county economy, and enhance its capacity to absorb the transfer of urban functions and promote rural development. By relying on the advantageous resources, efforts are needed to promote the intensive processing of agricultural products, rural service industries, and labor-intensive industries, explore new models for accepting industrial relocation, and integrate them into regional industrial chains and production networks. With county-level administrative regions as the basis and administrative towns as the fulcrum, efforts are needed to guide rural secondary and tertiary industries to concentrate in county towns, key towns and industrial parks, and set up a multi-level, wide-ranging, wide-covered service platform for the integrated development of rural primary, secondary and tertiary industries that covers a wide range of fields. Efforts are needed to strengthen the construction of municipal facilities and public service facilities such as education, medical care and culture in county-level cities, and improve their capacity for recycling and harmless disposal of waste. Efforts are needed to expand the autonomy of county development and improve their level of basic financial resources. Efforts are needed to provide more supports to counties and key towns in the central and western regions that have great development potential and large population.

3.3.4 How to better forward the path of new urbanization

To follow the path of new urbanization, it is necessary to understand the rules governing urbanization development. That is, through integrating the particularity of China's urbanization, efforts should be made to firmly establish the development concept with quality as the core, lower the threshold of urbanization, build inclusive cities and towns, improve the strategic pattern of urbanization, raise funds for urbanization through multiple channels, and deepen the institutional reforms.

3.3.4.1 Firmly establishing the development concept with quality as the core

The key to coordinating the development between urbanization speed and quality is to improve the quality of urbanization. In view of current situation, some issues should be resolved to further urbanization, since China's urbanization has entered a new stage characterized by promoting the in-depth population urbanization and urban-rural integration. First, put the people first and properly resolve the issue of "urban diseases". To do it, it is necessary to provide infrastructure and basic public services commensurate with economic development, give priority to resolving the issues such as employment, housing, education, medical care and transportation for urban residents, and improve their quality of life. Second, change the urban development mode and enhance the sustainable development capacity of cities and towns. To do it, it is necessary to strengthen the control over different types of urban and rural space, vigorously promote the development of low-carbon ecological cities and the intensive and compact development of cities and towns. It is necessary to speed up the development of urban service functions by promoting the soft power of urban development. It is necessary to strengthen the comprehensive urban management, establish a unified, coordinated, efficient and reasonable urban management system, and improve the level of urban management and services. Third, promote urbanization in pace with industrialization and agricultural modernization. To do it, it is necessary to adapt to the requirements of new industrialization, actively explore the path and pattern of new urbanization. It is necessary to explore the mechanisms, channels and approaches for industry to nurture agriculture and cities to support rural areas, and properly resolve the issues relating to agriculture, rural areas and rural people. Fourth, establish an evaluation system for urbanization development to ensure the sound development of urbanization. It is necessary to formulate an index system for evaluating the quality of urbanization in a scientific way, take the quality of urbanization into consideration when the appraisal of government performance and the supervision over major events are concerned, and strengthen the role of urbanization in the economic and social development.

3.3.4.2 Lowering the threshold for urbanization

It is necessary to lower the conditions and costs for rural migrant workers to settle down in cities, and turn eligible migrant workers into urban residents through providing equal public services. First, appropriately lower the conditions for rural migrant workers to become urban residents, and allow eligible rural migrant workers to become urban residents. Based on the scale and comprehensive carrying capacity of a city, and their different status such as the years of employment, residence and urban social insurance, all cities must set fair and just standards for rural migrant workers to settle down. Second, unswervingly adhere to real estate regulation, guide the sound development of the real estate market and the rational return of real estate prices, and resolutely curb high housing prices. In the meantime, it is necessary to improve the multi-level and diversified housing security system, and gradually increase the proportion of affordable housing in urban housing supply. Third, actively establish and improve a public service system that integrates urban and rural areas. To do it, it is necessary to gradually establish a nationwide unified public service system that covers education, employment, medical and health care, the elderly care, housing and basic living allowances. To meet the requirements of high mobility of migrant workers, it is necessary to realize the smooth transfer and continuity of social insurance rights and interests as soon as possible. Fourth, accelerate the reform of education and medical systems, and effectively resolve the problems faced by urban residents in education and medical care. In addition, by improving the employment capacity and income level of migrant workers, it means lowering the threshold of urbanization.

3.3.4.3 Building inclusive cities and towns

To build inclusive cities and towns, emphasis must be put on the balance and unity of urban development in the fields of economy, society, governance and culture, the internal consistency of fairness and efficiency in the process of urban development, and the homogeneity and equality of development rights of different urban subjects. Firstly, the key to building inclusive cities and towns lies in developing a high-level public service system. Among them, the popularization and equalization of public services is the core issue of bettering the public service system. Secondly, it should follow the endogenous operation rules governing the social system of urbanization, gradually reduce or eliminate the inappropriate interference that dominations the process of urbanization, and deal with the incoordination and imbalance among economy, politics, society and law under the principle of rule of law. Finally, gradually eliminate all the exclusionary systems that are not conducive to inclusive development, promote the urban acceptance and integration of rural migrant workers and other urban migrants, and enable the urban poor, including migrant workers, to enjoy equal rights.

3.3.4.4 Actively improving strategic pattern of urbanization

The strategic pattern of urbanization influences the direction of urbanization development and thus is an important part of development strategy of China's modernization. Therefore, it is necessary to formulate medium- and long-term planning and comprehensive policies and measures for the development of China's urbanization under the national modernization strategy and the guidance of Xi Jinping Thought on Socialism with Chinese Characteristics for a New Era and the new development philosophy. It is necessary to reasonably determine the functional orientation, industrial layout and development boundaries of large, medium and small cities and small towns, and form a new urbanization pattern featuring integrated basic public services and infrastructure and network development. In particular, it is necessary to guide the population flow and industrial transfer with reliance on large cities and focus on small- and medium cities, and by following the rule governing urban development, and the carrying capacity of different scale and different type of cities and towns. Thus, it can gradually form urban clusters with great radiation effect, promote a scientific layout of large and medium cities and small towns, and accelerate efforts to improve the urbanization strategy of "two horizontal, three vertical"[1] pattern. It is necessary to well plan the functional orientation and industrial layout of cities in urban clusters, strengthen the industrial functions of small- and medium cities, and enhance the public services and residential functions of small cities and towns. It is necessary to tap the development potential of the established small- and medium cities, and give priority to developing those with distinct geographical advantages and strong carrying capacity of resources and environment.

3.3.4.5 Raising funds for new urbanization through various channels

The number of farmers in China is extremely large and the total cost of farmers' urbanization particularly high. Obviously, how to effectively raise huge funds for

[1] The Yangtze River Economic Belt connects the Eurasia Continental Bridge Corridor and the Yangtze River channel as two horizontal axes, and the coastal Beijing-Harbin Beijing-Guangzhou and Baotou-Kunming channels as three vertical axes. This economic belt has gradually formed a strategic pattern of "two horizontal and three vertical" urbanization, supported by major urban clusters and with other areas on the axis as important components. —*Tr.*

developing new urbanization has become a major issue. To do it, it is necessary to raise funds for new urbanization through various channels. Apart from increasing investments by governments at all levels, it needs to encourage farmers to pool money together for building cities, and adopt other forms or channels, such as land leasing, paid transfer of land use rights, reasonable distribution of value-added income from using land, joint venture development, issuing bonds, investment in shares, loans and so on. It also needs to implement various preferential policies to attract and raise more funds including public and private funds, foreign capitals, and farmers' investment.

As far as how to effectively raise funds for urbanization is concerned, the key lies in resolving the issue that who should bear the costs or the funds for the citizenization of migrant workers, as it is now the focus of urbanization. So, who should bear the costs? For sure, it should not be borne mainly by migrant workers, as they have low incomes and cannot afford it and it is unreasonable for them to bear it. Also, it should not be borne by urban residents, as such costs are not brought about by urban residents. Therefore, the cost of citizenization of migrant workers should be borne mainly by the governments at all levels, apart from part of the costs borne by the enterprises that employ migrant workers as well as directly by migrant workers themselves. The reason is that equal rights, responsibilities and interests can ensure fair, reasonable and effective systems. As the low wage of migrant workers brings low costs and high profits to enterprises, they are supposed to treat rural migrant workers with equal salary, welfare and treatment. Moreover, the citizenization of rural migrant workers can remove their worries to settle down in cities and towns, set their mind at rest in the enterprises, meet the demands of enterprises for labor force, especially skilled labor, and ease or eliminate the shortage of migrant workers. Therefore, enterprises should bear part of costs of citizenization of migrant workers. These costs mainly includes partial expenses for job training, social security and living in cities.

On the surface, it seems unreasonable that the cost of citizenization of migrant workers is not borne mainly by migrant workers. Actually, it is mainly borne by migrant workers themselves, though nominally by governments at all levels and enterprises. The reason is that the costs borne by governments at all levels and enterprises mainly come from the labor value created by migrant workers, and such costs account for only a small proportion of profits created by migrant workers with low wages. Nevertheless, enterprises should not pay much more than they can bear, otherwise they will suffer from damaging their interests, which is not conducive to expand investments and economic development. Furthermore, it is actually borne indirectly by the migrant workers though nominally by governments at all levels. The reason is that such capitals provided by governments at all levels mainly come from the profits and taxes that are created from the value transfer by migrant workers. Among the costs of citizenization of migrant workers borne by the governments at all levels, it includes partial funds from industry to feed back agriculture, which is the essential compensation for the farmers' great contributions and sacrifice to industrial development, or the return of the value created by farmers.

In general, the sources or channels of raising funds needed for the citizenization of migrant workers mainly include fiscal expenditure from government, land value-added income, expenditure from enterprises that employ migrant workers, direct payment of migrant workers, and compensation from the transfer of contracted land by migrant workers. For sure, the funds from the government should be utilized in key areas, such as social security and urbanization. Now, the government needs to increase investments particularly in such areas to achieve multiple results with one stone. As for the infrastructure construction that the government has invested much on, more private investments should be encouraged to do it.

3.3.4.6 Actively deepening institutional supply-side structural reform

Urbanization needs the advancement of series of public policies, as the sound development of urbanization can not be achieved without institutional innovations. Over 40 years of rapid development of China's urbanization is inseparable from the innovation of system and institution, and the existing contradictions and issues are directly related to the imperfection of system and institution. To promote the sound development of urbanization in the coming period, great importance should be attached to deepening institutional supply-side structural reform, and make breakthroughs in key areas and links, such as land system, household registration system, employment system and social security system. To deepen the reform of household registration system, it needs to take de-benefit, urban-rural integration and free migration as the goal and direction. Under the unified planning of the central government, the welfare function attached to the household registration system should be stripped away, the due function of the household registration system should be recovered, and meanwhile other dual systems embedded in household registration system should be reformed to push forward the whole process.

To deepen the reform of land management system, first of all, it is necessary to follow the principle of clarifying and protecting land real rights, make the ownership visualized, strengthen contract rights, and establish a system of farmland property rights with contract rights as the core. Second, it is necessary to strictly define land for public welfare purposes and for commercial construction purposes, gradually narrow the scope of land acquisition, improve the compensation system and the compensation standard for land acquisition. Third, it is necessary to keep the red line of 120 million hectares, release the market transaction of rural collective construction land, ensure that farmers become the main players of rural collective land transaction, and make the rural collective construction land and urban construction land utilized with the same rights and prices. By doing so, it helps form the land supply dual-track system of rural collective land and state-owned construction. Fourth, it is necessary to appropriately formulate overall planning for land use and urban development planning, establish preferential policies for economical and intensive use of land, and improve the intensity of land use.

To deepen the reform of fiscal, taxation and financial systems, first of all, it is necessary to build and improve public service capacity, adjust fiscal expenditure structure, strengthen the government's responsibility for providing basic public services, and build a basic public service system that includes rural migrant workers. Second, it is necessary to intensify transfer payments from the central budget, and gradually increase the proportion of the central budget on compulsory education, the elderly care, medical care and other basic public services. Third, it is necessary to accelerate efforts to develop local taxation system to foster stable sources of local revenue, and introduce property taxation to enhance local governments' capacity to provide basic public services. Fourth, it is necessary to determine the distribution proportion of land transfer income reasonably among different subjects, bring the government's land transfer income into public finance, improve the efficiency and utilization of land transfer income, and reduce the local governments' dependence on land finance. Fifth, it is necessary to establish a diversified and multi-channel mode of fund supply according to the different situations of urban infrastructure and public services. In addition, it is necessary to reform the urban systems, and improve the social management capacity, and form an intensive and efficient administrative management system with reasonable layout and complete functions.

3.4 Poverty alleviation: important mission for building China into an economic powerhouse

It is an essential requirement of socialism and an important mission for building China into an economic powerhouse to eliminate poverty, improve people's livelihood and achieve common prosperity. In 2015, the Fifth Plenary Session of the 18th CPC Central Committee proposed that by 2020, all rural residents living below the current poverty line will have been lifted out of poverty, and poverty eliminated in all poor counties and regions. All Chinese people must fully understand the decisions and arrangements of the CPC Central Committee, work hard to win the battle against poverty, and ensure all poverty-stricken areas and poor people to enter the moderately prosperous society together by 2020. In the report to the 19th CPC National Congress in 2017, Xi Jinping pointed out: "we must take tough steps to forestall and defuse major risks, carry out targeted poverty alleviation, and prevent and control pollution, so that the moderately prosperous society we build earns the people's approval and stands the test of time." The Report on the Work of the Government 2018 clearly stated that efforts should be intensified in targeted poverty alleviation to lift another more than 10 million rural impoverished population out of poverty, and relocated 2.8 million from inhospitable areas to places with better economic prospects that year. On the whole, as the battle against poverty became more and more difficult, the poverty reduction target of another 10 million people was more tough than that of the previous two years, and more precise and targeted measures are needed to achieve this goal. It is obvious that winning the battle against poverty is an important historical mission for building China into an economic powerhouse.

3.4.1 Significance of winning the battle against poverty

"Poverty is not socialism." Socialism with Chinese characteristics means to lift the poor out of poverty and achieve common prosperity. It is an essential requirement of socialism and an important mission for building China into an economic powerhouse to eliminate poverty, improve people's livelihood and achieve common prosperity. Since the 18th CPC National Congress, the central authorities have included the work on development-driven poverty alleviation in the "Four-pronged Comprehensive Strategy", vigorously implemented the targeted poverty alleviation, constantly enriched and expanded the development-driven poverty alleviation path with Chinese characteristics, and constantly created a new environment for development-driven poverty alleviation. This fully embodies the firm determination and strong confidence from the new central collective leadership to achieve the First Centenary Goal, and the strengths of socialism with Chinese characteristics as well. As Xi Jinping pointed out, "We cannot declare that China has completed the building of a moderately prosperous society in all respects, while tens of millions of people still live below the poverty line. Otherwise, it will not only affect the people's recognition of building a moderately prosperous society in all respects, but also affect the recognition of the international community." Winning the battle against poverty was a major and urgent task during the 13th Five-year Plan period. Therefore, importance should be attached to poverty alleviation from a political, overall and strategic perspective, and realize the goal of poverty alleviation proposed in the Recommendations of the CPC Central Committee for the 13th Five-Year Plan for Economic and Social Development.

3.4.1.1 Winning the battle against poverty is an essential requirement of socialism

Lifting all the poor out of poverty is a symbolic indicator for completing the building of a moderately prosperous society in all respects and a major strategic task during the 13th Five-year Plan period. Realizing a moderately prosperous society in all respects by 2020 was the first goal of Two Centenary Goals. It is a solemn promise made by the CPC to the people and history. By 2020, if China's GDP and per capita income of urban and rural residents were doubled compared with that of 2010, its per capita GDP would reach about US$12,000, approaching the level of high-income countries according to the current World Bank's standard, and basically bypassing the middle-income trap. Here, "Bypassing the middle-income trap" is evaluated in terms of gross domestic product. As is known, the goal of building a moderately prosperous society covers all respects, which will benefit more than a billion people, shorten the income gap, improve people's living standards and qualities, and realize significant achievements in regional coordinated development between urban and rural areas, ecological progress, social equity and justice and so on. Compared with these requirements, there remained gaps in some aspects. Among them, the most prominent issue is to raise all the rural population out of poverty and eliminate regional overall poverty. The key to realizing the goal of building a moderately prosperous society in all respects depends on resolving the issue of raising all the rural population out of poverty. As Xi Jinping pointed out, "to achieve initial prosperity in the countryside, it is essential to raise rural living standards and particularly those of impoverished villagers." The goal of building a moderately prosperous society in all respects should benefit all the people and leave no one behind. No single impoverished area or poverty-stricken population should be excluded in achieving this goal. In the process of realizing a moderately prosperous society in all respects, poverty alleviation was the most arduous task. Therefore, the key and the fundamental goal for realizing moderate prosperity is to complete the task of poverty elimination as scheduled. If China has not won the battle against poverty, it can hardly be said that the country has won success in realizing a moderately prosperous society in all respects, and gained people's sense of satisfaction and the recognition of the international community.

Eliminating poverty, improving people's livelihood, and gradually realizing common prosperity is an essential requirement of socialism. Regardless of great achievements made over 40 years of reform and opening up, it can hardly be said that China have realized common prosperity, if a large number of poverty-stricken population still live in poverty and the issue of poverty alleviation remain unresolved. Poverty is often the root cause of many social contradictions and issues. No one can stay aloof when there are still large poverty-stricken areas. Therefore, Xi Jinping pointed out: "To resolve poverty alleviation in rural areas, it means that no ethnic minority group or region can be left behind, and that 1.3 billion Chinese people can be guaranteed to share the fruits of building a moderately prosperous society in all respects." Poverty alleviation through development must take poverty elimination as the top priority, improve people's livelihood as the basic goal, and achieve common prosperity as the fundamental direction. This will enable people in need to live a happy life with dignity and feel warmth from their hearts, and fully demonstrate the strengths of China's socialism. Ensuring that all the people share the fruits of reform and development is the Party's basic philosophy in governing the country. Xi Jinping further pointed out, "The Chinese dream is ultimately the dream of Chinese people, which can be realized by the people and must bring benefits to the people all the time." Currently, the people's living standards, their income level and their social security level have continued to improve, but there remain some issues such as a large income gap, increasing social contradictions, some people leading a difficult life and so on. Therefore, it is necessary to ensure that development is for the people, by the people, and shared by the people, and uphold social fairness and justice. To resolutely win the battle against poverty, this means to improve people's living standards and truly practice the vision of common prosperity.

3.4.1.2 Winning the battle against poverty is new driving force for economic growth

China's development has now entered the new normal and been in a transition with new growth drivers replacing traditional ones. To maintain a medium-to-high economic growth towards a medium-to-high level of development, it is necessary to foster new growth drivers and expand new space for development. However, there is a large gap between poor areas and other areas in terms of regional development and the people's income, as the vast poor areas include 14 contiguous poverty-stricken areas accounting for about 40 percent of China's land coverage. So, it should be noted that China's economic development has huge potential and space to move forward, especially in terms of poverty-stricken areas and population.

In terms of consumption, increasing income in these regions can expand effective consumption demand and win time for industrial restructuring and upgrading. In terms of investment, strengthening infrastructure and public services in poverty-stricken areas will not only increase effective investment demand, but also help absorb excess capacity. Poverty alleviation can foster new engines for economic growth, and advance sound economic development. Many poor areas are rich in natural resources, land resources and labor resources, and have unique natural conditions, lush mountains and lucid waters, beautiful environment and no soil pollution. If these advantages are converted into diversified products, it can stimulate potential investments and activate new consumptions. This will be conducive to promote the sound, steady economic development and enhance people's wellbeing. Accelerating the development of poor areas will create new poles of economic growth and win more space for China's economy. Through close coordination between the east and the central and western regions, it will promote the industrial transfer to the central and western regions, help the labor force get local employment and boost the local economic growth.

3.4.1.3 Winning the battle against poverty is the guarantee for maintaining long-term stability

As the Chinese saying goes, those who win the hearts of the people win the world. The fundamental purpose of the CPC is to serve the people wholeheartedly. Only when the Party adheres to the philosophy of people-centered development and the fundamental purpose of serving the people, and truly delivers benefits to the people, can it build a solid foundation for its governance. Only when all the people live a good life can the Party consolidate the foundation of its governance. In the midst of drastic changes in the international situation, why did the CPC and China's socialist system stand firm, while the Soviet Union and Eastern European countries collapsed like dominoes? The reason is that the routes, guidelines and policies of the CPC have brought benefits to hundreds of millions of people. That the purpose of the CPC's governance is to deliver benefits to the people makes the foundation for the CPC's governance stay as solid as a rock. Since the founding of the People's Republic of China in 1949, the CPC and its central government have attached great importance to poverty elimination and constantly intensified poverty alleviation through development. In particular, since the reform and opening up in 1978, under the leadership of the CPC Central Committee and the State Council, poverty alleviation through development has achieved remarkable results and won the support and recognition of the people. Remarkable results have been achieved in intensifying poverty alleviation in poverty-stricken population, improving infrastructure and public services, promoting economic development in poverty-stricken areas and so on. The new central collective leadership has adopted the strategy of targeted poverty alleviation and vowed to win the battle against poverty. This further demonstrates the confidence and resolve of the CPC to govern for the people.

Poverty tends to be the deep root cause of social contradictions, social conflicts and social turbulence. In the human history, affluence has been accompanied by stability, and poverty will inevitably lead to turbulence. Therefore, getting rid of poverty bears on an overall situation of national stability and social harmony. Many current mass events that trigger social contradictions and issues, such as employment, income distribution, education, medical treatment, ecology, social security, are mainly caused by insufficient development. So, accelerating development and eradicating poverty are the basis for ensuring that the people live and work in peace and contentment, and the society is stable and harmonious. Therefore, since the reform and opening up in 1978, the CPC has been seizing the development, unswervingly and tirelessly implementing the strategy for the development of China's western regions, accelerating the development of western regions, and eliminating poverty as soon as possible. This is of great significance to safeguard ethnic unity, national unity, national sovereignty and territorial integrity, and realize the long-term stability of the country. During the 13th Five-year Plan period, poverty alleviation through development should focus not only on improving the production and living conditions of the poor, but also on improving the public services in education, medical treatment, culture and other aspects, so that they can catch up with the pace of realizing moderate prosperity in all respects. Only when all the people live and work in peace and contentment can the society be harmonious and stable, and the country in long-term stability.

3.4.2 Making real efforts to targeted poverty alleviation

Xi Jinping pointed out that to achieve tangible results in poverty alleviation, the key is to find the right path, build an effective system and institution, and focus on key areas, overcome obstacles, and grasp the focus of poverty alleviation work. Empty slogans, being overambitious and unrealistic, no planning in mind, blind arrangements would not work. Spraying preferential policies of poverty alleviation indiscriminately, scratching the surface of problem, doing work with little care and caution, and bombing fleas with a hand grenade would also not work. What really matters is to make real efforts in policy-making, take targeted measures to help the poor and lift them out of poverty, and deliver tangible results in implementing targeted poverty alleviation.[1] Therefore, Xi Jinping made it clear that efforts should stay focused on targeted poverty alleviation and poverty elimination, and improving the efficiency of the battle against poverty. The key is to find the right path and build an effective system and institution.

3.4.2.1 Defining the goals of poverty alleviation and poverty elimination

According to the Decision of the CPC Central Committee and the State Council on Winning the Tough Battle Against Poverty, by 2020, poverty alleviation targets would have been guaranteed with adequate food and clothing, and provided access to compulsory education, basic medical care and safe housing for impoverished rural residents. The growth rate of rural per capita net income in poor areas would surpass the national average. The major indicators of basic public services in poor areas would approach the national average, and the targets were set to help all rural population under the current standards out of poverty, and help all impoverished counties out of poverty, thus eliminating regional overall poverty. Here, the goal of targeted poverty elimination set by the Central Committee — Two Assurances, Three Guarantees and Two Priorities — is an integral whole, among which the rapid growth of rural real income above the poverty line is the basis, and the "Two Assurances, Three Guarantees" is the most critical. To define whether rural residents are in poverty or not, or they have shaken off poverty, it depends on whether their rural income exceeds the poverty line. This requires to investigate their rural income, expenditure and household property, verify their income through expenditure, define their poverty status from the property, and resolutely put an end to the falsification of data of poverty alleviation. More importantly, it depends on whether impoverished rural residents have achieved a reasonable living standard of adequate food and clothing, and have actually gained access to compulsory education, basic medical care and safe housing.

3.4.2.2 Identifying the target of poverty alleviation and poverty elimination

For many years, the monitoring of poor population in China has been based on the household sample survey conducted by the National Bureau of Statistics of China. Poverty monitoring plays an important role in grasping the total amount of poor

---

[1] Xi Jinping's Speech at the Central Conference on Poverty Alleviation and Development, Nov. 27, 2015.

population and analyzing its trend. Due to its internationally comparable statistical classification, solid foundation of survey methods and continuously accumulated historical data, it was and remains to be a legal data reflecting the total amount, structure and basic trend of poor population in China. However, it should be noted that the statistical monitoring data are calculated by a small number of household sample survey, and can not be applied to calculating all specific individuals. Therefore, it is necessary to take the overall data of statistical system as the basis and register poor population by households and families through setting up files to grasp more accurate details of people in need. It is necessary to fully promote democracy and mobilize the masses to participate in identifying targets of poverty alleviation and registering their files. It is necessary to carry out in-depth and detailed poverty investigation from village to village and from household to household, and meanwhile make the investigation transparent and open. It is well enough to let rural residents living in the same village identify "whom to help" according to their own "standards", and make the identification of poor households transparent, open and relatively fair.

3.4.2.3 Defining the main body responsible for poverty alleviation and poverty elimination

To fully complete the historic mission of poverty elimination by 2020, it was crucial to identify the main body responsible for the work, and place responsibility on individuals in charge of it. The central government has made it clear that the working mechanism of poverty alleviation is that the central government makes overall planning, provincial authorities take overall responsibility, and municipal and county level play the main role to put the work into effect. The Party committee and the government of poverty-stricken county bears the main responsibility, with the Secretary and governor being the first responsible persons. The Party committee and the government at the county level should shoulder heavy responsibilities, clarify targets and specify responsibilities, and implement policies tailored to households to win the decisive battle against poverty as scheduled.

China is a socialist country, and it is the common responsibility of the society to eradicate poverty. As Xi Jinping pointed out, the central government has mobilized the whole society to participate in poverty alleviation, given full play to China's institutional strengths, built a poverty alleviation pattern through the joint efforts of government, society and market, and formed a multi-disciplinary social assistance system with cross-regional, cross-departmental and cross-unit social participation. Many hands make light work. At present, government-sponsored projects, industrial programs, and corporate and societal assistance supplement each other. A new poverty alleviation pattern is now in place. From "fighting alone" to "clenching fists" through integrating resources from all parties, this highlights the concept of targeted poverty alleviation. Targeted poverty alleviation can mobilize extensive participation of private enterprises, social organizations and individual citizens to create a new pattern of multi-dimensional social assistance.

3.4.2.4 Accurately taking targeted measures to poverty alleviation and poverty elimination

Xi Jinping stressed that how to implement poverty relief needs to take "Five Measures for Poverty Eradication"[1] according to the different situations of poverty-stricken areas and population. It is necessary to take targeted measures and find a new path of poverty alleviation and poverty elimination based on actual situations of poor rural areas and households. It is necessary to clarify the way how to lift them out of poverty household by household, define priorities and specific measures, and resolve the problems to the end, based on the national policy of poverty alleviation and the conditions of villages and households. As we know, lifting poor areas out of poverty as scheduled is inseparable from the steady development of local economy and the continuous growth of rural income. Of course, it was important to take overall measures and routine measures to promote the development of poor areas. To do it, the key is to help rural households out of poverty by truly delivering the "Two Assurances, Three Guarantees". The two aspects should be better integrated to achieve overall development and, more importantly, to lift people in need out of poverty household by household.

3.4.2.5 Accurately evaluating when and how to deregister those who has come out of poverty

Then, a very important link is how to deregister rural households that have been shaken off poverty, and ensure procedure-based, rational and orderly exit from the registered files in the national poverty alleviation information system. In this regard, first, through careful review and public supervision, identify whether those impoverished households and individuals have truly stayed free from poverty, never let those still in need drop out of poverty, and prevent those who have emerged from

---

[1] This refers to boosting the economy to provide more job opportunities, relocating poor people from inhospitable areas, compensating for economic losses associated with reducing ecological damage, improving education in impoverished areas, and providing subsistence allowances for those unable to shake off poverty through their own efforts alone.

poverty from keeping the label to continue accessing preferential treatment; second, a "grace period" is allowed for previously impoverished households, during which poverty alleviation policies continue to encourage them to further cultivate and consolidate their capacity for self-development until they are secure and safe away from returning to poverty; Third, evaluate poverty relief with clear provisions on the standards and procedures for deregistering the list of poor counties, villages, and individuals, and enhance the credibility of poverty alleviation performance.

3.4.3 Taking multiple measures to promote better economic and social development in poor areas

To implement the spirit of the National Conference on Poverty Alleviation and win the decisive battle against poverty as scheduled, it is necessary to redouble efforts to targeted poverty alleviation and the performance in every specific link, and meanwhile take multiple measures to further promote a comprehensive and better economic and social development in poor areas. China has entered a new normal of economic development, which is also the new environment for poor areas. Against the backdrop of growth speed shifting, structural optimization, and growth drivers shifting, how to promote the comprehensive economic and social development in poor areas lies in fully implementing the philosophy of innovative, coordinated, green, open, and inclusive development in all aspects of poverty alleviation to promote sound and rapid economic development in poverty-stricken areas.

3.4.3.1 Strengthening infrastructure construction in impoverished areas to lay solid foundation for poverty alleviation

Infrastructure is the "lifeline" for economic development and poverty alleviation in impoverished areas. Efforts are needed to strengthen the integral and coordinated development of infrastructure, and balance the relationship between the part and the whole, the present and the future, the priority and the non-priority. Priorities should be given to resolve the problems such as poor transport links, and shortage of drinking water and electric power etc. to make the economic artery and the bloodline of agricultural rural development smooth, and improve production and living conditions in impoverished areas. First, strengthen the construction of transportation, water conservancy and electric power. Effective measures should continue to be taken to accelerate the major transportation projects and build road networks in impoverished areas, so that it can make it convenient for poor people to travel and transport. Measures should be taken to accelerate water conservancy projects which are directly related to the work and life of people in impoverished areas, and consolidate and improve safe water projects to comprehensively resolve the problem of shortage of drinking water in rural areas. Measures should be taken to upgrade rural power grids in impoverished areas and ensure that poor people have access to electric power. Second, promote the construction of information infrastructure. It is crucial for poor areas to eliminate the "digital divide" and seize the "digital opportunity" to catch up with better economic level in other regions, as information construction in impoverished areas may trigger a new pattern of poverty alleviation. Efforts are needed to accelerate the pace of informatization, introduce Internet thinking into poverty alleviation, increase financial investment, and achieve full coverage of broadband network in impoverished villages through PPP application and entrusted operation. A typical example is the sale of green and high-quality agricultural products by the poor mountainous areas in Hunan Province to the cities through the Internet. It not only helps people out of poverty and work hard for a better life, but also enables urban residents to enjoy safe and healthy products. Third, speed up the construction of cultural infrastructure. Lifting people out of poverty should first endeavour to help them access to education and build up aspirations. So, the positive role of culture to nurture and enrich the people should be brought into full play to promote an all-round economic and social development in poor areas. A network that integrates fixed, mobile and digital facilities with each other should be built. Public libraries, cultural centers and other public cultural facilities at the county level should be built to improve its weakness and fill in the gaps. Basic public cultural service projects should be promoted to meet with the required standards and cover all rural areas with counties as the basic units.

3.4.3.2 Developing characteristic industries in impoverished areas to create an engine for poverty alleviation

Efforts should be intensified to implement the strategy of innovation-driven development, and motivate the overall economic and social development in impoverished areas. Through fostering and innovating new growth drivers to trigger leading development that leverages the first-mover advantage, it can truly present its own uniqueness, advantages and characteristics. First, more efforts to promote the development of characteristic industries. The key measures to achieve targeted poverty alleviation and increase rural income of poor people lie in developing characteristic industries and implementing poverty alleviation through developing industries and businesses. So, it is necessary to formulate plans for developing characteristic industries in impoverished areas according to their actual conditions, strengthen policy supporting, carry out the campaign to promote the industry of "one village, one product" in poor villages, and support and develop a number of distinctive agricultural bases with high participation that highly benefits poor people. For example, in areas with vast barren mountains and deserts and abundant light resources, the development of photovoltaic power generation will allow rural households to use electricity for free, and the surplus electricity will be put on sale online. Second, continue to optimize the industrial structure. As a reasonable industrial structure is the basis for long-term development of impoverished areas, efforts are needed to adjust and optimize the industrial structure in impoverished areas, and vigorously develop competitive industries with local characteristics and broad market prospects. Supports should be provided to impoverished areas in developing local resources in an orderly and rational way, actively developing emerging industries, undertaking industrial transfer, and accelerating the integrated development of primary, secondary and tertiary industries, so that poor households can share more value-added benefits of the entire agricultural industry chain and value chain. Third, vigorously promote agricultural modernization. As the way out for agricultural development lies in its modernization, efforts should be made to speed up the extensive application of modern science and technology in poor areas, make agricultural operations efficient and agriculture a promising industry. Efforts should be made to foster farmers' cooperative organizations in impoverished areas, encourage enterprises to engage in agricultural industrialization, explore the mechanism for integrating interest between enterprises and poor farmers to promote a steady increase in rural income of poor households. Efforts should be made to explore ways to invest financial funds in assets generated by projects such as facility agriculture and large-scale aquaculture, and give its quantified shares to poor villages and rural households, so that they can share the dividends of agricultural modernization.

3.4.3.3 Enhancing ecological protection and development in impoverished areas to safeguard development-driven poverty elimination

Efforts should be intensified to earnestly implement the philosophy of green development and combine poverty alleviation with building a beautiful China. Strengthening ecological environmental protection and development in poverty-stricken areas is now not only a targeted measure to achieve poverty alleviation, but also an approach to strengthening its foundation for eliminating poverty in the long run. Efforts should be made to promote harmony between man and nature, protect the environment just like how to treat our eyes and lives. Efforts should be made to encourage impoverished areas to adopt a new development pattern and way of life through the philosophy of green development, and work together to make China prosperous, strong and beautiful. First, compensate impoverished residents for eco-environmental protection. For areas with poor living conditions and in need of improvement and restoration, efforts should be made to combine ecological and environmental protection and improvement, and explore new ways of poverty alleviation through developing ecology to make poor areas benefit more from ecological and environmental protection. Second, vigorously develop ecological industries. More efforts should be made to build an ecological industrial system, support the development and utilization of renewable energy in poor areas, develop clean energy such as solar, wind and biomass energy in light of local conditions, and turn ecological advantages into economic advantages. Third, effectively relocate impoverished households from inhospitable areas to areas with better economic prospects. For those who live in areas with poor living conditions, fragile ecological environment and frequent natural disasters, it is better to relocate them in compliance with the voluntary and prudent principles, and ensure that they are willing to move out of their hometown and settle down in new areas, and work hard to live a better life and become rich. Fourth, promote the development of beautiful countryside. More efforts should be made to integrate development-driven poverty alleviation with building beautiful villages through scientific planning, renovate dilapidated houses in poor villages and make rural houses more earthquake-resistant, and promote comprehensive environmental improvement in poor villages.

3.4.3.4 Deepening structural reform in impoverished areas and enhancing capacity for development-driven poverty alleviation

Coordinated development should be implemented to promote the organic unity between total volume and structure, quantity and quality, speed and efficiency. Pushing forward structural reform is an essential way to benefit and strengthen agriculture. Efforts are needed to boost the vitality of sustained economic growth in poor areas and promote their overall level of productive forces. First, advance supply-side structural reform in agriculture. The reason is that agricultural development is the key to promoting poverty alleviation. By finding out the root cause of agricultural development in poor areas, it can promote its structural adjustment through the reform on supply side, improve the quality and efficiency of agricultural supply system, and reduce ineffective and low-end supply while expanding effective and medium- and high-end supply, so as to make its supply structure more adaptive and flexible to changes in demand, and improve total factor productivity. Second, advance structural reform of resource income distribution in impoverished areas. Policies on income distribution from resource development will be adjusted and improved to let poor people share more fruits of reform. Take for example, in areas rich in resources such as hydropower, coal, and oil and gas, circular economy bases at a high level should be built to benefit rural people by turning occupied resources into farmers' equity; in areas with favorable natural and unique cultural environments, rural tourism should be developed to turn agricultural products into tourist products, farmhouses into tourist facilities, and lucid waters and lush mountains into invaluable assets for rural people to get rid of poverty and become rich. Third, increase the supply of public services in impoverished areas. Compared with other regions, impoverished areas have large gaps in residents income, public services and social programs. So, Lifting people out of poverty and eliminating overall regional poverty need to strengthen the weak links in public services. For example, priority should be given to contiguous poverty-stricken areas for major projects to address the prominent contradictions and issues that restrict development, strengthen their capacity for supporting economic and social development, and create favorable conditions for poor people to develop production and improve their lives.

3.4.3.5 Promoting self-reliance, hard struggle and enterprising spirit to stimulate internal driving forces for development-driven poverty alleviation

As a Chinese saying goes, teach a man to fish and you feed him for a lifetime. Poverty alleviation aims to motivate poor people to work hard for better life and become rich through endogenous vitality instead of charity and relief. To do so, it is necessary to follow the philosophy of people-centered development, do what we can do according to current conditions, turn small victories into big success, motivate the enthusiasm of poor people in poverty-stricken areas, and work towards the goal of common prosperity for all. First, respect the principal role of poverty alleviation targets. Poor people are not only the targets of poverty alleviation, but also the main players in eliminating poverty to live a better life. The fundamental way for poverty alleviation is to enhance their capacity for self-improvement, as getting rid of poverty and moving towards common prosperity depends on their own hard work. Therefore, it is necessary to guide all those who are capable to work to be self-reliant, find employment and start businesses, and encourage them to create a better life with their own efforts. Second, attach importance to leveraging the pioneering role of grassroots cadres and masses. As a Chinese saying goes, as long as one has faith in the heart, loess will be turned into gold. Efforts are needed to publicize, educate, train and organize cadres and people in impoverished areas, guide them to develop the idea that they would rather work hard than endure hardship, support them to actively explore ways and approaches to poverty alleviation, and create favorable environment and conditions for them to leverage their talents and achieve their results. Third, boost the morale of people in need in impoverished areas. Poverty alleviation aims to help people in need become rich and initiative. Poverty does not mean no way out for people in need to stay free from poverty. If they have no desire or aspiration to work hard to lift themselves out of poverty, no poverty alleviation funds can boost effects that help them shake off poverty. Therefore, it is necessary to guide development-driven poverty alleviation through comprehensive people-centered development, advocate the spirit of hard struggle, enrich cultural activities in poor areas, and strengthen social development in these areas.

3.5 Improving socialist market economy with the people-centered philosophy

As the socialist market economy in China needs to improve, it requires the Party and the government to develop market economy from the standpoint of taking people as the centre. Since the 18th CPC National Congress in 2012, the Party Central Committee with Xi Jinping as its core has placed prominent position to people-centered philosophy in its governance. This is a remedy for deviating the people's interests in some local economic and social development, a red line to maintain for developing and improving socialist market economy, and an important compliance for developing a powerful economy.

3.5.1 Developing socialist market economy that fully reflects people-centered philosophy

Socialism follows the values of fairness and justice, which is one of the reasons why people accept socialism. However, the problem has not been satisfactorily resolved in the course of developing socialist market economy, and great efforts are still needed to resolve some problems.

3.5.1.1 Reflecting people-centered philosophy in fairness

When Deng Xiaoping contemplated and put forward that market economy can also be implemented in socialist country, and determined the reform towards socialist market economy in 1992, he was wary of whether market economy would produce the contradiction between fairness and efficiency. In 1992, Deng Xiaoping said pertinently, "Polarization will arise if the rich are getting richer and the poor getting poorer, and the socialist system should and can avoid polarization." He further pointed out that reform would fail if it led to polarization.

As to the efficiency and fairness among income distribution, Decision of the CPC Central Committee on some Issues Concerning the Establishment of a Socialist Market Economy System in 1993 clarified a principle of policy arrangement adapting to national conditions at that time, that is, "establish an income distribution system according to one's performance, in which distribution plays the main role with priority to efficiency and due consideration to fairness. Encourage some people and some areas to get rich first and follow the road of common prosperity for all". For many years, this basic policy orientation has been implemented to eliminate low efficiency and absolute egalitarianism under planned economy, and thus to adopt the concept of policy and the idea of institutional design in reality. Although it had historical rationality and achieved obvious results in liberating productive forces and promoting economic development, after all, this policy orientation had great defects and limitations. In fact, it is a "second best choice" under the specific historical conditions.[1] As China has entered a new stage of development, it will be difficult to resolve the unbalanced, uncoordinated, unsustainable problems, if it continues to implement the policy of "priority to efficiency and due consideration to fairness" to develop economy and handle social relations. This is because the policy orientation implies that efficiency can be improved at the expense of fairness. Obviously, this is not in line with the requirements of the new era.

From the whole process of realizing fairness, it includes a fair start, fair process and then fair result, which follow in turn and influence each other. In a modern market economy, if the start and the process are fair, then the consequent result can be regarded as a competition conforming to the principle of fairness, and people will recognize and accept this result to a large extent. Therefore, fairness from the start to the process is put at the core in the process of building a fair society.[2] Expert research believes that what really counts is to make the start and the process fair, otherwise the result they bring will

---

[1] Jin Bei, "Deepening Reform Based on Consensus about Market Economy", *Social Science Front*, 2014(11).

[2] Hu Jiayong, "On the Innovation and Development of Socialist Market Economy Theory", *Economic Research Journal*, 2016 (7).

not be recognized by the society.

To realize social fairness and promote economic efficiency, first of all, it is necessary to ensure that the start and the process are fair. For a fair start, it is important to ensure that all sectors of society, especially children from low-income families, have equal access to education. For a fair process, it requires fair and transparent competition rules, open competition opportunities, and equal access to factors of production. On this basis, the competition results should be properly corrected through social security, subsidies for low-income groups, poverty elimination and other measures to achieve results at a higher degree.

The transformation to market economy indicates a process of conceptual conflict and conceptual transformation. Foreign experience shows that if the principle of market economy is in conflict with the original concept, the introduction of market mechanism will lead to social unrest, and be very likely to cause large-scale political conflicts. In China, after the transition from planned economy to market economy, many new rules adapting to market economy are bound to conflict with some widely-accepted concepts which has been rooted in the old system. When market exchange replaces planning as the decisive coordinated mechanism of resource allocation, it will endanger the basic survival and vested interests of people who depend on and recognize the rationality of the original mechanism, causing widespread social unrest. This requires the government to provide help for these people to adapt to the new mechanism, instill the concept of market economy into the public mainly by means of persuasion and with the backing of coercive force of the state, popularize the rule of market economy in the society, and gradually legalize them and make them law-based.[1] Although the market can improve the efficiency of resource allocation, especially that of scarce resources, the market itself has its limitations and cannot resolve all issues concerning fairness and justice. As China's socialist market economy needs to improve, the government needs more efforts to remedy its defects and compensate for its deficiencies in many aspects. This means that it is necessary to let the market play the decisive role in resource allocation from the standpoint of the people, while staying committed to giving full play to the government to properly address the issues concerning efficiency and fairness, and prevent the excessive gap between the rich and the poor.

In the process of transitioning from planned economy to market economy, political

---

[1] Pei Xiaoge, "Step up Efforts to Improve the Socialist Market Economy from the Standpoint of the People", *Theoretical Investigation*, 2014 (5).

democratization should follow the pace with the improvement of people's autonomous consciousness and capacity for self-management. It should gradually adapt to the new concept of democratic administration of market economy that replaces the traditional concept of authoritarian governance, promote the administrative system restructuring, and shape the overall responsibility of the government. A democratic government that adapts to market economy holds that the power of government comes from the people, and the people are the main players in social management; that the power of the society is controlled and restricted by the multiple dominators; that the authority of government derives from the institutionalized dialogue between the government and the people. The government should take responsibility for steering and serving rather than controlling and regulating, and should act on people-oriented demands rather than self-oriented needs.

3.5.1.2 People-centered philosophy of development is an essential requirement for developing socialist market economy

Why is it said that people-centered philosophy of development is an essential requirement for developing socialist market economy? This is determined by the status and role of the people in the process of economic development, as the people are the main players and play a decisive role in the economic development. Under the socialist market economy, upholding the principal status of the people means that the main players of social practice go to the people, rather than capitals or anything else. However, due to relatively weakness of productive forces in the primary stage of socialism, it is urgent to change the backward economy by introducing and developing capitals. As Marx said, like any other Western European countries, the Soviet suffered from both the development of capitalist production and its non-development in other aspects. So, the urgency of economic development and realistic demands for capitals led to the ignorance of the people's role in developing socialist market economy, and the aspiration for economic development led to one-sided pursuit of GDP index to a large extent. As a result, more value was put on capitals than on people's demands in the process of developing economy.[1] From the perspective of practice, people's demands have been objectively ignored, although great economic achievements have been made in China. Therefore, timely putting forward the people-centered philosophy of development can reverse this trend, and make the development of socialist market

[1] Han Dong, "Adhering to the People-centered Philosophy is the Necessity for the Development of Socialist Market Economy", *Reformation and Strategy*, 2017 (1).

economy as people-centred development, and really give full play to the role of people as they are the main players of social practice in developing socialist market economy.

Under the socialism, people has capacity for mastering rather than being enslaved. As the most positive and active factor, they can consciously promote the development of productive forces. In addition, it is necessary to timely adjust production relations and have a new understanding of people as the fundamental driving force for developing productive forces, as this is the key to resolving overcapacity and promoting supply-side structural reform. As the most positive and active factor in developing productive forces, people play an indispensable role in developing science and technology, management innovation, and business start-ups and innovation. Therefore, under the socialism, the development of the people determines that of production. Unleashing the creativity and innovative spirit of the people can create an inexhaustible driving force for economic development and resolving any difficulties. Putting the people first and relying on the people for development affirm that the people are the biggest driving force for economic development, and play a major role in developing productive forces. As long as the enthusiasm of the people for development is fully mobilized, the socialist market economy can maintain the driving force for sustained development.

Since the reform and opening up in 1978, China has made remarkable achievements in the economic development, and become the world's second largest economy. However, compared with "China's miracle", relatively slow social construction has become a weak link in its economic and social development. Since the 18th CPC National Congress, the CPC has clearly put forward the thinking of "guarding bottom line, highlighting key areas, improving institutions, and guiding public voices" in its work to improve people's livelihood. The CPC has put more stress on people's basic livelihood, low-income groups, and building institutions, and made new progress in improving social security and people's livelihood. In 2015, China basically achieved the United Nations Millennium Development Goals and became the first developing country in the world to realize the goal of poverty reduction set in the MDGs, thus making great contribution to global poverty reduction. So, Xi Jinping has repeatedly stressed that reform is an ongoing process, ensuring people's wellbeing never comes to an end, implementing the mass line never comes to stop, and the character of "not claiming credit but always making sure to contribute their share to the success of the cause" should be advocated. These important expositions have directed the path for China to follow people-centered development, and ensure and improve people's wellbeing in the new situation.

3.5.2 Socialist market economy serves the people in a wider context

An important characteristics of China's socialist system lies in the fact that China has developed a socialist market economy. Therefore, it is necessary to establish a people-centered market economy, and serve the people in a wider context.

First, implement the requirements for completing the building of a moderately prosperous society in all respects, constantly enhance the capacity for effective development, and strive to improve people's wellbeing according to the Five-sphere Integrated Plan. Accelerated efforts are needed to strengthen weak links, provide timely assistance, further alleviate poverty through development, and implement the strategy of targeted poverty alleviation and elimination. Accelerated efforts are needed to implement the strategy of people-centered new urbanization, promote coordinated development between urban and rural areas, and resolve the problems of the "three 100-million-people tasks"[1], and constantly promote the process of granting urban residency to rural migrant workers, and raise the level of urbanization among the registered population. Efforts are needed to implement the strategy of comprehensively promoting balanced development among all population, constantly improve social security, and provide access to education, employment services, basic medical care and other public services at a higher level. Efforts are needed to better implement the vision of green development, and provide people with cleaner water, fresher air and more food supply security.

Second, implement the requirements for comprehensively deepening reform, act in accordance with the characteristics of governance by the CPC, the development of socialism, and the evolution of human society, and constantly strengthen the endogenous impetus for development to bring more tangible benefits to the people. At present, China's economy has entered a new normal, with the growth rate shifting from high speed to medium-to-high speed, and various cyclical and structural economic problems more prominent. Therefore, during the 13th Five-year Plan period and beyond, it was necessary to grasp the requirements for comprehensively deepening reform, earnestly follow the rules governing the economic development, sustainable development and social inclusive development, and give full play to economic reconstructing as a driving force. It was necessary to make great progress in supply-side structural reform, boldly

[1] The "three 100-million-people tasks", that is, to enable the 100 million migrant farmer workers to settle down in cities and become real city residents by 2020; to accelerate the urbanization process of the central and western regions, guiding 100 million farmers to enter the nearby towns and cities voluntarily; to concentrate on rebuilding the run-town areas and unsafe buildings in cities to solve the housing problem for 100 million people. —*Tr.*

release and develop forces of production, strengthen the endogenous impetus for economic development, make the "cake" of economic development growing larger. By doing so, it will lay a solid economic foundation for the people to seek welfare.

Third, implement the requirements for comprehensively governing the country by the rule of law, seek to modernize governance system and governance capacity, and constantly enhance law-based market economy, so that people can truly feel the fairness and justice, which are the common aspiration and pursuit of human society, as well as an important guarantee for upholding the people-centered philosophy of development. To achieve this, it should stay committed to modernizing China's governance system and governance capacity, and accelerating efforts to modernize China's systems. In particular, efforts are needed to accelerate law-based socialist market economy. In essence, law-based socialist market economy lies in confirming the principal status of the people's market, as it is for the people. Therefore, continuous efforts should be made to let people feel a sense of fairness and justice in every judicial case, and constantly improve law-based socialist market economy.

Fourth, implement the requirements for comprehensively exercising full and rigorous governance over the Party, consolidate the mass foundation for the Party's governance, and constantly enhance the Party's governance capacity, so that people have greater confidence. The Party holds the key to the success of China's undertakings, and to implementing Xi Jinping's philosophy of people-centered development. It is necessary to take new steps in comprehensively strengthening self-discipline over the Party, just as what has been done in the past years to build close bonds and ties with the people, and share bitterness, joys and destiny with the people. It is necessary to listen to the voices and suggestions of the people, experience the people's happiness, anger, sorrow and joy, and accurately grasp the pulse of the masses. It is necessary to enable officials to hold the people in awe, rely on the people, and serve the people, so that people have a greater sense of fulfillment and happiness, and confidence in the governance of the Party and the government.

Chapter 4
The Guarantee and Support for Developing a Powerful Economy

4.1 The CPC's leadership as an important guarantee for developing a powerful economy

History has proved that it is of vital significance to strengthen the CPC's leadership for China's revolution, development and reform. As China has entered the new normal of economic development, the CPC must unite with and lead the Chinese people of all ethnic groups with greater resolve in reform, more practical measures for development and more superb leadership, and play a greater role in developing a powerful economy.

4.1.1 The significance of the CPC's leadership in developing a powerful economy

Over 40 years of reform and opening up, China's economy has made remarkable achievements and created a miracle in the history of world economy. This is inseparable from the important role played by the leadership of the CPC. Now, China has undoubtedly become a world major economy, yet not a powerful economy. Indeed, developing a powerful economy can make it possible to achieve the great rejuvenation of the Chinese nation. To do it, the leadership of the CPC is the key to running China's affairs well, China's institutional strengths compared with other countries', and the fundamental guarantee for the success of all the work of the Party and the country.

4.1.1.1 The core of the CPC leadership has stood the test of history

A mature Marxist political party is bound to form a leadership core in the course of its development. Engels pointed out profoundly in his article On Authority that authority and obedience are determined objectively by social development rather than subjectively by the people's wishes. Lenin stressed that historically no class could have achieved authority without its political leaders and advanced representatives who are good at organizing and leading movements. In retrospect, it has always been a major subject of political party construction for Marxism to safeguard authority in the world history of socialism development.

In the history of the CPC, a leadership core at the three levels has been gradually formed, that is, the core of the Party's leadership, that of the Central Committee and that of the Party's top leaders. The core of the Party's leadership, in terms of external relationship, means that the Party leads all economic, social and cultural undertakings, the armed forces and all other organizations. In a nutshell, it commands the overall situations. The core of the Central Committee's leadership, in terms of internal relationship, means that among the Party's organizations at all levels, the CPC National Congress, the CPC Central Committee elected by the National Congress, and the Political Bureau, the CPC Standing Committee of the Political Bureau and the General Secretary elected by the Central Committee account for the positions of leadership. The leadership core of the Party's top leaders, in terms of the central collective leadership, means that a single leader is the centralized embodiment of the Party's leadership and the personification of the central leadership at its core. The leaders, the Central Committee and the CPC form a concentric circle, which constitutes the entity strength of the core of the CPC leadership.[1] Seen from the history of the CPC, forming its core of leadership has played an extremely crucial role in advancing the great cause led by the Party.

The core of leadership at the three levels is the inevitable result of China's national situations and its political operation logic, as well as the inevitable conclusion of summing up the experience and lessons of the Party's construction. Without the CPC as the core, China would lack the backbone for all its undertakings, and it would be difficult to integrate various forces to accomplish the historical task of building China into an economic powerhouse. Without the CPC Central Committee as the core, its political party, which is composed of millions of the Party's organizations and members, would lack unity. Without the Party's leader as the core, senior leaders of the Party may make inconsistent decisions, and even face the risk of separatism when it comes to major events, resulting in a passive situation in which power is tied down and nothing is done.

In the history of the CPC, it has been particularly important for the Party and the country to form a strong central collective leadership and maintain its authority in practice. Before the Zunyi Conference in 1935, as the Party failed to form a mature central committee, it led to several setbacks in its cause, and even faced the danger of failure. After Mao Zedong's leading position in the Red Army and the CPC Central

[1] Zeng Jun, "Why is the Leadership Core Important to a Political Party", *Policy*, 2017 (1).

Committee was established in the Zunyi Conference, the CPC began to form a strong core of leadership. Since then, the Chinese revolution has taken on a new look. It is due to the strong leadership of the CPC Central Committee, and the efforts by generations of Chinese Communists to unite and lead the Chinese people in their continuous struggle that China has made remarkable achievements in its revolution, development and reform. When it comes to the core of leadership, Mao Zedong once said that just as a peach has a hard core at its centre rather than several cores, a core of leadership should be established to oppose "one country, three leaders to govern". Deng Xiaoping also said that every leading group must have a core of leadership, and the leadership without a core is unreliable. The core of the CPC leadership has profoundly revealed the Marxist theory on the Party's construction, and well sum up the fine tradition and unique strengths of the CPC formed in the long-term practice, which is of great significance for China's development and building China into an economic powerhouse.

By examining the development of many modern countries, it can be found that a political party plays an important role in the development, and it has become an important feature for a country to modernize governance with a political party as its main body. From a theoretical perspective, the governance by a political party emphasizes the enhancement of governance capacity, and the realization of institutionalized and authorized power operation, thus achieving its goal of integrating society, forming good governance and enhancing vitality. In China, since the CPC became the ruling party and realized its long-term governance, the CPC governance has been deeply integrated into the national governance. In the process of gradually realizing the prosperity of the people and of the country, the governance of the CPC has effectively promoted the realization of the governance of contemporary China.

Socialism with Chinese characteristics has many features, but the most essential attribute is to adhere to the leadership of the CPC. Strengthening and comprehensively improving the Party's leadership over economic work, is not only an essential requirement for staying committed to democratic centralism, but also the strength of China's political system. The Party commands the overall situations, coordinates all aspects and take full leadership over economic work as its central work in state governance. If the central work is seized, other undertakings can be better carried out.[1]

---

[1] *Excerpts from Xi Jinping's Treatise on Socialist Economic Construction*, Beijing: Central Party Literature Press, 2017, p.308.

4.1.1.2 The CPC's leadership as a must for developing a powerful economy

In an era when the global pattern has made profound adjustments with increasingly fierce international competition, and in an important period when comprehensively deepening reform and advancing development are domestically carried out, China is now confronted with the "Four Tests" and "Four Risks"[1] within the Party's construction. The burden and difficulty of governing the country are beyond imagination. Therefore, to carry out the great struggle with many new historical features, advance the great cause of socialism with Chinese characteristics, modernize China's governance system and capacity, and enhance China's international status and influence, a strong core of leadership has been a must more than ever before.

The 18th CPC National Congress proposed to ensure the completion of building a moderately prosperous society in all respects by 2020, and the Fifth Plenary Session of the 18th CPC Central Committee put forward new goals and requirements, made comprehensive arrangements, and defined the 13th Five-year Plan period as a decisive period for building a moderately prosperous society in all respects. According to the proposal, a moderately prosperous society in all respects should cover more communities, benefit all the people, and be shared by all the people. Building a moderately prosperous society in all respects emphasizes the concept of "in all respects", which is more important and more difficult to achieve, as the concept implies the balance, coordination and sustainability of development. Therefore, the focus and difficulty lies in how to address the weak links of unbalanced, uncoordinated and unsustainable development. First, it is necessary to ensure the quality and efficiency of economic development. Under the new normal, China's economic development is mainly characterized by the transformations in speed, mode, structure and driving force. As these transformations are the inevitable process of China's economic evolution to a stage of higher shape, better division of labor and more reasonable structure, it poses great new challenges to realize such extensive and profound changes. Second, it is necessary to address the issues of unbalanced, uncoordinated and unsustainable development. The reason is that unbalanced, uncoordinated and unsustainable development is the weak links in realizing a moderately prosperous society in all respects. Third, it is necessary to improve the awareness and capacity for risk prevention and control. The 13th Five-year Plan period was a period in which various risks would

[1] The Four Tests refer to exercising governance, carrying out reform and opening up, developing the market economy and responding to external development. The Four Risks refer to lack of drive, incompetence, disengagement from the people, and inaction and corruption. —*Tr.*

accumulate and even become concentrated in China's development. If major risks occurred, China's national security may face major risks and the process of building a moderately prosperous society in all respects may be interrupted. Therefore, it is necessary to fight against a tough battle for preventing and defusing major risks. To do with such risks and challenges, it needs to strengthen the Party's leadership and enhance its capacity and level of building China into an economic powerhouse.

In the first decade of the 21st century, China's per capital income increased from less than US$1,000 to over US$4,000. According to the standard of the World Bank, China has stepped into the ranks of upper middle-income countries from lower middle-income countries since 2010. Although China's economic growth has slowed down somewhat since then, its per capital income had reached US$8,836 by 2017, nearly doubling that of 2010, which has stepped into a new historic stage in building a moderately prosperous society in all respects. From the international experience, the most important economic transition is to move from a low-and middle-income economy to a high-income economy. This is to say, it reflects a transitional stage where the economy is moving forward from extensive to intensive growth, the industrial structure upgrading from low-to high-end, and the social structure transforming from "dumb bell shape" to "olive shape". If the transition succeeds at this stage, it will help a country to overcome the "middle income trap". However, if the transition fails, it will lead a country to fall into the "middle income trap". Since the Second World War, Japan, Republic of Korea and Singapore have been among those few countries that have successfully crossed the "middle income trap".

In view of *People's Tribune* magazine, which solicited the opinions of 50 Chinese experts and scholars, it is believed that countries falling into the "middle income trap" generally have ten characteristics, including economic growth falls or stagnation, democratic chaos, polarization between the rich and the poor, corruption, excessive urbanization, shortage of social and public services, employment problems, social unrest, loss of beliefs, and fragile financial system. Anyway, with the strong leadership of the CPC, the Chinese people have great confidence and capability to overcome the middle income trap. Objectively speaking, when the social transformation come to a period during which various social resources become diverted, social forces dispersed, social ideological trends differentiated, social organizations divided, and social contradictions frequently occurred, it needs a strong ruling party to resolve these issues. So, the key to overcoming the "middle income trap" is to give full play to China's strengths and unleash its potential. And the only way out is to deepen reform, which objectively requires the strong leadership of the CPC. The CPC has the scientific theories that consciously grasp the law governing the development of socialism with Chinese characteristics, lofty character that selflessly and fearlessly benefit the nation and the people, strong capability for organizing, mobilizing, planning and coordinating, strong will to reform and innovate, and rich experience to govern. All this has provided strong concept, thought and organizational guarantee for China to comprehensively deepen reform and overcome the "middle income trap".

4.1.2 Strengthening the CPC's leadership over economic work

The exposition of "the CPC Central Committee with Xi Jinping as its core" not only reflects the continuity of the political tradition of the Communist Party of China, but also contains its developmental aspects. It must be understood against the backdrop of the great rejuvenation of the Chinese nation and the requirements of building China into an economic powerhouse. Bettering the economic work needs to strengthen and improve the Party's leadership over it. The direct purpose of establishing the leadership core is to safeguard the authority of the Central Committee, the unity of the Party and the centralized and unified leadership. Nevertheless, this is not the ultimate goal. The ultimate purpose is to better gather all positive factors, seize more opportunities, overcome actual and potential risks, and promote the goal of building China into an economic powerhouse into practice.

4.1.2.1 Guided by Xi Jinping Thought on Socialist Economy with Chinese Characteristics for a New Era

Xi Jinping Thought on Socialist Economy with Chinese Characteristics was put forward for the first time on the Central Economic Work Conference, which was held from December 18 to December 20, 2017. The Conference made it clear that Xi Jinping Thought on Socialist Economy with Chinese Characteristics for a New Era, crystallizes the experience of China's economic development over the past five years, and the latest achievement and spirit of the socialist political economics with Chinese characteristics, and that the Thought is the valuable asset of the Party and the country, and must be upholded for a long time to come and constantly enriched. Its main connotation can be summarized as "seven persistences": In terms of basic direction of China's economic development, the country must remain committed to strengthen the Party's centralized and unified leadership over economic work to steer the development of China's economy on the right course, and improve the Party's leadership over economic systems and institutions. In terms of value orientation of China's economic development, the country must remain committed to the people-centered philosophy of development, and integrate the people-centered approach into the Five-Sphere Integrated Plan and the Four-pronged Comprehensive Strategy. In terms of assessing the new situation and trend of economic development and its countermeasures, the country must remain committed to adapt to and steer the new normal of economic development, take into consideration the broad views and follow the rules governing its development. In terms of pursuing the direction of economic restructuring, the country must ensure that the market plays a decisive role in resource allocation and the government performs its functions better, and resolutely remove institutional obstacles to economic development. In terms of major tasks in the present and future stage of China's economic work, the country must adapt to changes in the main contradictions facing China's economic development and improve its macro control, make discretionary choices, and issue corresponding solutions, take supply-side structural reform as the major tasks of China's economic work, and provide the right solutions to China's economic transformation and upgrading as well as sound and sustained development. In terms of formulating and deploying economic development strategies, the country must take a problem-oriented approach in developing new strategies for economic growth. Key strategies adopted include the innovation-driven strategy that emphasizes stimulation, the collaborative development strategy of the Beijing-Tianjin-Hebei region, the development strategy of the Yangtze River Economic Belt, the Belt and Road Initiative, the strategy of "bringing in" and "going global", the strategy of comprehensively opening China's economy to the outside world to create a new pattern, the strategy of rural revitalization, and the strategy of targeted poverty alleviation and elimination etc. These strategies have exert profound influence on China's economic growth and transformations. In terms of the tactics and approaches that guide the economic work, the country must have sound tactics and approaches, pursue progress while ensuring stability, maintain strategic resolve, think about worst-case scenarios, and promote solid progress in all economic work. In general, Xi Jinping Thought on Socialist Economy with Chinese Characteristics for a New Era has achieved another new development and the sublimation of the Party's guiding ideology for developing a powerful economy. Accurately understanding and grasping its rich connotation and spiritual essence is of great significance to accelerate the strategy of developing a powerful economy.

4.1.2.2 Strengthening the CPC's leadership over the institutional development of economic work

Since the 18th CPC National Congress, the CPC Central Committee has strengthened working mechanism of the Central Leading Group for Financial and Economic Affairs, improved its institutions, strengthened its strengths, focused on key areas, and put emphasis on implementation. The economic work has achieved notable results under the leadership of the Standing Committee of the Political Bureau of the CPC Central Committee. Led by the CPC Central Committee, a system has been established to conduct quarterly analysis and research on the economic situations, while regularly studying and making arrangements for major strategic issues. In recent years, special studies has been conducted on fiscal and tax reform, urbanization development, food security, water security, energy security, innovation-driven development, and the Belt and Road Initiative etc., which has played an important guiding role in developing a powerful economy. In March 2018, the CPC Central Committee issued the Plan for Deepening the Reform of the Party and State Institutions, reorganizing the Central Leading Group for Financial and Economic Affairs into the Central Commission for Financial and Economic Affairs (CCFEA), which is responsible for the top-level design, overall layout, overall coordination, advancement and supervision of implementing major financial and economic affairs. On April 2, 2018, Financial and Economic Commission of the CPC Central Committee held its first meeting, deliberating on the ideas and measures to fight against the three critical battles, and approving the Work Regulations for the Central Commisions for Financial and Economic Affairs.

4.1.2.3 Enhancing the CPC's leadership over law-based economic work

In essence, the socialist market economy is operated under the rule of law, and economic disorder mostly results from the fact that laws are not observed and violations are not prosecuted. Therefore, it is necessary to stay committed to the mentality of the rule of law, strengthen the concept of the rule of law, and regulate and govern the economy according to the rule of law. It is necessary to resolutely abandon the way the economy is managed by administrative orders and so on, change the way the enterprises and projects were blindly pushed forwards to promote the development beyond the rule of law, and the way how to achieve revenue by outdated planning and coercion. The essential requirement of economy governed by the rule of law is to grasp and respect the law governing the economy. Since the 18th CPC National Congress, the Central Committee has placed special emphasis on handling affairs according to the rule of law, and consciously applied the mentality and approach of the rule of law to deepen reform, promote development, resolve conflicts, and maintain stability.

4.1.2.4 Strengthening the professional capacity of the CPC's leadership over economic work

Since the great economic development has been achieved in China, it requires the professional capacity of the leadership to support the economic work. To be competent in the work, the leading officials must make great efforts to improve their knowledge structure, increase their practical capability and compensate for what they need to improve. They must not only learn more about political, economical and societal areas, but also acquire more knowledge on international, strategic and psychological aspects. They must cultivate the spirit of scientific research from the macro- and micro-perspective. Also, continued efforts should be made to carry out the theoretical training with practical experiences, and train and select a large number of leading officials who are politically reliable, professionally competent in economy and management to strengthen the leading groups at all levels.

4.2 Modernizing national governance as the direction to move forwards in developing a powerful economy

The level of national governance represents an important symbol to test whether the socialist system is perfect and well-defined or not. Obviously, to develop from a major economy to a powerful economy, it is inseparable from the support of a stable and mature system. National governance system and capacity is the centralized embodiment of a country's system and capacity to implement. Since the 18th CPC National Congress, the CPC Central Committee with Xi Jinping at its core has adopted a series of major measures in governance, comprehensively raised the Party's capacity to govern the country at a new level, and formed a new concept on governance.

4.2.1 Modernizing national governance as a must for developing a powerful economy

A sound governance system and capacity is not only the basic conditions for a country to operate and develop in an orderly, sound manner, but also an important guarantee for the people to live and work in peace and contentment, for the society to keep stable and orderly, and for the country to maintain lasting peace and stability. What is more important, they are the essential way for a country to develop a powerful economy.

4.2.1.1 Modernizing national governance as an inevitable choice for China's transformation development

Reviewing the development history of socialism, there is no successful precedent for governing socialist society in the exploration and practice of socialism in the world. Marx and Engels put forward many important propositions on socialist construction, but they are lack of corresponding practice. Lenin also failed to explore this issue deeply. Although the Soviet Union has gained practical experience in governing socialist society, it has made some serious mistakes. Strictly speaking, it was not a successful case. Since the founding of the People's Republic of China in 1949, the CPC has led the people to constantly explore ways to govern socialist society. Although it encountered serious twists and turns and took many detours, it has accumulated rich experience, and achieved great results in the national governance system and capacity, especially remarkable progress in the past 40 years since the reform and opening up. China's splendid achievements in the economic and social fields stand in stark contrast to the chaos in some regions and countries in the world. This reflects the fact that China's governance system and capacity have generally adapted to China's national situations and development requirements.

However, it should be soberly realized that the socialist modernization with Chinese characteristics has reached a new stage of development after 40 years of reform and opening up. The reform has entered a period of overcoming difficulties and deep issues, the economic development has stepped into a period of readjustment, and social issues are frequently occurred. There remain many deficiencies and much room for improvement in China's governance system and capacity to live up to the expectations of the Chinese people, the increasingly fierce international competition, and the goal of realizing a moderately prosperous society in all respects and China's dream of national rejuvenation. If the state does not carry out comprehensive reforms, and crack various hidden dangers in national governance from the institutional level, the problems China are now encountering may further worsen, and even affect the ruling position and foundation of the Party. Due to these reasons, it is necessary to carefully summarize the experience and lessons of other countries in the world, extract the successful experience of China's reform and opening up, and let the government play a better role while giving full play to the decisive role of the market in resource allocation. In this sense, modernizing China's governance system and capacity is the general trend of the times as well as the imperative of the situations.

4.2.1.2 Modernizing national governance as an important guarantee for economic transformation and upgrading

China has now entering a new normal of economic development in a period of shifting economic growth speed, adjusting economic structure and digesting stimulus policies. Since the reform and opening up, China has entered a "golden period of economic development" with an average annual growth rate of nearly 10%, which has profoundly changed the world economic pattern. In 2013, China's GDP accounted for about 12.3% of the world's total, only next to that of the United States, and China has become the world's second largest economy, the largest industrial country, and the largest trader of goods and holder of foreign exchange reserves. China's overall national strength and that in science and technology have reached a new level, and its international status and influence are increasing. However, the issue of unbalanced, uncoordinated and unsustainable development has not been fundamentally addressed. Economic and social risks are growing; population, resources and environmental constraints are becoming tighter, and the pressure to ensure and improve people's livelihood has increased. China's economy is still facing downward pressure, although it has entered a stage of medium-to-high growth speed within an appropriate range. There has overcapacity in the traditional manufacturing sector, the core competitiveness of strategic emerging industries is weak, and the development of the service sector lags behind. In the meantime, the traditional demographic dividend, globalization dividend and system transition dividend are gradually removing. With the appreciation of renminbi, China's comparative advantage in the world industrial division of labor is rapidly weakening. In terms of development model, China's economy is essentially a "three-dimensional" market economy—in which it is necessary to balance the relationship among the strategic central government, corporatized local government and competitive enterprises. However, the government, especially the local government, intervenes excessively in the economic operation and plays an important role in resource allocation, which affects the full play of the market mechanism and leads to the deformity of the growth mode. Therefore, it is urgent to reform the growth mode as it has come to an end.

4.2.1.3 Modernizing national governance as an intrinsic requirement to eliminate social contradictions

It is fair to say that since the reform and opening up, China has made remarkable economic achievements and people's livelihood has greatly improved. However, social transformation and economic development have not been synchronized, and there remains much room for improving people's sense of happiness. First, the gap between the rich and the poor is rapidly widening. At present, China's Gini coefficient is above 0.46 and still at a relatively high level. The issue of uneven distribution is more prominent when the difference in the stock of property is taken into account. Second, social stratification is accelerating. After years of development, China has formed different social interest groups, such as original urban residents and immigrants, urban residents and rural residents, and residents in large cities and small and medium-sized urban residents. In particular, with the rapid advancement of urbanization, various conflicts of interests become increasingly serious. This shows that China are facing new and unprecedented challenges. In a word, the rapid social changes call for the improvement of national governance, which is indispensable for China to develop a powerful economy.

4.2.1.4 Modernizing national governance as an objective need to meet the public demands of the people

In view of Adam Smith, in the early stage of economic development, the state is responsible for nothing but to ensure national security, and provide justice and infrastructure. Nevertheless, as economic activities become more complex, the people have more demands on the state and the level of national governance. In the early days of reform and opening up, the Chinese people's demands were to resolve the issue of ensuring people enough food and clothing, which was essentially to meet the basic needs of survival. At that stage, the people's demands on the government are relatively low. They can resolve their basic needs through their own labor, as long as the government creates relaxed external environment. However, when the basic survival needs are met, their demands for public services, such as education, medical care, social security and ecological environment are rapidly increasing, and so are their demands on the government. In particular, with the prominent public issues, such as climate warming, global public security and international cooperation, there are increasing demands to improve the level and system of national governance. Therefore, it is an objective need to modernize national governance to meet the public demands.

4.2.1.5 Modernizing national governance as an integral part of addressing various risks and challenges

From a global perspective, the global financial crisis that broke out in 2008 has had a profound impact on the world economy. Accordingly, the world has entered a period of profound transformation and adjustment. Up to now, the economic prospects of the United States, Japan and Europe are not optimistic, the economic growth in emerging market countries tends to decline, and the global economy remains sluggish. Global issues, such as the increasing various protectionism, climate change and energy security, are becoming more prominent. The Trans-Pacific Partnership Agreement (TTP) and Transatlantic Trade Investment Partnership (TTIP), championed by the US, seek to reformulate the rules for the world. A new round of scientific and technological revolution and industrial transformation has taken shape. This is a "double-edged sword" for China, representing both important opportunities and severe challenges. If China does not respond properly, it will not only fail to achieve "leapfrog development", but also widen the gap with developed countries. How to cope with the increasingly complex international competition, enhance China's capacity to participate in international governance, and provide global public goods, this is a new topic for China.

4.2.2 The relationship between modernizing national governance and developing a powerful economy

Modernizing government governance serves as the foundation of modernizing national governance. Therefore, the Third Plenary Session of the 19th CPC Central Committee pointed out that it is necessary to remove the institutional and mechanism deficiencies that restrict the market to play a decisive role in resource allocation and the government to function better. Centering around the high-quality development, efforts should be made to develop economic modernization, strengthen and improve the government's role in economic regulation, market supervision, social management and public service functions, and ecological environment protection, adjust and prioritize the functions of government institutions, comprehensively improve government efficiency, and build a service-oriented government that the people are satisfied with. According to what is stated in *World Development Report 1997*: *The State in a Changing World*, what government is good at is not limitless, and the key to an effective government is to do what government is good at, rather than infinitely expand the scope under its control. In order to achieve effective governance, first of all, it is necessary to determine what role the government should play and what the government can do and what cannot do. Therefore, the key to modernizing national governance system and capacity is to improve the governance capacity of the government. This is the difficulty of transforming from traditional national governance system to modern national governance system. Therefore, to improve the government's governance capacity, it is necessary to understand and reconstruct the relationship between government and market, government and enterprises, government and the people, government and society, government and government, promote the modernization of government governance, and then boost China to develop a powerful economy.

4.2.2.1 Striking a balance between the role of the government and that of the market to ensure their due roles

The key to economic restructuring lies in striking a balance between the role of the government and that of the market. This is actually a question of whether the market or the government should play a decisive role in resource allocation. In the countries with modern market economy, the market makes effective resource allocation by examining the relationship between supply and demand through price. Throughout more than 40 years of reform and development in China, the core issue is how to understand and balance the relationship between the government and the market. Objectively speaking, Chinese people have made a profound understanding of the market's strengths in resource allocation. It is due to the accurate understanding of the power of market and then stimulating the vitality of market that China has made such notable economic achievements. It can be said that the function and conditions of China's market allocation of resources have been gradually formed. However, it should be noted that the relationship between the government and the market needs to be improved. On the one hand, the administrative intervention on the performance of economic operation is overdue, and the administrative means is intensified rather than weakened over a period of time. The government has excessively controlled the market, performing some functions that should have been undertaken by the market and enterprises. On the other hand, both market vitality and market competition are insufficient. And, the enterprises have not played its due role as the main players of market economy, relying too much on the government's support and the preferential policies. Therefore, Xi Jinping pointed out at a province- and city-level meeting held in Wuhan in July 2013, "we should speed up the transformation of government functions and properly balance the relationship between the government and the market". In the Explanatory Notes for Decision of the CPC Central Committee on Some Major Issues Concerning Comprehensively Deepening the Reform, Xi further said, "to better balance the relationship between the government and the market, the key lies in whether the market or the government should play the decisive role in resource allocation."

To properly strike a balance between the role of government and that of market, it is necessary to trust and respect the market and let the market play the decisive role in allocating resources. What the government should do is to play the function of "let go", that is, the "visible hand" of the government should give way to the "invisible hand" of the market in allocating resources. With the rapid progress in science and technology and the complex market environment, the government is confronted with the situation of limited information and decision-makings, which may increase the probability of making errors. As it is enterprises that truly understand the market, the government should reduce its intervention in the micro economy and return to the way the market is going. In the meantime, the government should withdraw its "visible hand" from areas where it was not supposed to do, address deep-rooted issues in institutions and systems, break the barriers of entrenched interests, make new strides in institutional development and innovation, move faster to form a unified, open market system with orderly competition, improve the efficiency of resource allocation, and give better play to the market.

While recognizing and affirming the positive role of market, one should not ignore the negative effects caused by unbalanced market. As the famous economist Samuelson said, "The market has no heart; the market has no brain." That is, the market cannot effectively resolve issues such as externalities, public goods, monopoly, information asymmetry, unreasonable preferences, income distribution etc. It is due to the imbalance and failure of the market that the government needs to play a complementary role. This is the basic reason for the government to intervene in market economy as the eliminator of external effects, the supplier of public goods, the supervision and sanction of monopoly, the provider of perfect information, the corrector of preference, the regulator of fair distribution and so on. Xi Jinping pointed out, "the market plays a decisive role in allocating resources, but is not the sole actor in this regard." What implies is that the market cannot do everything, and its natural defects determine that the development of market economy cannot be separated from the appropriate regulation of the government.

4.2.2.2 Improving the level of economic governance and unleashing the vitality of enterprises

In 2017, China's GDP reached US$12.2503 trillion, accounting for about 15% of the world's total. It is fair to say that China's economy has deeply embedded in the world economic system, and its governance is quite different from what it was in the early days of reform and opening up. Objectively speaking, China has basically established the macro control system under the socialist market economy. Nevertheless, it is urgent to reform the traditional and outdated means of regulation and control in comparison to the complexity of macro economy and the demands to develop a powerful economy. It is necessary to improve the macro control system, further withdraw from the micro-economic areas, maintain the balance of economic aggregate, promote the coordination of major economic structures and the optimal distribution of productive forces, mitigate the impact of economic cycle fluctuations, safeguard regional and systemic risks, stabilize market expectations, prevent major fluctuations, and achieve sustained and sound economic development.

Therefore, it is necessary to stay committed to market-oriented reform, significantly reduce the government's direct allocation of resources, minimize the central government's management of micro-affairs. It is necessary to resolutely implement the "Three Shoulds" proposed at the Third Plenary Session of the 18th CPC Central Committee. That is, for all economic activities that can be effectively regulated by the market mechanism, the government review and approval should be abolished. For all economic and social matters which are directly addressed to the community level, large in quantity and extensive in scope, they should be delegated to local governments and organizations for more convenience and effective management. To deepen the reform of investment systems, all investment projects should be decided by enterprises in accordance with laws and regulations, except for those significant for national security, ecological security, the distribution of major productive forces, and the development of strategic resources and major public interests. On this basis, further efforts should be made to cancel more government review and approval for some items or delegate power to local governments, reduce and standardize preliminary review and approval, and lessen qualification permits and administrative fees. Furthermore, efforts should be made to encourage governments at all levels to implement list-based management of administrative review and approval, establish standardized and transparent procedures for items on the list, and provide efficient and quality services. Thus, the market and non-government entities can make their own decisions in accordance with the law. Enterprises can leverage their rights by the rule of the law, and the government cannot do anything unauthorized by the law. In the meantime, intensified efforts should be made to delegate power to local governments to further leverage the comparative advantages of local governments in occupying information and fully mobilize the initiatives of both the central and local governments.

4.2.2.3 Strengthening market regulation to ensure and improve people's wellbeing

When the market plays a decisive role in resource allocation, the market competition will become more intense. Consequently, the government governance needs to be improved, and the function of government supervision be strengthened. That is, strengthening supervision must go hand in hand with streamlining administration and delegating power. While reducing administrative review and approval drastically, the government should strengthen the formulation and implementation of development strategies, planning and policies and standards, and supervision over market activities. In terms of supervision process, supervision during the process and after the event are treated with different focus. The supervision during the process should focus on strengthening the monitoring of market order, production safety, product quality, capital and credit, and timely identify issues and take appropriate measures to correct and nip them in the head. The supervision after the event should focus on strengthening the evaluation of implementing the items, and deal with violations of laws and regulations. In terms of supervision responsibility, governments at all levels share the regulatory responsibilities. The central government focuses on strengthening the guidance of laws and policies, while local governments strive to remove various local protection barriers, unify market rules, maintain market order, eliminate market blockades and fragmentation, and create a fair market competition environment. In the coming future, it tends to strengthen the market supervision in cities and counties. In terms of supervision forms, both comprehensive supervision and sampling supervision should be integrated with each other. On the one hand, big data, cloud computing and other modern information technologies should be fully employed to address inefficient regulation in some industries. On the other hand, sampling supervision should be conducted to randomly check some enterprises, and impose heavy fines on those that make counterfeit and shoddy products, and put them on a blacklist to increase the economic and social costs of violations of laws and regulations.

In recent years, China has made remarkable economic achievements, and significantly contributed to global economic growth, becoming an important engine of world economic growth. However, it should be noted that due to the blind pursuit of GDP, environmental pollution has become increasingly serious in some areas, and people's sense of happiness has not kept pace with economic development. At the sixth group study session of the Political Bureau of the 18th CPC Central Committee, Xi Jinping pointed out, "to balance the relationship between the economic development and ecological environment protection, it is necessary to establish the concept that protecting the ecological environment signifies protecting productivity, improving the ecological environment signifies developing productive force, and further promote green development, circulation, low carbon development, and never at the expense of the environment for economic growth." Theoretically, as one of the basic public services, the ecological environment belongs to the public goods provided by the government and shared by the whole people. So, against the background of serious environmental protection, the Third Plenary Session of the 18th CPC Central Committee included ecological environmental protection as one of the government's functions, which further highlighted the necessity and urgency for the government to provide good ecological products for the people, and reflected the new connotation of government functions in the new era. From May 18 to May 19, 2018, the National Ecological and Environmental Protection Conference was held in Beijing. Undoubtedly, it is of great significance since this is the first national conference on environmental protection since the 18th CPC National Congress. At the conference, Xi Jinping elaborated on the significance of promoting ecological progress, laid out the important principles for developing ecological progress, and made comprehensive plans for strengthening environmental protection and fighting the tough battle against pollution.

4.2.2.4 Deepening fiscal system reform to enrich the people and ensure the prosperity of the country

National governance must be conducive to improve the people's wellbeing, enrich the people and ensure the prosperity of the country. The Third Plenary Session of the 18th CPC Central Committee proposed that the starting point and ultimate goal of comprehensively deepening reform is to promote social equity and justice and improve people's well-being. That is, it is intrinsically unified to make a country prosperous and enrich the people towards developing a powerful country. One should not neglect that the glory brought by a strong country will not last long if a country is economically strong and its residents are not wealthy. Conversely, one country cannot do much on the international stage if its residents are wealthy and it has a weak government finance. Therefore, it is essential to balance the relationship between enriching the people and making the country prosperous in order to improve the government's governance capacity. It should be realized that the lower river is full when the upper river flows, and the big river will not dry when the source river streams. In terms of public economics, there is a contractual relationship between residents and the government. Residents pay taxes to the government in exchange for public services they cannot provide effectively.

That is to say, finance is the important link between residents and the government. All in all, the fiscal system reform is crucial for the residents and the government. On the premise of ensuring the normal development of national undertakings, more consideration should be given to the affordability of enterprises and residents, so that residents can share a greater proportion of the pie of wealth, and the government functions can be forced to shift from an economical development-oriented and corporate-oriented government to a service-oriented and law-based government.

The Third Plenary Session of the 18th CPC Central Committee pointed out that public finance is the foundation and an important pillar of state governance, and that sound fiscal and taxation systems provide an institutional guarantee for optimizing resource allocation, maintaining market unity, promoting social equity, and realizing enduring peace and stability of the country. In other words, fiscal and taxation systems have been playing a fundamental, institutional and supportive role in national governance. The underlying reason is that the financial system reflects the basic relationship between the government and the market, the government and society, the central and local governments, and deeply influences the areas such as economy, politics, culture, society, ecological civilization, national defense etc. Through deepening the financial and fiscal system and establishing a modern financial system, it will lay a foundation for promoting the modernization of national governance system and marching towards developing a powerful economy.

4.2.2.5 Innovating social management and promoting harmonious society

To improve China's governance capacity, it is necessary to give full play to the interactive governance by multiple entities and realize the positive interaction between government governance, social self-regulation and self-governance of residents. This reflects the progress of the state, society and residents from contradiction to win-win cooperation. Through innovating social management, it can contribute to realizing positive interactions between the government, society and residents, and thus promoting social equity, justice, harmony and stability. It is necessary to foster a spirit of citizenship, mobilize their enthusiasm for participating in political life, promote efforts to separate government administration from social activities, open up market access, and hand over to social forces as much as possible what society can do, so as to give full play to the positive role of social forces. Full play should be given to the local governments, so that they can carry out their work in accordance with the new requirements of the people in the new period; meanwhile the grassroots organizations should be strengthened. It is necessary to increase social functions in self-regulation, and give full play to the role of social norms in coordinating social relations, constraining social behavior, and safeguarding the interests of the people. It is necessary to deepen self-governance of residents and carry out democratic governance with self-management, self-education, and self-service as main purposes.

So, efforts should be made to reform the management system of social organizations and stimulate social vitality. Direct registration of social organizations, such as professional associations in chambers of commerce, science and technology, public welfare and charity organizations, and urban and rural community services, will be implemented to maximize the initiative of all types of organizations and stimulate social vitality. It is necessary to further delink the trade associations and chambers of commerce from administrative bodies, establish a multi-department joint law enforcement mechanism, investigate and punish illegal activities of social organizations in accordance with the law, and resolutely ban illegal social organizations. It is necessary to actively promote government purchase of services. In real life, providing public services for residents does not need to be entirely undertaken by the government. The government can achieve the same effect by delegating power to the society and purchasing public services, and improve the quality and efficiency of people's livelihood services by expanding the main bodies of governance. In the areas of general public services, social organizations can undertake whatever is suitable for them through competitive selection. In the areas of basic public services, such as education, employment and health care, the government must redouble efforts to purchase services. The main task of the government is to formulate standards for purchasing public services, conduct assessments and publicize the results to the public in a timely manner.

For one thing, new approaches and methods should be developed to address social contradictions and issues; meanwhile regular management should be integrated with dynamic management to identify and address them as soon as possible or promptly. For another, new approaches and methods should be developed to maintain public security; meanwhile special rectification activities should be integrated with long-term management to improve the multi-dimensional system for preventing and controlling public security, and maintain social stability. Through innovating social management and improving the level of governance, it will promote efforts to form a sound development pattern in "building a strong government and a strong society".

4.2.2.6 Mobilizing the two initiatives and effectively motivating governments at all levels

The key link in the national governance system is to balance the relationship between the role of the central government and that of local governments. So, it is crucial to leverage the enthusiasm, initiative and creativity of local governments, while maintaining the authority of the central government in national governance. The Third Plenary Session of the 18th CPC Central Committee clearly pointed out the importance of properly balancing the relationship between the central government and local governments, stressing that the initiatives of both the central and local governments should be brought into play. At present, one of the important reasons affecting the "initiative" of local governments is the mismatch between authority of office and responsibility of expenditure. In recent years, the expenditure responsibility undertaken by local governments has been increasing, but the local disposable financial resources has changed little. The widening financial gap needs to be alleviated to some extent by means of transfer payments. Therefore, it is particularly important to further adjust and optimize the expenditure responsibility of governments at all levels when the financial structure of the central and local governments remains basically stable. And the basic principle to define expenditure responsibility lies in the compatibility of the externality of public goods, the complexity of information and the incentive compatibility, and leveraging the comparative advantages of the central government and local governments.

So, the central government should strengthen its macro control responsibility and capacity, and strengthen its functions, such as formulating development planning, studying and evaluating the trends of economic development, designing systems and institutions, managing overall issues, and coordinating overall institutional reforms. Local governments should strengthen their responsibilities in public services, market supervision, social management and environmental protection, and better leverage their advantages of being close to the masses, grassroots units and having access to information.

Apart from the expenditure responsibilities that obviously belong to the central or local governments, most of them belong to the common rights of the central and local governments. These rights include public goods and services that have the advantage of regional management information but have a greater impact on other regions, such as developing and maintaining major trans-regional projects. On the basis of clear responsibility of the authority of office, the central government bears the expenditure responsibility of the central authority, the local governments bear that of the local authority, and the central and local governments share that of the common authority according to the regulations. The central government may entrust local governments with some of the responsibility for government expenditure by arranging transfer payments. Through the rational distribution of the authority of office and expenditure responsibility, it can fully mobilize the initiatives of both the central and local governments, and then promote China to achieve the strategic transformation from a major economy to a powerful economy.

4.3 A better role of the government to develop a powerful economy

The government must perform its functions in modern society, just as a modern society needs the government to manage. The key lies in determining the optimal level of government intervention between the two extremes: one is the central planned economy, in which the government claims to represent national interests and make all economic decisions on behalf of the public; the other is "laissez-faire" economy, in which the government is constrained to do what market cannot do and what society needs. How to meet the balance between the two extremes poses challenges for economists and policymakers alike.[1]

4.3.1 Correctly understanding the relationship between market and government to develop a powerful economy

Judging from the history of the development of western countries, the government and the market interplay with and interpenetrate each other, there no longer exists the so-called pure market economy where does not need the government to play its role. In the middle of the 18th century, the capitalist economy was becoming increasingly mature with the market mechanism perfected and the primitive accumulation of capital completed. Then, western countries advocated the theory of "limited government", believing that the government safeguards the role of the market and the best government least intervenes the market. Nevertheless, after the great crash of capitalism in 1929, Keynesians believed that perfectly competitive markets did not exist in real life. Since the "invisible hand" cannot automatically guide the economy to a stable state, the government should take partial responsibility for regulating the relationship between

[1] Vito Tanzi, *Government Versus Markets: The Changing Economic Role of the State*, Chinese Edition, translated by Wang Yu et al., Beijing: The Commercial Press, 2014.

supply and demand, thus entering the stage of "full government intervention". But the "stagflation" in the 1970s and the two oil shocks showed that the government can sometimes be out of brake. Hence, the neoliberal economic theory became the dominating economics officially, emphasizing that the market mechanism should be the basic adjustment mechanism in the economic operation, thus strengthening the role of the market. However, the financial crisis in 2008 showed that the neoliberal economic theory was not a panacea, and then the new comprehensive market theory gradually took the mainstream position. The new comprehensive market theory holds that modern market economy should be an organic combination of modern market mechanism and modern government regulation and control, and their mutual cooperation, mutual compensation and mutual correction are the structure of normal economic operation and the basic force of maintaining economic order. The market failure caused by the deficiencies of the market itself can only be remedied by the limited government conforming to the internal economic requirements of the market. In addition, the government itself also has its boundary function, and inherent externalities and defects. The effective restrictions on the government are the basic requirement of modern civilized society, but its basic restriction mechanism comes from the maturity and development of market economy. In essence, modern capitalism has entered the stage of "mixed economy", in which neither the market nor the government can perform well by its individual role. Moderate government intervention should be carried out to achieve the best combination of the market and the government.

Looking through the development of China's "progressive" reform, it has always been centering around the core issue of how to understand and balance the relationship between the role of the government and that of the market. China's economic development has been undergoing different stages of exploration in the "progressive" reform, and the role of the market in allocating resources has been constantly enhanced, but the role of the government in different stages of reform and development has always been emphasized and brought into play to achieve the basic "symmetry" and balance between the two alternative forces. In the 1980s, it began to reduce government planning and cultivate market players. It emphasized planned economy supplemented by market regulation at first, and later the socialist planned commodity economy with the state regulating the market and the market guiding enterprises. In 1992, the 14th CPC National Congress stipulated that China's economic restructuring aimed at establishing the socialist market economy, allowing the market to play a basic role in allocating resources under the state's macro control. This major theoretical breakthrough played an extremely important role in guiding China's reform and opening up and its economic and social development.

After the 21st century, the socialist market economy has gradually improved, emphasizing "giving greater play to the basic role of the market in resource allocation" as well as "improving the state's macroeconomic regulation and the government's functions of social management and public services". In November 2013, the Third Plenary Session of the 18th CPC Central Committee further stated, "the focus of deepening reform comprehensively is economic restructuring, and the underlying issue is how to strike a balance between the role of the government and that of the market, and let the market play a decisive role in resource allocation and the government perform its functions better." This was the Party's new thoughts on developing socialist market economy and new understanding of the relationship between the government and the market. The role of the market was newly positioned with its "basic role" in allocating resources revised by its "decisive role". That the market plays a decisive role in allocating resources and the government performs its functions better is integrated with and cannot be separated from each other. It can be seen that in the process of economic restructuring it tends to be market-oriented, and the government has been effectively leveraging its role. The difference is that the market plays an increasingly direct role in resource allocation, and the government is gradually withdrawing from the direct allocation of resources, and shifting to macroeconomic regulation of the market by economic and legal means achieving indirect regulation of resource allocation. During this period, the central and local government institutional reforms were carried out for several times, thus forming the basic framework of socialist market economy, promoting rapid economic development and ensuring social stability and national security.

4.3.2 Giving better play to the role of the government to develop a powerful economy

As China has implemented socialist market economy, it should continue to give full play to the superiority of socialist system and let the Party and the government perform their positive functions. The government should play a more vigilant and effective role in supervision and regulation more than ever before. The Decision of the CPC Central Committee on Some Major Issues Concerning Comprehensively Deepening the Reform (hereinafter referred to as the Decision) adopted at the Third

Plenary Session of the 18th CPC Central Committee has put forth clear requirements for improving the functions of the government, emphasizing that scientific macro control and effective government governance are intrinsic requirements for giving full play to the advantages of the socialist market economy. The Decision has also made plans for improving the system of macro economic regulation and control, comprehensively performing government functions, deploying the optimal structure of government organizations. It stresses that the main role and responsibility of the government is to maintain the stability of macro economy, strengthen and optimize public services, ensure fair competition, strengthen market supervision, maintain market order, promote sustainable development and common prosperity, and intervene in situations where market failure occurs.

4.3.2.1 Improving the level of macro regulation

The market may show certain blindness in allocating resources, as sometimes it cannot effectively balance the relationship between total supply and total demand of social production, and resolve the issues caused by the unreasonable industrial structure. It is prone to have cyclical economy fluctuations, regional and systemic economic risks, and excessive imbalance in regional development. By playing a guiding role, the government can indirectly influence resource allocation, maintain stable, balanced and sound development of macro economy, and promote economic transformation and upgrading. By improving the macro control system, the government can further withdraw from micro economy, maintain the balance of economic aggregate, promote the coordination of major economic structures and the optimal layout of productive forces, mitigate the impact of economic cycle fluctuations, safeguard regional and systemic risks, stabilize market expectations, and achieve sustained and sound economic development.

The premise for a country to form competitive advantages in domestic and international markets is to select technologies and develop industries according to the comparative advantages determined by factor endowment structure. What enterprises pursue is profit, and only when the price signals are formed under the full competitive, perfect and effective market system can enable entrepreneurs to choose technologies and industries according to the comparative advantages determined by factor endowment at that time. Thus, the whole country has competitive advantages. As economic development is a process of constant changes in technology, industry, infrastructure and institutional structure, accordingly, infrastructure and upper system must be constantly improved with continuous technological innovations and industrial upgrading. However, the improvement of infrastructure and upper system cannot be promoted merely by entrepreneurs, but by the government to organize and coordinate the investment of relevant enterprises or by the government itself. In addition, the government needs to compensate for the risks and uncertainties faced by the leading enterprises in the process of technological innovations and industrial upgrading. Then, it can continue to innovate and upgrade technologies and industries smoothly according to the changes of comparative advantages. Therefore, the successful development of a country must base on market economy, coupled with an effective government.[1]

The cyclical fluctuation of economic prosperity and recession is the inevitable outcome of market economy. The stronger the market power is, the more intense the cyclical fluctuation will be, and the more serious the economic and social turbulence will be. In the past century, the great global economic depression in 1929, the collapse of the Bretton Woods system under the international financial system in the early 1970s, and the outbreak of the international financial crisis in 2008, these cyclical fluctuations have led to severe economic and political turbulence, and even conflicts and wars in the world. Objectively speaking, there will be big cyclical fluctuations in China's economic operation, as well as the fluctuations deeply affected by the world economy with the deepening of marketization and internationalization. Once the resonance of the two fluctuations occurs, the adverse consequences are incalculable to the economy and the society. Although the central government bears the heavy responsibility to maintain macro economic stability, and has accumulated many useful experience, however, it needs the relevant state departments to establish highly coordinated systems and institutions in fiscal, finance, trade and industry, in an effort to slow the vibration of domestic economic cycle, and avoid or reduce the impact of the big global cycle fluctuations.

4.3.2.2 Strengthening market supervision

Market failures are widespread. Due to externalities, information asymmetry, incomplete competition, natural monopoly and other factors, the market cannot effectively resolve the issues such as the supply of public goods, fair distribution etc., the government needs to play a complementary role by strengthening market supervision, maintaining market order, promoting sustainable development and common prosperity, and intervening in situations where market failure occurs. As the government possesses

---

[1] Justin Yifu Lin, "Countries in Transition Need Efficient Markets and Effective Governments", *China Economic Weekly*, 2014 (6).

all social members and coercive power, it shows some salient features in correcting the market: power of taxation, power of prohibition, power of punishment and advantages of transaction cost (the government has certain advantages of transaction cost in some market failures).[1] These features support the function of government supervision over enterprises. When the market plays a decisive role in resource allocation, the market competition will become more intense, and the function of government supervision needs to be strengthened. That is, strengthening supervision goes hand in hand with streamlining administration and delegating power. After drastically reducing the administrative approval, the government should strengthen the formulation and implementation of development strategies, planning, policies and standards, and strengthen the supervision over market activities. From the perspective of supervision process, the government should make differentiated supervision during the process and after the event. Supervision during the process focuses on strengthening the monitoring of market order, production safety, product quality, capital and credit, and timely identify issues and take appropriate measures to nip them in the head. Post-supervision focuses on strengthening the evaluation of performance, and investigating and dealing with violations of laws and regulations. From the perspective of supervision responsibility, the governments at all levels undertake the responsibility jointly. The central government focuses on strengthening the guidance of laws and policies, while local governments strive to eliminate various local protection barriers, unify market rules, maintain market order, eliminate market blockades and fragmentation, and create a fair market competition environment. The future trend is to move down its focus to strengthen the supervision power in cities and counties. From the perspective of supervision methods, comprehensive supervision and sampling supervision are combined with each other. Big data, cloud computing and other modern information technologies will be taken full advantage to address the issues of inefficient supervision in some industries. In the meanwhile, sampling supervision will be conducted to check some enterprises randomly, impose heavy fines on those found to produce and sell counterfeits and shoddy goods, and put them on a blacklist to increase the economic and social costs of violations of laws and regulations.

4.3.2.3 Improving public services

When the members of the Standing Committee of the Political Bureau of the 18th

[1] Joseph Stiglitz, *Why does Government Intervene in Economy: The Economic Role of the State*, Chinese Edition, translated by Zhang Bingwen, Beijing: China Materials Publishing House, 1998.

CPC Central Committee met with Chinese and foreign journalists, General Secretary Xi Jinping said, "Chinese people love life. They look forward to better education, more stable jobs, more income, more reliable social security, better medical and health services, more comfortable living conditions and a more beautiful environment. They want their children to grow up better, work better, and live better." Here, it involves the issue of public services, such as education, employment, social security and health care, whereby the government has the responsibility to address. Therefore, the government should shift its role to strengthening and improving public services, and ensure that the fruits of development benefit all the people in a more equitable manner. First, the boundary between government, society and market should be clarified. The government must focus on invigorating the market to offset downward economic pressure, and develop a tightly woven and sturdy safety net of basic public services, which covers the entire population to provide basic security for people's lives; meanwhile better leverage the role of the market and society in providing non-basic public services. Second, the government should do its best and do what it can do to provide public services. Although the government cannot provide the same level of public services as that in developed countries at this stage, it can proceed to do its best without going beyond the possibilities based on reality and national conditions. It can do more to help those in need to make things better, and ensure better basic public services now and sustainable for the future. Third, the government should innovate service contents and methods. It is necessary to change the way the government does all the work, guide non-government forces to participate in public services, provide more personalized and specialized public service products, and form a multi-level, multi-mode, and diversified pattern of public service supply. Fourth, it is necessary to actively promote government purchase of services. In principle, a competitive mechanism should be introduced to deal with the transactional management services, which can be purchased from the society through contracts and entrustments.

4.3.2.4 Strengthening environmental protection

In recent years, China's economic achievements have attracted worldwide attention and become an important driving engine for the world's economic growth. However, it should be noted that due to the blind pursuit of GDP, environmental pollution has become increasingly serious in some areas, and people's sense of happiness has not improved in accordance with the economic development. Xi Jinping pointed out at the Sixth group study session of the Political Bureau of the 18th CPC Central Committee:

"We should properly balance the relationship between economic development and ecological environment protection, firmly establish a concept that protecting the ecological environment means protecting productivity, and improving the ecological environment means developing productivity, more consciously promote green development, circulation, low carbon development, never at the expense of the environment for economic growth." Theoretically, the ecological environment belongs to the public goods shared by the whole people and one of the public services provided by the government. The Third Plenary Session of the 18th CPC Central Committee proposed to include environmental protection as one of the government functions, which further highlighted the necessity and urgency of the government to provide good ecological products for the people, and reflected the new connotation of government functions in the new era. The ninth part of the report to the 19th CPC National Congress made top-level design and systematic arrangements for accelerating institutional reforms for ecological progress and building a beautiful China. Then, the National Conference on Ecological and Environmental Protection made comprehensive planning for strengthening ecological and environmental protection and fighting against the critical battle of pollution prevention and control.

Market economy does not exclude the role of government, and through the role of government it can construct the social and political environment on which market economy depends. Market economy requires the government to perform its most fundamental function, which is to guarantee property rights and economic freedom. To establish an effective government, it is necessary to realize constitutional government, the rule of law, separation of powers and checks and balances, judicial independence, and provide basic institutional guarantee for people to participate in the administration, discussion and supervision of state affairs. In the history, the most serious infringement is by the government, the most serious corruption is by the power, and the most inefficient economy is to control economy. Therefore, constructing the government by the rule of law and service-oriented government is the inherent requirement for leveraging the advantage of the socialist market economy system.

4.3.3 Issues when operating government function

Government function refers to the responsibilities and functions that state administrative organs should undertake when managing national political, economic and social affairs according to the rule of law and the needs of social environment and social development. In short, government function is the responsibilities and functions when the government manages national affairs. Since the reform and opening up, the transformation of government functions has been constantly improved to adapt to extensive and profound changes that China's economic foundation has undergone. This provides an important guarantee for the reform, opening up and modernization drive. However, on the whole, the transformation of government function is still lagging behind. To be specific, the government remains direct resource allocation in large scope, intervenes much in micro economic subjects, provides insufficient public services, and remains relatively weak in market supervision and social management.

4.3.3.1 Process of adjusting government function

The evolution of the transformation of China's government function revolves around the word "transforming functions". In order to avoid repeating the old path of the reform of government institutions, that is, "streamlining—expanding—streamlining again—expanding again", in October 1987, the 13th CPC National Congress put forward the proposal of transforming government function. According to this thought, the following seven major institutional reforms by the Chinese government all carried out the thought of transforming functions, with transforming government functions as the core and fundamental way of institutional reforms.

It started from the institutional reform in 1988. In October 1984, the economic restructuring was carried out in China with the focus of reform and opening up transferring from the countryside to the city. With the deepening of the economic restructuring, the government functions formed under the traditional planned economy have become an obstacle to economic development and reform. Therefore, the Decision of the CPC Central Committee on Economic System Reform clearly pointed out that the government's economic management institutions, functions, methods and personnel allocation need to be readjusted and designed in accordance with the requirements of the socialist commodity economy. In 1987, the 13th CPC National Congress proposed that the key to the reform of government institutions was to transform government functions. It was necessary to adapt to the requirements of economic restructuring and the separation of government administration from enterprise management, merge and reduce specialized administrative departments, transform the way of government administration, and improve the macro control capacity of the government.

Then, the institutional reform in 1993. In 1992, the 14th CPC National Congress put forward that economic restructuring aimed at establishing the socialist market economy, and comprehensively expounded the transformation of government functions to meet the requirements of establishing the socialist market economy. In March 1993, the Second Plenary Session of the 14th CPC Central Committee deliberated and adopted the Plan for Reforming the Institutions of the Party and the Government. Afterwards, it pointed out that China should focus on transforming government functions, streamlining internal institutions and personnel, strengthening macro control and supervision functions, and weakening micro management functions, so as to meet the demands of establishing the socialist market economy.[1] Its key point is to transform government functions, and the fundamental way to transform government functions is to separate government administration from enterprise management. Therefore, it is necessary to strengthen the macro control and supervision departments of the central government, strengthen the functional departments of social administration, and gradually remove and merge specialized administrative departments. It is necessary to reduce the specific reviews and approvals and the direct management of enterprises, and ensure the balance between its macro management and its micro management. It is necessary to firmly delegate power that belongs to enterprises and let them resolve problems that they should, as the administrative functions of the government mainly include overall planning, policy mastery, information guidance, organization and coordination, provision of services, inspection and supervision.

Then, the institutional reform in 1998. The report to the 15th CPC National Congress in September 1997 pointed out: It is urgent to address the issues such as bloated government institutions, overstaffed personnel, no separation of government administration from enterprise management, and serious bureaucracy, as they directly hinder in-depth reforms and economic development, and affect the relationship between the Party and the people. We should take all factors into consideration, organize specialized forces, promptly formulate proper designs and actively promote it. The exposition on the political system reform in the 15th CPC National Congress directly promoted a new round of reform of government institutions that was launched in 1998.

Then, the institutional reform in 2003. The report to the 16th CPC National Congress pointed out that improving the government functions of economic regulation, market supervision, social management and public service is the new situation caused by adapting to deepening reform and opening up, and the new requirements by transforming and standardizing government functions. To this end, it is necessary to

---

[1] Institutional Reform Plan of the State Council Adopted at the First Session of the 8th National People's Congress, Apr. 19, 1993.

deepen the reform of the administrative system and form an administrative system that is standardized in conduct, coordinated in operation, fair and transparent, and clean and efficient. According to the requirements of the report of the 16th CPC National Congress, the institutional reforms by the State Council in 2003 included the following five key points, that is, deepening the reform of state-owned assets management system, improving the macro control system, perfecting the financial supervision system, continuing to promote the reform of circulation management system, and strengthening the construction of food safety and production safety supervision system.

Then, the institutional reform in 2008. The main tasks for deepening the institutional reforms by the State Council in 2008 are as follows: First, rationally allocate the functions of macro control departments, coordinate development planning, fiscal and taxation policies and monetary policies, and form a scientific, authoritative and efficient macro control system. Second, integrate and improve industry management systems, and better leverage the role of industry management departments in formulating and implementing industrial policies, industry planning and national standards. Third, improve energy, resources and environmental management systems, and promote its sustainable development. Fourth, straighten out the market supervision system, integrate law enforcement and supervision forces, and resolve the issues of multiple and duplicate law enforcement. Fifth, strengthen social management and the development of public service sectors, improve the management system, strengthen service functions, and ensure and improve the people's livelihood.

Then, the institutional reform in 2013. In 2013, the Decision of the CPC Central Committee on Some Major Issues Concerning Comprehensively Deepening Reform (hereinafter referred to as the Decision) adopted at the Third Plenary Session of the 18th CPC Central Committee further defined the functions of the government, namely macro control, market supervision, public services, social management and environment protection. The Decision pointed out that government functions should be fully and correctly performed, and the government should make efforts to further streamline administration and delegate power, deepen the reform of administrative review and approval system, and minimize the central government's management of micro affairs. For all economic activities that can be effectively regulated by the market mechanism, the government review and approval should be abolished, and those items that are subject to government review and approval should be managed in a standardized and efficient manner. For all economic and social matters that are directly addressed to the grassroots level, large in quantity and extensive in scope, they should be delegated to local governments and organizations for more convenience and effective management. Indeed, the Decision put forward such an important assertion that the market should play a decisive role in allocating resources, and the government should perform its functions better, which has become an important guiding ideology for comprehensively deepening reform in the new stage.

Then, the institutional reform in 2018. The Third Plenary Session of the 19th CPC Central Committee deliberated and adopted the Decision of the CPC Central Committee on Deepening the Reform of the Party and State Institutions and the Plan for Deepening the Reform of the Party and State Institutions. The plenum pointed out that it was an important task to deepen the reform of the Party and state institutions by transforming government functions and optimizing the establishment of government institutions and its functional configuration. Resolute efforts should be made to remove the institutional drawbacks that restrict the market to play a decisive role in allocating resources and the government to perform its functions better. Revolving around the development of high quality, efforts should be made to develop economic modernization system, adjust and optimize government functions, rationalize the configuration of macro management functions, further deepen the reform of streamlining administration and delegating power, perfect market supervision and law enforcement system, reform the natural resources and ecological environment management system, improve the system for managing public services, strengthen supervision during the process and after business operations, improve administrative efficiency, comprehensively improve government effectiveness, and build a service-oriented government that the people are satisfied with.

4.3.3.2 Main issues in transforming government function

Great achievements have been made in China's economic restructuring. The transformation of government functions has greatly contributed to establishing and improving the socialist market economy and promoting the reform and opening up. Since the reform and opening up, with the continuous development of China's socialist market economy, government functions have correspondingly transformed, which mainly manifests in reducing the government's administrative control, exerting government functions and powers subject to more constraints of laws and regulations, and laying more emphasis on providing public services etc. However, government functions have not changed in its place. On the one hand, the government's monopolizing resources leads to anti-market practices, such as power economy, corruption of power-rent-seeking and so on. On the other hand, the government's abandoning some basic functions leads to the excessive marketization of public services, such as in education, health, infrastructure etc. Moreover, it was insufficient to implement some functions that the government was supposed to perform, such as establishing and improving sound legal system, unemployment security system, and protecting ecological resources and environment and so on. The contradiction between these problems and the development of socialist market economy is increasingly prominent, far from meeting the demands of building a harmonious society. The main issues that exist in China's government functions are presented as follows:

First, the "offside, dislocation and absence" of government functions. At present, the offside and dislocation of government functions is serious. Government departments still manage many affairs that they shouldn't do and they can't properly handle. The phenomenon that the government directly participates in the production and management of enterprises and intervenes in micro economic activities is serious and common. The government acts as the investor of state-owned enterprises, and meanwhile supervises and manages the production and operation of enterprises. It does not separate government functions from enterprise management, and government administration from state assets management, which is quite different from the government's commitment to create a harmonious environment for social organizations. For example, excessive government approval, as Li Keqiang mentioned, is suspected of rent-seeking. For another example, excessive intervention in land sales is a matter of "umpire participation in the game". The "offside" of government functions mainly manifests as follows: firstly, direct intervention in micro economic activities; secondly, many local protections for benefits; thirdly, the pursuit of short-term achievements; fourthly, overdoing social affairs. In contrast, there are a lot that need the government to play its due role in the market, such as food and drug supervision, cheap sale of state-owned assets, and various tax evasion by real estate developers. However, many local governments did not leverage its due role, seeking for no faults for service instead. That is, the "absence" of government functions mainly manifests as follows: firstly, out-of-place macro control and market supervision; secondly, inadequate protection of environmental resources; thirdly, insufficient overall planning and coordination; fourthly, insufficient supply and unfair distribution of public services.

Second, the government management system is not smooth. Due to the lack of advanced institutional design and arrangement, there appear some issues such as bloated government institutions, overfine division of labor etc. As a result, some departments have overlapping functions, unreasonable division of responsibilities and inconsistent responsibilities and powers, which has led to insufficient government management and low efficiency. For example, social security and insurance are managed both by civil administration and by social security departments; the health sector is managed by multiple departments. Due to the overcentralized power in some departments and posts coupled with lack of institutional norms, there appear inadequate and unchecked supervisions, thus creating space for rent-seeking and corruption. Due to the unclear powers between the central government and local governments, and between the local governments at all levels, especially in terms of the financial power and personnel power, there appear many contradictions that the local agencies are established highly corresponding to that of the central government, resulting in overlapping organizations and increasing administrative costs. Meanwhile, many central agencies co-exist with similar functions. As a result, the responsibilities at different levels are not clearly clarified, and they compete for managing affairs with interest and pass the buck to each other for not bearing their due responsibilities. This brought loss to the benefits of the people. For example, the central government institutions have excessive control over local affairs, such as funding arrangements, institutional setup and internal administrative division, while failing to manage the trans-regional issues such as the governance of major cross-regional rivers, which shows inadequacy in top-level design. Another is the issue of distribution system. The market is not almighty and the distribution of wealth must be optimized through institutions. Among more than 30 developed countries in the world, the gap between the rich and the poor in Japan, Republic of Korea, Germany, France and the Five Nordic countries is not large. However, the Gini coefficient represented by the United States and the United Kingdom is much larger, and several BRICS countries also have high Gini coefficient, which is closely related to their economic system, especially their economic distribution system. Lower taxes on capital, for example, will inevitably lead to a large gap between the rich and the poor, while doing little to boost economic growth.

Third, effective market supervision and governance are insufficient. Due to the imperfect laws and rules for regulating market order, some issues emerge in their implementation, such as lax law enforcement, lax management, lax discipline, and even sometimes disobeying the law and no punishment to the illegal cases. All these result in the government's off-sided or insufficient market supervision, making the existing laws, rules and systems only in name. Only with a well-regulated market order and strict supervision can it encourage true entrepreneurship, invigorate enterprises and enhance their social responsibility.

Fourth, the government has excessive intervention in micro economy, especially in state-owned enterprises, and an effective state-owned assets management system has not taken shape. The administrative review and approval system, which was formed during the period of planned economy and to some extent expanded in the period of economic transition to market economy, still exists widely. In particular, the administrative review and approval system in setting up enterprises, appointing and removing leaders, and developing investments and foreign trade etc., needs to be cleaned up and reduced. However, it should be noted that in the process of promoting the reform of state-owned enterprises, implementing some related policies has produced side effects of strengthening administrative review and approval and casework intervention. The irrational distribution of state-owned economy and the overstretched management remain prominent. A fair competitive environment has not taken shape due to many restrictions on non-public economy. The functions between the government's public management and the owner of state-owned assets remain confused without fundamental changes. Therefore, it has become an important and urgent issue to construct a new state-owned assets management and operation system for deepening the reform of state-owned enterprises.

4.3.4 Improving government governance

It is the intrinsic requirement to emphasize scientific macro control and effective government governance by giving full play to the socialist market economy. Government governance is the most important body of national governance, and the level of government governance directly determines the national governance performance. To modernize China's governance system and capacity and let the government perform its functions better, it is necessary to continue to improve the government governance.

4.3.4.1 Reducing administrative review and approval

The primary task of transforming government functions is to reduce administrative review and approval of items as a breakthrough, streamline administration and delegate power. The government should delegate power that should be delegated to, minimize its role in micro economic management, and refrain from getting involved in the economic activities that it can not manage well and should not fall within its purview, and that the market can regulate effectively. The government should let the market further play a decisive role in allocating resource, stimulate the creative vitality of market players, and strengthen the internal driving force for economic development.

Efforts should be made to adhere to market-oriented reform, significantly reduce the government's direct allocation of resources, minimize the central government's management of micro affairs. Efforts should be made to resolutely implement the "Three Shoulds" proposed at the Third Plenary Session of the 18th CPC Central Committee, that is, for all economic activities that can be effectively regulated by the market mechanism, the government review and approval should be abolished; for all economic and social matters that are directly addressed to the grassroots level, large in quantity and extensive in scope, they should be delegated to local governments and organizations for more convenience and effective management. To deepen the reform of the investment system, all investment projects should be determined by enterprises in accordance with laws and regulations, except those related to national security, ecological security, the distribution of major productive forces, the development of strategic resources, and major public interests. Efforts should be made to reduce and standardize preliminary review and approval, reduce qualification permits and administrative fees. Efforts should be made to encourage governments at all levels to implement inventory management for administrative review and approval, establish standardized and transparent procedures for items on the list, and provide efficient and quality services. The market and non-government entities will make decisions independently in accordance with the law. Enterprises can do what is not prohibited by the law, and the government cannot do what is not authorized by the law. In the meantime, efforts should be intensified to fully mobilize the two initiatives by delegating power to local governments and giving full play to the comparative advantages of local governments.

4.3.4.2 Performing due economic functions of the government

Efforts should be made to further separate government administration from enterprise management, government administration from state assets management, government administration from social affairs, government administration from social organizations, and take the "four separations" as the fundamental way to transform government functions. The separation of government administration from enterprise management, and government administration from state assets management mainly manifested in the separation between state-owned assets management and that of the government. In terms of reform, it is the separation of government administration from enterprise management, and government administration from state assets management that contribute to the achievements made by state-owned enterprises. However, the performance in this regard has not yet completed and needs to be vigorously pushed forward. Efforts should be made to further separate government administration from enterprise management and relax some market-based areas. For example, the reform of prices of factors, such as oil price, electricity price, interest rates and land prices, has not yet been fully market-based. Efforts should be made to further separate government administration from state assets management, and government administration from social affairs; and the investment and personnel rights should be further delegated to the central state-owned enterprises in accordance with the Company Law of the People's Republic of China. For example, the power to resolve the issue of integrating the profits of the central state-owned enterprises, including financial enterprises, into the state budget. In the reform of public institutions, more efforts should be made to both meet the requirements of category-based reform and separate government administration from state assets management, and government administration from social affairs. Apart from its performing administrative functions, the power should also be delegated to public institutions to promote the separation of state assets from non-operational state assets, such as those in the cultural, educational and health sectors. Efforts should also be made to separate government administration from social organizations and form a new mechanism for multiple parties to participate in transforming government functions. For sure, people have high expectations for transforming government functions, letting the government perform its functions better, and modernizing China's governance system and capacity. To improve government governance, it is indispensable to understand what the people think, respect their initiative, and mobilize their enthusiasm for government reforms, so as to form a new mechanism for multi-party participation in promoting the transformation of government functions. First, establish a mechanism for public participation in government reforms. It is necessary to extensively listen to the opinions and suggestions of the people, promptly summarize the fresh experience by the people on the front lines, so as to ensure that the transformation of government functions meets the expectations of the people. Second, establish a mechanism for coordinating interests. As the reform has entered a deeper water zone, the adjustment of government functions will inevitably be accompanied by the huge adjustment of the pattern of interests. Efforts should be made to handle interests that are complex and difficult to balance by opening up channels for expressing the opinions, improving the system of public hearings and building platforms for dialogue. Third, establish the mechanism for theoretical research, publicity and guidance. In the *Explanatory Notes for the Decision of the CPC Central Committee on Some Major Issues concerning Comprehensively Deepening Reform*, Xi Jinping pointed out, "in the process of comprehensively deepening reform, we should strengthen top-level design and overall planning, and strengthen the study to make various reforms more relevant, systematic and feasible." To improve the government governance, it is necessary to tackle theoretical problems and promote the development of think tanks, so as to enhance self-confidence and build consensus through rational, scientific research that suits China's national conditions. Through theoretical interpretation and public opinion guidance to create good atmosphere, it can make the improvement of government governance a process of participation, coordination and benefit sharing by all parties.

4.3.4.3 Improving legal administration

Xi Jinping stressed, "we should put more emphasis on developing governance capacity, enhancing awareness of handling affairs in accordance with the systems and the laws, govern the country well through the systems and the laws, and turn institutional strengths in all aspects into efficiency in governing the country."[1] To be specific, it is necessary to adapt to the contemporary changes, reform systems and institutions, and laws and regulations that do not adapt to the requirements of practical development, constantly build new systems and institutions, and laws and regulations, and build a law-based government in which its operation and conduct are subject to legal norms and constraints.

On the one hand, government functions must be clarified through legislation to balance the relationship between the government and the market, government and enterprises, government and society, government and citizens. On the other hand, the relationship between the central government and the local governments must be gradually institutionalized, and the scope of their respective powers, the manner of their power operations, their responsibilities and obligations and benefit allocation structure must be clarified through legislation, so as to form the legal power and interest relationship between the central government and the local governments, and their long-term stable trustable relationship rather than individual relationship on this basis.[2] It is necessary to balance the relationship between the central government and the local

---

[1] Xi Jinping, "We Must Unite our Thinking in the Spirit of the Third Plenary Session of the 18th CPC Central Committee", *People's Daily*, Jan. 1, 2014.

[2] Wang Puju, *The Role of Government in Economic System Transformation*, Beijing: Xinhua Publishing House, 2001.

governments, define government functions by enumeration to make it as detailed, comprehensive and accurate as possible, and improve the institutionalization, standardization and legalization of government governance, so as to provide legal guarantee for the government to perform its functions better. In addition, it is necessary to strengthen the restraint of administrative law enforcement, prevent the abuse of power, improve the capacity of governments at all levels to apply law-based thinking and approaches, so as to promote the government functions to transform from "management" to "governance".

4.3.4.4 Optimizing the configuration of government institutions

Indeed, the reform of government institutions should be deepened to improve the government governance and transform government functions. It is necessary to optimize the configuration of government institutions and government functions in accordance with the requirements that decision-making, execution and supervision powers are restricted and coordinated with each other. The reason is that new issues caused by the "absence, offside or dislocation" of government functions may appear, especially after the great achievements made by comprehensively deepening the reform. Accordingly, it is necessary to revamp processes and tighten performance management. Efforts should be made to establish an administrative system in which institutions are set up in a reasonable and efficient manner, and departments have a sound responsibility system with appropriate staff scale, reasonably-divided government responsibilities at the upper and lower levels, clear boundaries of different powers, well-matched financial affairs, consistent powers and responsibilities, reasonable division of labor, scientific decision-making, smooth implementation, powerful supervision and unimpeded decrees.

Next, the system of large government departments should conform to the principle of streamlining, unity and efficiency, which is beneficial to optimize the allocation of administrative resources and improve administrative efficiency. Therefore, efforts should be made to actively yet prudently implement the system of large government departments, straighten out the relationship between their responsibilities, and reduce overlapping responsibilities and disputes among them. With the continuous improvement of IT application, it is possible to explore and promote the reform of county (city) system under direct provincial administration. Efforts should also be made to strictly control authorized strength, appoint leading officials and cadres in accordance with the prescribed posts, reduce the number of organizational units and posts of officials, and control the total number of personnel supported by government finance.

4.4 Conducting in-depth studies on developing a powerful economy after realizing a moderately prosperous society in all respects

The goal of building a moderately prosperous society in all respects can be achieved during the 13th Five-year Plan period. When the goal has been realized by 2020, China, as a civilized and developing socialist country with a long history, will become a country that has basically realized industrialization, that has significantly enhanced comprehensive national strength, and that has ranked the top among countries in the world in terms of its overall scale in the domestic market. China has become a country where the people are getting richer, the quality of people's life has dramatically improved and the ecological environment is sound. It has been the foothold and starting point for Chinese people to move forward to develop China into an economic powerhouse after completing the building of a moderately prosperous society in all respects by 2020. Under this situation, a rational analysis is a must.

4.4.1 The situations facing China's economic development after realizing a moderately prosperous society in all respects

After completing the building of a moderately prosperous society in all respects, China will still facing both opportunities and challenges; meanwhile, the world will witness a rapidly rising China that is more confident, powerful and open wider. China will further development, expand international influence, and enter an important period of developing a powerful economy. All in all, China has stood up at the center of the world stage with its future development still in an important period of both strategic opportunities and increasing risks and challenges.

From the international perspective, under the general trend of world peace and development, China still has favorable conditions for sustained development during the important period of strategic opportunities. In recent years, China has made significant progress in its relationship with major countries, neighboring countries and developing countries, constantly deepened its interdependence with the world and increased its influence in the world. For one thing, China has become the principal trading partner of over 130 countries in the world. China's development has provided opportunities to the world, and most of countries in the world look forward to benefiting from China's development and sharing development and prosperity with China. For another, the constant changes in global economic governance have provided opportunities for China to participate in formulating international rules. The global economic downturn and the financial crisis in developed economies have provided opportunities for China to expand its overseas interests.[1] People in the world have a growing desire for peace and development, and the possibility of world war or local war is very tiny. China has greatly increased its military strength, economic strength and political influence as well. In a word, China will embrace new opportunities for common development with the rest of the world.

From the domestic perspective, China has entered the new normal in economic and social development. Over 40 years of reform and opening up, China's progress has laid an important foundation for its future development. The Chinese people have already made a historic leap from poverty to basic food and clothing, and then to overall prosperity, and accumulated abundant material wealth and scored remarkable achievements in all areas of development. The national economy has rapidly developed, economic strength constantly enhanced, and people's living standards significantly improved. Science and technology are advancing by leaps and bounds, and national defense has made major achievements. China's overall national strength has significantly increased and its international standing has increasingly improved. China has been steadily growing in its economic aggregate since 2010, ranking the second in the world, surpassing that of Japan and next only to that of the United States, and now far higher than that of Japan and European countries and other traditional developed countries. In the meantime, China's economic development remains and will maintain a medium-high growth rate for a long time to come, far ahead of other major economies in the world, and the gap with the world's largest economy, the United States, is getting smaller and smaller. Steady progress has been made in developing new urbanization, and coordinated development among regions has become more reasonable and scientific. The Belt and Road Initiative, the Beijing-Tianjin-Hebei Coordinated Development strategy, and the Yangtze Economic Belt strategy have been implemented to create new growth poles of the regional economy. Efforts have been made to adhere to the overall regional strategy of developing western China, revitalizing northeast China, promoting the rising of central China, and taking initiative in developing eastern China, and a

[1] See China Center for International Economic Exchanges, A Thorough Research on "the Development after Finishing Building a Moderately Prosperous Society in all Respects", 2016.

number of new regional centers are emerging.

4.4.1.1 Favorable factors for China's economic development

First, China has at least two stable basic support conditions for economic development. One is that China has huge market demand, which is determined by the fact that China has the largest population in the world, thus creating huge space for its economic development. A large population directly supports economic development at least in three aspects: The first is equal demand. There are significant differences between urban and rural areas and between regions in terms of actual access to production, consumption, individual needs or public services, and filling such gaps means huge market space. The second is the process of transformation. As China is now undergoing a transformation from a developing country to a relatively developed one, the supply brought by industrialization, urbanization and IT application will create huge space for its economic development. The third is the substitution between internal and external. If the domestic market can provide more high-quality products, it can realize not only the substitution for products produced by foreign enterprises, but the substitution of Chinese consumers' buying products abroad, which also means huge market space. Another is that China has the strong CPC leadership over management and organizational capacity, which is determined by the basic national situations of China's socialist system. This not only enables the Chinese people to pool strengths and resources to overcome difficulties and handle emergency treatment, but helps to encourage innovation in supply and expansion in demand on the whole, effectively suppress interference and grip, and promote the allocation of resource elements in a wider range, as well as inter-regional and inter-enterprise cooperation. It is due to the two basic supporting conditions that have underpinned China's steady economic growth and made all the predictions over the decades about China's economic collapse false or nonsense. Unless influenced by special non-economic factors, China's economic development that are supported by these two basic conditions will not experience great ups and downs in the future.

Second, there are many positive factors that support China's economic progress while maintaining stability. One is that the related policies can gradually release effects under its intergrated forces with rich contents. In recent years, a series of major policies, reforms, projects and programs have been introduced with an aim to ensure steady growth, adjust economic structure and improve people's livelihood, which cover a wide range of areas and are highly targeted. The supporting effects by these major measures on economic development will gradually come into play. Another is that China has deepened economic transformation, and accelerated the development of new economy and the efforts to fostering new growth drivers on the basis of innovations. The new energy of economic development continues to be accumulated and will gradually occupy dominant position. On the whole, all these will be conducive to better further economic development, and there are sufficient and strong favorable conditions to support steady economic progress and improvement.

4.4.1.2 The environment facing domestic economic development

Due to over years of accumulated economic and social problems, social contradictions in China are on the rise. The unbalanced, uncoordinated and unsustainable development remains serious, the innovation capacity for science and technology weak, the industrial structure irrational, the mode of development extensive, and the gaps between urban and rural development and between individual income distributions wide. The social contradictions have significantly increased. On the whole, China is facing unprecedented strategic challenges for further development, although it has made great achievements and experience over 40 years of reform and opening up, and a new system has taken shape.

Firstly, the seriousness of the concentrated issues. Since the reform and opening up, the historical process of developing industrialization, IT application, urbanization, marketization and internationalization has been concentrated in a short period. This caused the concentrated issues and contradictions in a relatively short period in China, which emerged in different development stages in developed countries within two or three hundred years. As China has entered a new historical stage of comprehensively deepening reform and opening up after entering a moderately prosperous society, these difficulties, issues and contradictions may become more obvious, prominent, acute and serious, putting unprecedented pressure on comprehensively deepening reform and opening up as well as economic and social development.

Secondly, the complexity brought by multiple interwoven contradictions. In the course of comprehensively deepening reform and opening up, China will face difficulties, contradictions and issues that have not been fully resolved in the previous development or newly emerged in the course of new development, some of which are caused by the influence of the original system factors, some formed by the system reforms, and some produced and to be produced in the process of improving new system. It matters not only for the coordinated development of economy, politics, culture, society and ecology, but for strengthening the Party's self-construction and governing capacity. This makes the present and future development face extremely complex contradictions.

Finally, the risks caused by the increasing difficulties of interest coordination. To deal with various difficulties, issues and contradictions, and maintain sustainable development, it is necessary to coordinate deep interest relations in different aspects, different areas, different regions and different groups, coordinate the comprehensive relationship between deepening economic restructuring and deepening the reforms of political system, cultural system and social system, coordinate internal links in systems, coordinate the relationship between breaking the original system and improving new system, coordinate the relationship between deepening the system reform and promoting economic development, political development, cultural development, social development and ecological progress, coordinate the relationship between improving systems, promoting development, maintaining stability and opening wider to the outside world, promoting the development of world peace, and so on. It is obvious that the difficulties of coordinating these issues and contradictions have greatly increased, and any imprudence may cause adverse reactions to further deepen reform in certain or larger scope. In a sense, the risks facing new developments are no less than ever before.

4.4.2 Policies and proposals for developing China into economic powerhouse

When it comes to China's economic development, a prominent feature is that it moves constant stride towards a new stage of development. Therefore, it is of great significance to grasp the attributes and characteristics of developing China into an economic powerhouse after completing the building of a moderately prosperous society in all respects and establish the corresponding development strategies.

4.4.2.1 Making in-depth review of characteristics of developing China into economic powerhouse

History is the mirror of success and failure. Since the 15th century, Portugal, Spain, Netherlands, the United Kingdom, France, Germany, Japan, Russia and the United States have successively become the world's economic powerhouses. Although the United States, Japan and Germany have been so-called economic powerhouses in the world, colonial expansion and wealth plunder and other violent ways accompanied by their rising process. Nowadays, against the backdrop of current economic globalization and the world pattern of multi-polarization, the era when the rising of an economic powerhouse by relying on foreign colonial expansion has passed. However, major research topics should be made to generalize the inherent regularity and inevitability of the rising of an economic powerhouse and its beneficial enlightenment. By doing so, it can deepen the understanding of developing China into an economic powerhouse to achieve our goal.

4.4.2.2 Putting forward the strategic vision of developing China into economic powerhouse

We should have a rational understanding of the negative voices in the international community, and fully understand the concerns over building China into an economic powerhouse in the domestic theoretical and policy circles. However, it should be realized that China has entered a critical period from a major economy towards developing an economic powerhouse, and there is no choice but to do it. In terms of economic strategy, realizing the Chinese Dream means accelerating efforts to realize the strategic goal from a major economy to an economic powerhouse on the basis of realizing a moderately prosperous society in all respects. In other words, the strategic vision and goal of building an economic powerhouse really concretes China's Dream in the economic field, which is in line with China's Dream.

4.4.2.3 Speeding up implementing innovation-driven strategy

Strong innovation capacity in science and technology provides a strategic support for developing an economic powerhouse. Therefore, it must be placed at the core of developing an economic powerhouse. Indeed, China has implemented the "863" Project, the national support plans for science and technology, and major scientific and technologic projects, and set up the technologic innovation funds for small and medium-sized enterprises, venture capital funds for small and medium-sized enterprises etc. However, objectively speaking, China's industrial competitiveness is not strong enough to reverse the passive situation of its core technologies. It is suggested that efforts should be made to strengthen the source support for enterprise technological innovation, and encourage enterprises to set up research and development institutions based on market demands; efforts should be made to strengthen supports for developing scientific and technologic service industry, so as to provide market-oriented services from product research and development to consumer terminals; efforts should be made to strengthen open scientific and technological innovation, and plan and promote innovation from a global perspective.

4.4.2.4 Speeding up China's industrial development

A world economic powerhouse is bound to have a high-end industrial structure.

From a global perspective, a country will thrive when its industry thrives, and a country will become strong when its industry is strong. From the perspective of China's basic national situations, it has vast population but limited arable land, which makes its agricultural industry uncompetitive in the world, whereas its service sector can greatly develop only when the country has reached a high level of economic development. So, it is suggested that measures and policies should be further implemented to develop strategic emerging industries; various policy objectives should be further carried out to develop advanced manufacturing industries; various measures should be further implemented to accelerate the transformation and upgrading of traditional industries and promote the growth and expansion of productive service sectors.

4.4.2.5 Speeding up China's financial development

One of basic connotations for being an economic powerhouse goes to that the currency of a country can be freely convertible and accepted by international exchanges, and become the foreign exchange reserve currency of other countries; meanwhile, it has relatively large-scale financial assets and a developed, stable financial system. So, it is suggested that accelerated efforts be made to develop international financial centers in China's core cities, and support the establishment of international financial centers in metropolises, such as Shanghai and Beijing. Accelerated efforts should be made to promote interest rate liberalization and exchange rate market reform, and achieve the goal of developing China from a major country to one country powerful in finance, so as to provide strategic supports for developing China into an economic powerhouse.

4.4.2.6 Fully implementing the strategy of developing China through science and education

An economic powerhouse in the world is bound to be a country powerful in human resources. As the largest developing country with the largest population in the world, China has already been a large country rich yet not powerful in human resources. Therefore, it is important to respect labor, knowledge, talents and creation, and accelerate efforts to establish the strategy of training competent personnel as a priority to build a large contingent of such personnel, and turn China from a country with large human resources into one with a large pool of competent professionals. It is suggested that comprehensive reform should be further deepened in the field of education and innovate the personnel training systems and mechanisms of universities and research institutes. The reform of medical and health care system should be further deepened to promote the vertical flow of high-quality medical resources, and improve the nutritional supply of the Chinese population.

4.4.2.7 Speeding up China's maritime development

The ocean is the bloodline and bridge that connect the world's economies. It is a historical rule that "when oceans thrive, then the world gains its strength and flourishes". Throughout the development history of the world powerhouse, it is in essence the history of the rising of maritime powerhouse. It is suggested that the Marine economy should be developed to make it new growth force. The maritime administration system and maritime law enforcement system should be strengthened. Efforts should be made to encourage Marine science and technology to be innovation-led, and resolutely safeguard China's maritime rights and interests.

4.4.2.8 Actively developing China into a country powerful in trade

The rising of the world's economic powerhouses shows that no country can exemplify its rising in a closed economic system. Actually, the important external factors that affect the rising of the great powerhouses are open global markets, in-depth development of free trade, the formation of the world economic system, and the linkage of international industrial structure. It is suggested that equal importance should be attached to export and import to form new advantages in the export competition with technology, brand, quality and services as the core. Accelerated efforts should be made to build the Silk Road Economic Belt and the Maritime Silk Road, and free trade zones such as Shanghai Free Trade Zone, Guangdong Free Trade Zone, Tianjin Free Trade Zone, Fujian Free Trade Zone, Liaoning Free Trade Zone, Zhejiang Free Trade Zone, Henan Free Trade Zone, Hubei Free Trade Zone, Chongqing Free Trade Zone, Sichuan Free Trade Zone, Shannxi Free Trade Zone etc. Full efforts should be made to develop Hainan province into a pilot free trade zone, and support it for gradually exploring and steadily advancing the development of a free trade port with Chinese characteristics.

Bibliography

[1] Amartya Sen, *From Growth to Development*, Chinese Edition, translated by Wu xiaoying, et al., Beijing: China Renmin University Press, 2015.

[2] Aoki Masahiko, Wu Jinlian, *The Chinese Economy: A New Transition*, Chinese Edition, translated by Yao Zhimin, et al., Jiangsu: Yilin Press, 2014.

[3] Ayres Robert, *Turning Point: The End of Growth Paradigm*, Chinese Edition, translated by Dai Xingyi, Huang Wenfang, Shanghai: Shanghai Translation Publishing House, 2001.

[4] Bi Jiyao, Zhang Zheren, and Li Wei, "Create a New Round of High-level Opening Up", *Qiushi*, 2017(7).

[5] Cai Fang, "Adhering to the People-centered Development Philosophy", *People's Daily*, Aug. 3, 2016.

[6] Cai Fang, Chinese Economy: How to Cross the "Low Middle Income Trap", *Journal of Graduate School of Chinese Academy of Social Sciences*, 2008(1).

[7] Cai Fang, "Conditions of Narrowing Income Gap: The Theory of Economic Development and Chinese Experience", *Gansu Social Sciences*, 2007(6).

[8] Cai Fang, *Demystifying the Economic Growth in Transition China*, Beijing: China Social Sciences Press, 2014.

[9] Chang Xiuze, *Inclusive Reform Theory*, Beijing: Economic Science Press, 2013.

[10] Chang Xiuze, *Innovation Strategy for National Construction*, Beijing: Xue Xi Press, 2013.

[11] Chen Jiagui, Huang Qunhui, et al., *National Conditions of the Large Industrial Country and Strategy of the Powerful Industrial Country*, Beijing: Social Sciences Academic Press, 2012.

[12] Chi Fulin, *Bonus from Reforms*, Beijing: China Economy Publishing House, 2013.

[13] Chi Fulin, *The Second Reform: the Path to a Stronger China in Future 30 Years*, Beijing: China Economy Publishing House, 2010.

[14] Chi Fulin, *A Decisive Choice to Advance Economic Transition 2020: Trends of and Challenges for China's Economic Transition and Upgrading*, Beijing: China Economy Publishing House, 2015.

[15] Compiling Group, *Major Monographic Study on the 13th Five-year Plan Proposal*, Beijing: China Market Press, 2016.

[16] Department of Economics Teaching and Research, National Academy of Governance, *China's New Normal of Economy*, Beijing: People's Publishing House, 2015.

[17] Department of Economics Teaching and Research, National Academy of Governance, *China's Supply-side Structural Reform*, Beijing: People's Publishing House, 2016.

[18] Department of Economics Teaching and Research, National Academy of Governance, *New Orientation of China's Economy*, Beijing: People's Publishing House, 2017.

[19] Fan Gang, *Changes Brought by System for China*, Beijing: China CITIC Press, 2014.

[20] Fan Jida, "Enhance Capacity for Primary-level Governance: Pave the way for China towards Economic Powerhouse", *China Economic Times*, Dec. 31, 2013.

[21] Feng Qiaobin, "Urgency of Establishing Management System of Local Government Debt", *China Reform*, 2013(11).

[22] Gao Peiyong, *Reform of Fiscal System and Modernization of State Governance*, Beijing: Social Sciences Academic Press, 2015.

[23] Gu Shengzu, *Innovation-driven Strategy and Economic Transformation*, Beijing: People's Publishing House, 2013.

[24] Han Changfu, "We Shall Deepen Agricultural Supply-side Structural Reform", *Farmers' Daily*, May 13, 2016.

[25] Han Kang, *Research for Chinses Market Model*, Beijing: Economic Science Press, 2010.

[26] Han Kang, "The Decisive Role of Market in Resource Distribution", *The Journal of Shanghai Administration Institute*, 2014, 15(3).

[27] Han Kang, "We Need to be Ready for a Protracted War on Pains in China's Economic Transition", *Journal of Chinese Academy of Governance*, 2016(2).

[28] Hong Yinxing, "China's Transformation of Economic Development Mode

after becoming World's Big Economy", *Contemporary Economic Research*, 2010(12).

[29] Hong Yinxing, *Order and Norm of Market*, Shanghai: Truth & Wisdom Press, Shanghai SDX Joint Publishing Company, Shanghai People's Publishing House, 2015.

[30] Hu An'gang, *China in* 2030: *March Toward Common Prosperity*, Beijing: China Renmin University Press, 2011.

[31] Hu An'gang, *Chinese Political and Economic History* (*1949-1979*) (Second Edition), Beijing: Tsinghua University Press, 2012.

[32] Hu An'gang, *Modernization of China's Governance*, Beijing: China Renmin University Press, 2014.

[33] Hu An'gang, Zhou Shaojie, and Ren Hao, "Supply-side Structural Reform: The Strategic Innovations Towards Adapting to and Leading China's New Normal Status", *Journal of Tsinghua University* (*Philosophy and Social Sciences*), 2016, 31(2).

[34] Huang Qunhui, "Deepen Industrial Supply-side Structural Reform Substantially", *Economic Daily*, Apr. 28, 2016.

[35] Hua Sheng, *The Right and Undone of China's Reform*, Beijing: The Oriental Press, 2012.

[36] Jia Kang, Su Jingchun, *New Supply-side Economics*, Taiyuan: Shanxi Economy Press, 2016.

[37] Jiang Bixin, "Promote the Modernization of National Governance System and Governance Capacity", *Guangming Daily*, Nov. 15, 2013.

[38] Jian Xinhua, He Zhiyang, and Huang Kun, *China's Urbanization and Characteristic Road to Urbanization*, Jinan: Shandong People's Publishing House, 2009.

[39] Jian Xinhua, Huang Kun, "Empirical Analysis and Forecast of the Level and Speed of Urbanization in China", *Economic Research Journal*, 2010, 45(3).

[40] Jin Bei, "Study on the New Normal of Chinese Economic Development", *China Industrial Economics*, 2015(1).

[41] John C. H. Fei, Ranis Gustav, *Growth and Development from An Evolutionary Perspective*, Chinese Edition, translated by Hong Yinxing, Zheng Jianghuai, Beijing: The Commercial Press, 2014.

[42] Justin Yifu Lin, "Miracle of China's Economic Development Will Continue", *Qiushi*, 2012(8).

[43] Justin Yifu Lin, *New Structural Economics*, Beijing: Peking University Press, 2012.

[44] Justin Yifu Lin, *There's No Textbook Paradigm for Interpreting the Chinese*

Economy, Beijing: Social Sciences Academic Press, 2008.

[45] Justin Yifu Lin, Cai Fang, and Li Zhou, *China's Miracle: Development Strategy and Economic Reform*, Shanghai: Truth & Wisdom Press, 1994.

[46] Kissinger, Henry, *On China*, Beijing: China CITIC Press, 2002.

[47] Kissinger, Henry, *World Order*, Beijing: China CITIC Press, 2015.

[48] Kong Jingyuan, "The International Background, Causation Illustration and China Solution of Middle Income Trap", *Reform*, 2011, (10).

[49] Kuang Xianming, "'Middle Income Trap' is Essentially 'Reform Trap'", *South Daily*, Nov. 22, 2011.

[50] Li Guanghui, "Speed up the Implementation of China's strategy to the Free Trade Area", *Study Times*, Apr. 12, 2017.

[51] Li Jinzao, *Farewell to the GDP Worship*, Beijing: The Commercial Press, 2014.

[52] Li Keqiang, "Implement Urbanization is a Strategy Crucial for Modernization", *Administration Reform*, 2012(11).

[53] Lin Zhaomu, "China's Economic Transformation and Upgrading is Imperative", *Reality Only*, 2013(10).

[54] Liu He, *Comparative Study on the Two Global Crisis*, Beijing: China Economy Publishing House, 2013.

[55] Liu Shijin, "Shift in China's Phase of Economic Growth and Transformation of Development Mode", *Journal of Chinese Academy of Governance*, 2012(2).

[56] Liu Shucheng, "China's Economy is in Medium and High Speed Growth Phrase", *People's Daily*, Oct. 24, 2013.

[57] Liu Shucheng, Fan Mingtai, "Analysis on China's Economic Fluctuation", *China Industrial Economics*, 2000(5).

[58] Li Yang, Zhang Xiaojing, "The New Normal: the Logic and Perspective of Economic Development", *Economic Research Journal*, 2015, 50 (5).

[59] Li Yining, "On Meddle Income Trap", *Economic Perspectives*, 2012(12).

[60] Lou Jiwei, *Rethinking of Intergovernmental Fiscal Relations in China*, Beijing: China Financial & Economic Publishing House, 2013.

[61] Lu Ming, *China's Development Road to Great Power Economy*, Beijing: Encyclopedia of China Publishing House, 2008.

[62] Maddison, Angus, *Chinese Economic Performance in the Long Run: 960-2030 AD*, Shanghai: Shanghai People's Publishing House, 2016.

[63] Maddison, Angus, *The World Economy: Historical Statistics*, Chinese Edition,

translated by Wu Xiaoying et al., Beijing: Peking University Press, 2016.

[64] Ma Jiantang, "Much Remains to be Done for China to Comprehensively Become an Economic Powerhouse", *China Collective Economy*, 2011(4).

[65] Ma Jiantang, "On the World Economy and Chinese Economic Development", *Statistical Research*, 2013, 30(1).

[66] Ma Kai, "Take a Path to Urbanization with Chinese Characteristics", *Journal of Chinese Academy of Governance*, 2012(5).

[67] Ma Xiaofang, "Promote China's Economy with Opening-up Strategy", *China Economic Times*, Jul. 26, 2013.

[68] Mu Haiping, Zhang Zhanbin, "Reform is the Biggest Dividend for China", *Guangming Daily*, Jun. 14, 2013.

[69] North, Douglass C, *Structure and Change in Economic History*, Shanghai: Shanghai SDX Joint Publishing Company, 1991.

[70] Party Group of National Development and Reform Commission, "Openness and Development is the Sure Way to Make Our Country Strong and Prosperous", *Qiushi*, 2016(3).

[71] Party Literature Research Center, CPC Central Committee, *Important Selected Works Since The 18th CPC National Congress* (Volume I, Volume Ⅱ, Volume Ⅲ), Beijing: Central Party Literature Press, 2014, 2016, 2018.

[72] Pei Changhong, Li Chenghua, "Theoretical Innovation and Practical Significance of Xi Jinping's Economic Thought", *Nanjing Journal of Social Sciences*, 2015(2).

[73] Piketty Thomas, *Capital in the Twenty-first Century*, Beijing: CITIC Press Group, 2014.

[74] Qiu Baoxing, *Urbanization and Urban-rural Coordination Development*, Beijing: China City Press, 2012.

[75] Qiu Xiaohua, Guan Qingyou, *New Normal Economy*, Beijing: China CITIC Press, 2015.

[76] *Selected Works of Chen Yun* (Volume Ⅲ), Beijing: People's Publishing House, 1986.

[77] *Selected Works of Chen Yun* (Volume Ⅱ), Beijing: People's Publishing House, 1984.

[78] *Selected Works of Deng Xiaoping* (Volume Ⅲ), Beijing: People's Publishing House, 1993.

[79] *Selected Works of Deng Xiaoping* (Volume Ⅱ), Beijing: People's Publishing

House, 1994.

[80] *Selected Works of Hu Jintao*, Beijing: People's Publishing House, 2016.

[81] *Selected Works of Jiang Zemin*, Beijing: People's Publishing House, 2006.

[82] *Selected Works of Karl Marx and Friedrich Engels*, Beijing: People's Publishing House, 1972.

[83] *Selected Works of Liu Guoguang*, Beijing: Xue Xi Press, 2003.

[84] *Selected Works of Mao Zedong*, Beijing: People's Publishing House, 1991.

[85] *Selected Works of Wang Mengkui*, Beijing: Xue Xi Press, 2003.

[86] Simmons, Randy T., *Beyond Politics: The Root of Government Failure*, Chinese Edition, translated by Zhang Yuan, Beijing: Xinhua Publishing House, 2017.

[87] Tian Pengying, "Global Implications of the China's Reform and Opening up", *Studies on Marxism*, 2015(5).

[88] Wang Shaoguang, *Inspiration from American Progressive Era*, Beijing: China Financial & Economic Publishing House, 2002.

[89] Wang Yiming, "Working for an Upgraded Version of the Chinese Economy", *Macroeconomic Management*, 2013(6).

[90] Wang Yiwei, *Opportunities and Challenges of the Belt and Road*, Beijing: People's Publishing House, 2015.

[91] Wei Liqun, "Development Strategies under the Transition from a Big Economy to a Strong Economy". *Xinhua Digest*, 2013(18).

[92] Wei Liqun, Han Kang, *China's System of Administrative Control for Recent* 60 *Years*, Beijing: National Academy of Governance Press, 2009.

[93] Wei Liqun, Lin Zhaomu, and Zhang Zhanbin, *Transformation from Largest Economy to Economic Powerhouse*, Beijing: People's Publishing House, 2015.

[94] Wei Liqun, "Reform and Opening up Broadens the Road of China's Development", *Qiushi*, 2015(21).

[95] Wen Hua, "Advance Reforms Resolutely", *Qiushi*, 2017(3).

[96] Wu Jinglian, *The Choice of China's Growth Model*, Shanghai: Shanghai Far East Publishers, 2013.

[97] Xi Jinping, *Speech at the Conference Celebrating the* 40*th Anniversary of Reform and Opening up*, Beijing: People's Publishing House, 2018.

[98] Xi Jinping, *The Governance of China* (Volume Ⅰ), Shanghai: Foreign Language Press, 2014.

[99] Xi Jinping, *The Governance of China* (Volume Ⅱ), Shanghai: Foreign Language Press, 2017.

[100] Xu Yaotong, "On Deng Xiaoping's Thought on Reform and Opening Up", *Studies on Socialism with Chinese Characteristics*, 2014(4).

[101] Yang Zhengwei, "New Engine for Economic Globalization", *People's Daily*, Apr. 23, 2017.

[102] Yu Keping, *On Modernization of China's Governance*, Beijing: Social Sciences Academic Press, 2014.

[103] Yu Pinhua, "On the Significance and Influence of Reform and Opening Up", *Leading Journal of Ideological & Theoretical Education*, 2016(7).

[104] Zhang Youwen, Xu Mingqi, *Economic Power: The Trend and Objective of China's Peaceful Rise*, Beijing: People's Publishing House, 2004.

[105] Zhang Zhanbin, *China's Dream to Be Economic Powerhouse*, Shijiazhuang: Hebei People's Press, 2014.

[106] Zhang Zhanbin, *China-style Rising*, Beijing: National Academy of Governance Press, 2007.

[107] Zhang Zhanbin, "Connotations and Requirements of New Urbanization", *People's Daily*, Jan. 9, 2014.

[108] Zhang Zhanbin, *Governance of Great Power Economy*, Beijing: National Academy of Governance Press, 2014.

[109] Zhang Zhanbin, *New Layout of China's Economy*, Beijing: People's Publishing House, 2018.

[110] Zhang Zhanbin, *New Starting point of Chinese Reform*, Beijing: People's Publishing House, 2017.

[111] Zhang Zhanbin, *Releasing of Reform Dividend*, Beijing: SDX Joint Publishing Company, 2014.

[112] Zhang Zhanbin, "Strategies for China to Cross 'Meddle Income Trap'", *Review of Economic Research*, 2012(56).

[113] Zhang Zhanbin, "The Strategic Significance and Reform Challenges of New Urbanization", *Journal of Chinese Academy of Governance*, 2013(1).

[114] Zhang Zhanbin, "Upgrade the Chinese Economy and Strive to Achieve Chinese Dream of Economic Powerhouse", *China Economic Times*, Sep. 11, 2013.

[115] Zhang Zhanbin, Zhou Yuehui, "Basic Approach and Strategic Priorities to Distribute Dividends of the Economic Structural Reform", *Journal of China Executive Leadership Academy Yan'an*, 2013, 6(5).

[116] Zhang Zhanbin, Zhou Yuehui, *The Economic Aspects of Great Power under*

the New Normal, Changsha: Hu'nan People's Press, 2015.

[117] Zhang Zhanbin, Zhou Yuehui, "Two One-hundred Strategic Nodes and the Research of China's Economic Power Dream", *Journal of Chinese Communist Party History Studies*, 2014(1).

[118] Zhang Zhuoyuan, "A Breakthrough Is Needed in the Current Economic Reform", *Theoretical Trends*, 2012(17, 19).

[119] Zhang Zhuoyuan, *Top-level Design for China's Reform*, Beijing: China CITIC Press, 2014.

[120] Zhao Zhenhua, "How to Exert the Guiding Role of Economic System Reform", *Guangming Daily*, Dec. 3, 2013.

[121] Zheng Bingwen, "'Middle Income Trap' and China's Path Development: In Perspective of International Experiences and Lessons", *Chinese Journal of Population Science*, 2011(1).

[122] Zheng Yongnian, *Uncertain Future: How to Continue the Reform*, Beijing: China CITIC Press, 2014.

[123] Zhou Tianyong, *Chinese Dream and Chinese Road*, Beijing: Social Sciences Academic Press, 2013.

[124] Zhou Zhenhua, *Research on the Development of Modern Service Industry*, Shanghai: Shanghai Social Science Press, 2005.

[125] Zong Han, "China: From Large Economy to Economic Powerhouse", *The Chinese Spirit*, 2012(19).

[126] Zou Dongtao, *Basic Experience from China's Economic System Reform*, Beijing: China Renmin University Press, 2008.

This book is the result of a co-publication agreement between Economic Science Press (China) and Paths Publishing Group LTD. (U.K.).

Title: The Road to China's Economic Powerhouse
Author: Zhang Zhanbin
Translated by Lin Jihong
ISBN: 978-1-80589-011-9
Ebook ISBN: 978-1-80589-012-6

Paths Publishing Group LTD.
Published in the United Kingdom
www.pathspublishinggroup.com

www.ingramcontent.com/pod-product-compliance
Lightning Source LLC
LaVergne TN
LVHW081043250726
843429LV00022B/130